WEL

Welcome to the world of free computing

There's a lot of mystery surrounding Linux. Until recently, it was an operating system used exclusively by geeks who knew how to control a computer by typing unfathomable commands such as 'sudo apt-get install pkgnames emerald'.

The good news is that Linux is now as good-looking, easy to install and simple to use as Windows. What's more, it's absolutely free – you'll find your copy of Ubuntu on the back page of this book ready for you to try out straight away. You can install it on as many computers as you like, try as many different versions as you want and download thousands of free applications to use with it.

In this book, we'll show you how to do everything in Linux that you can do in Windows, such as browsing the internet, sending emails, organising and editing your photos, creating a spreadsheet, listening to music (and transferring it to your MP3 player), watching DVDs and much more.

So whether you're building a computer from scratch or you're simply fed up with how slow your current Windows PC is, this book is for you.

Jim Martin, Editor

THE COMPLETE LINUX MANUAL

Contents

Find out how to do everything in Linux just as easily as you can in Windows – and all for free!

CHAPTER 1

Introduction to Linux
Find out why this free OS is better than Windows

Why should I use Linux?	6
How to get Linux	8

CHAPTER 2

Installing Ubuntu
Our step-by-step guide to installing your new OS

Installing Ubuntu	12
Welcome to the Ubuntu desktop	16
Adding peripherals	18
Installing software	22

CHAPTER 3

Getting to know Linux
Finding your way around is simple with our help

Getting started	28
Transferring files to your new computer	32
Configuring Ubuntu	36
Installing a dock	38
Creating user accounts	39

CHAPTER 4

Basic desktop tasks
It's just as easy to do everything in Linux that you do in Windows, as you'll soon discover with our step-by-step guides

Using OpenOffice	42
Burning CDs and DVDs	44
Connecting a digital camera	46
Getting started with Gimp	48
Improving your photos using Gimp	50
Organising your photos with Picasa	52
Connecting a video camera to your PC	54
Editing video	56
Playing DVDs	58
Playing music files with Rhythmbox	60
Connecting an MP3 player	62
Connecting an iPod	64
Synchronising a mobile with Linux	66
Using Google Desktop	68

CHAPTER 5

Internet on Linux

Find out how to get your web browser, email, instant messaging and VoIP working

Getting connected	72
Controlling the web	76
Configuring email	80
Using VoIP	84
Using instant messaging	86
Connecting a webcam	88
Firewalls and internet security	91
Storing files online	96
Uploading files with FTP	98

CHAPTER 6

System health

Linux is as vulnerable to system faults as any other operating system. In this chapter we'll show you how to protect it – and your data

Choosing a backup destination	102
Making backups	104
Making an image of your system	109

CHAPTER 7

Network storage

Why not use Linux to turn an old PC into a NAS?

Making your own NAS	116
Configuring FreeNAS	120

CHAPTER 8

Troubleshooting

Stuck? Our guide will help you fix any problems

Troubleshooting	126
How to use your free Ubuntu 9.10 CD	128

THE COMPLETE LINUX MANUAL

CHAPTER 1

Introduction to Linux

The Linux operating system is a great alternative to Windows. As you'll learn over the next few pages, there are plenty of reasons to use it other than the fact that it's free.

One important point to note about Linux is that there are many different versions, or distributions, as they're known. Each version is based around a kernel (the core part of the operating system), but they vary when it comes to the interface and software they include.

Ubuntu is one of the most popular and easy-to-use distributions, and it's the one we'll use throughout this book. You'll find a copy of the latest version of Ubuntu on the free disc on the back page. Of course, you can try any other distribution you like: Linux Mint, Mandriva, Debian, Fedora and Qimo are all popular choices.

Why should I use Linux?	6
How to get Linux	8

CHAPTER 1

Why should I use Linux?

There are many reasons to use Linux beyond the fact that it's free. Here we'll explain why it's a viable alternative to Windows

Linux really will cost you nothing. Well, nothing more than price of this book, of course, but beyond that, you shouldn't need to spend a single penny. Not only is the operating system itself free, but all the software and utilities you'll need are either included as part of Linux, or you can install them with just a few clicks, all for free.

For another thing, it couldn't be easier; we've even stuck a CD in this book so you can try it immediately. All you need to do is pop it into your CD or DVD drive and boot from it; you don't even need to install it.

If you're still not convinced, here are another eight reasons why you should switch operating systems and use Ubuntu instead.

1 All the programs that you have to buy for Windows are free in Linux. It can be incredibly frustrating when you get your new PC home, set it up and go to load Microsoft Word. You'll either find that you've got a trial version that can be run 25 times, or that it isn't installed at all. You won't have that problem with Ubuntu. OpenOffice is installed by default, and has compatible versions of Word, Excel, PowerPoint and Outlook. That means you can create letters, presentations and spreadsheets immediately, and start sending and receiving email.

There's plenty else besides: photo-editing software, music and video players, instant messaging and disc-burning utilities – the list goes on and on. You'll find guides to many of these applications in chapter 4.

2 Ubuntu will run on just about any computer. Whether you have the latest quad-core PC or a relic with hardly any RAM, Ubuntu will work. In fact, it will use the full power of both those machines, so whatever you have, it isn't wasted by running Ubuntu on it. Because Ubuntu is a very lightweight operating system, older computers can be given a new lease of life. Instead of feeling sluggish and taking 10 minutes to boot up, they can feel snappy simply by swapping a clogged-up version of Windows with Ubuntu.

3 Viruses and malware are virtually non-issues. Because most computers run Windows, the vast majority of viruses are written to target that operating system. There are almost no cases of Linux suffering from virus attacks, and as Ubuntu is updated regularly, potential security holes are patched very quickly.

Extra reassurance comes from the fact that, unlike Windows, the main computer user doesn't

■ Whether your PC is heading for the scrapheap or has the latest quad-core processor, Linux will make the most of it

INTRODUCTION TO LINUX

have administrator rights. In simple terms, this means that there's a limit to the parts of the operating system that can be accessed, and this provides greater safety from malware.

4 Updates are easy. Ubuntu has a central update manager that manages updates for all the programs you've installed. This means there's just one place you need to go to get new versions, and one program to run. Windows, on the other hand, doesn't manage updates for third-party software. A typical Windows PC is littered with programs that run constantly, checking to see if a new version of the program is available. This uses up system resources and makes your computer run more slowly.

5 You don't need a second monitor. In Windows, you have only one desktop. Open more than a few windows and you'll soon become tired of juggling them all. In Ubuntu, you have multiple workspaces, which are like virtual monitors. Click on an icon, and you switch to a new, clean desktop. It's so easy to flip between workspaces that you'll never be able to go back.

6 There's no shareware, adware or serial numbers. If you want to install extra programs, you do it through Ubuntu's Package Manager. There are thousands of applications to choose from, and all are free. If you like it, you can keep using it. If not, you can simply uninstall it. You'll never have to enter your details, nor will you be bombarded by emails.

7 It's just like Windows. If you know how to use Windows, you'll be right at home with Ubuntu. Almost everything works the same way, from the 'start' menu to navigating through files and folders. Tooltips will pop up to help you learn what each icon and button does, plus there's the comprehensive Help Center.

8 Hardware support is much better than it used to be. One reason many people haven't tried Linux is because they think it won't work with their hardware. The truth is that, unless you have a really obscure bit of kit, Ubuntu is likely to work with it. You'll probably find that most of your computer's functions work as soon as Ubuntu is installed, from wireless networking to your memory card reader.

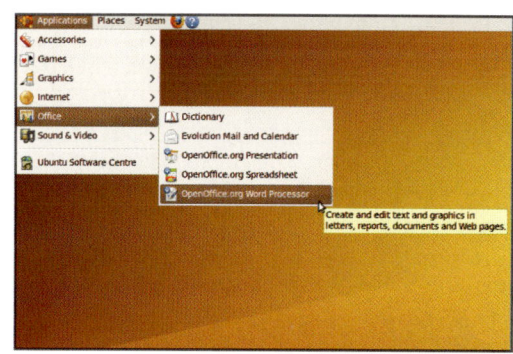

■ Ubuntu is really easy to use, and provides help at every turn

WHAT CAN'T LINUX DO?

There are many games available for Linux, but you won't be able to play the latest titles that you'll see available for Windows. This is Linux's only real weak area. However, you can run Ubuntu alongside Windows – a technique known as dual-booting – so you can still enjoy Call of Duty, Colin McRae: Dirt 2 or whatever your favourite games are on the same computer.

If we're honest, though, Linux does have other failings. Although it includes a heady array of applications, there are a number of small omissions; for example, Ubuntu needs a codec to be installed manually to record music in MP3 format. Hardware support, as we've said, is very good, but it's possible that some things may not work on your computer. In the process of writing this book, we installed Linux on many PCs and laptops; some worked perfectly, while others caused headaches. Problems ranged from major issues such as not being able to boot after installing Ubuntu on a Sony Vaio laptop to niggles such as unreliable wireless networking.

You may also find that buttons on laptops such as brightness and volume controls don't work. The good news is that someone is bound to have hit your problem before, and you're highly likely to find the solution in a forum such as **http://ubuntuforums.org**. If not, ask in the forum, and you're sure to get an answer.

■ Help for trickier problems is always at hand through friendly community forums

CHAPTER 1

How to get Linux

Now that you're ready to give Linux a go, we'll outline the different versions on offer

Hopefully you're now convinced that Linux is worth trying. The trouble is, how do you choose between the multitude of different distributions? Each distro, as they're called, has a particular kind of user in mind, and if you're just starting out with Linux, it's best to choose one that's specifically tailored to new users.

There's another consideration, though: the type of computer on which you want to run it. There are distros for desktop PCs, laptops and netbooks. The latter, though, deserve special attention. While most distros will happily work on a desktop or laptop, some may be too much for a netbook. It may be a question of resources, such as RAM, screen resolution or hard disk space, but whatever the reason, a cut-down Linux distro could be the answer.

DIFFERENT DISTROS

A version of Ubuntu for netbooks, called the Netbook Remix, is optimised to run on the low-powered, internet-centric devices. Its user-friendly interface makes it incredibly easy to get online, watch a video, edit your photos or create documents. You can find out more at www.canonical.com/netbooks. You may find there's a version of Linux for your specific netbook. Easy Peasy, for example – which used to be called UbuntuEee – was designed for Asus EeePC netbooks. Now you can use it on all netbooks; download it from www.geteasypeasy.com.

If you plan to run Linux on a PC or laptop, there's a wide selection of user-friendly distros. The most obvious difference between them is the number and type of programs they include. Linux Mint, for example, is based on Ubuntu but has a start menu much like Windows Vista's. The installer shows screenshots and ratings of

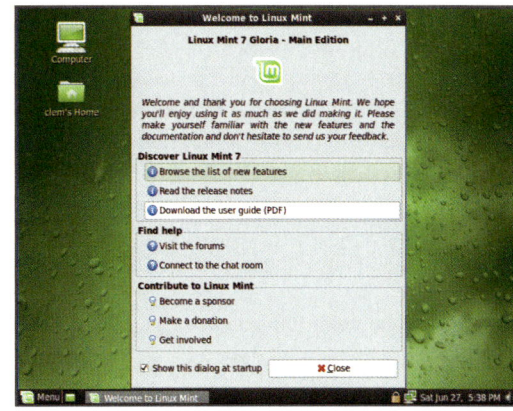

■ Linux Mint is the best-looking distribution. It has a Vista-style Start menu, complete with a search bar

applications, plus user reviews, which makes it easy to decide whether a package is what you're after. Adobe Flash and Sun Java are installed by default, so most websites containing music and video, such as YouTube, work straight away. You can download it from www.linuxmint.com.

If you're after a distro for the whole family, try Qimo (www.qimo4kids.com). It's also based on Ubuntu and has a friendly interface and built-in parental controls for controlling internet access. It even comes with educational games.

Fedora (http://fedoraproject.org) and Debian (www.debian.org) are more mainstream choices, and aren't quite so user-friendly. Fedora prides itself on having the latest versions of applications, while Debian is exceptionally stable and has an enormous choice of software available through its package manager.

However, we think the best distro for most people is Ubuntu. Its look and feel is very close to Windows, and unfamiliar aspects such as the Package Manager and virtual desktops are hidden away. It's because of this that Ubuntu has become the most popular Linux distribution.

INTRODUCTION TO LINUX

ALL ABOUT UBUNTU

Ubuntu has excellent compatibility, which means it will run on just about any hardware. It also optimises itself for your computer, including setting the correct screen resolution for your monitor and finding your home wireless network. In fact, Ubuntu can be even easier to use than Windows on occasion. Connect an external monitor to a laptop, for example, press the function key combination on the keyboard to enable it and Ubuntu will automatically set the right resolution and configure an extended desktop to the side of your laptop's screen.

Ubuntu is updated every six months. Some versions have the letters 'LTS' after the version number, which stands for long-term support that lasts for three years. Standard releases have support for 18 months. Upgrading to a new version is simple and can be done from the Update Manager. In between releases are constant minor updates, so your PC always has the latest versions of applications installed.

Boot times are fast, and you'll realise just how slow Windows is when you see your desktop appear in under 30 seconds. As well as OpenOffice, Firefox is preinstalled, so you can get online straight away.

■ If you're looking for a version of Linux that can be used by all the family, give Qimo for Kids a try

INSTALLATION OPTIONS

For most people, installing Ubuntu will be a breeze. Simply pop the CD that comes with this book into your computer's drive and press the power button. It's then just a case of following the onscreen instructions. You'll find our complete guide to installation in Chapter 2.

■ The Netbook Remix is a special version of Ubuntu for low-powered computers

We realise, though, that not every computer has a CD or DVD drive. In this case, all you need is a 1GB USB flash drive, plus a computer running Windows. This method should work for all modern computers made in the past two or three years. If you don't have a flash drive, you can buy one for a couple of pounds from high-street stores such as PC World or WH Smith.

First, go to **www.ubuntu.com/getubuntu** and choose whether you want the Desktop Edition or Netbook Remix. Choose your location from the menu and click Begin Download (if you want the 64-bit version, click on the Custom Options section at the bottom of the screen first).

While the 700MB file is downloading, plug in your USB drive, go to **http://unetbootin. sourceforge.net** and click Download for Windows. When it's downloaded, run the application. As we're downloading the latest version of Ubuntu, there's no need to select the distribution from the menu. Instead, select Diskimage.

Once Ubuntu is downloaded, click the ... button to the right of Disk Image and navigate to the Ubuntu ISO file. Finally, choose the correct drive letter for your USB flash drive (check in Windows Explorer if you're unsure) and click OK. This will copy Ubuntu to your flash drive and configure it so your computer can boot from it.

Plug the flash drive into the computer on which you wish to install Ubuntu and turn it on. If it doesn't boot from the USB drive, you'll need to change the boot options in your computer's BIOS. Restart your computer and press Delete, F1 or F2 (or look for a message telling you which key to press to enter Setup). Look for the boot options and change the settings so that the first boot device is either an External drive or a USB drive. Save your changes and reboot.

THE COMPLETE LINUX MANUAL

CHAPTER 2

Installing Ubuntu

Installing Linux is incredibly easy. Once your computer has booted from the CD (or USB flash drive), the step-by-step instructions explain everything. In this chapter we'll show you what to expect and give you some tips on how to make sure things run smoothly.

Although Ubuntu looks a little different to Windows, its desktop should still be familiar, but we'll give you a whirlwind tour of where everything is on page 16.

We'll also show you how to check whether your hardware is working correctly and, if not, how to install the components that aren't. Finally, on page 22, you can find out how to install any additional software that you might need, such as Adobe's Flash plugin for Firefox.

Installing Ubuntu	12
Welcome to the Ubuntu desktop	16
Adding peripherals	18
Installing software	22

CHAPTER 2

Installing Ubuntu

It's just as easy to install Linux as it is to install Windows. Here, we'll show you what to do with a step-by-step guide

You've probably already found the CD stuck to the inside of this book. We've included it to save you the hassle of downloading the 700MB file yourself. It's the Desktop Edition of version 9.10, which was the latest at the time of writing.

Linux is regularly updated, so check the website www.ubuntu.com/getubuntu to see if there's a newer version, or if you want to install a different version, such as the 64-bit edition. If you do download one of these ISO (disc image) files, you'll need to burn it to a CD before you can use it. We recommend using CDBurnerXP, which is a free download from http://cdburnerxp.se. Alternatively, you can use the free Unetbootin utility (see page 9) to create a bootable USB flash drive with the ISO image.

You don't need to commit to using Linux at this stage; if you just want to give it a try, you can run it directly from your installation disc (see Step 2 for more details).

1 Put the Ubuntu CD you just created into your optical drive and wait for the 'Press any key to boot from CD' message. If you miss this, you'll have to restart your computer to load the Ubuntu installation routine. The first Ubuntu install screen should appear very quickly; you'll just need to select the installation language.

2 You'll then be presented with an installation menu and a handful of options. The default installation option is to try Ubuntu without making any changes to your computer. This simply loads Ubuntu from the CD and doesn't write any files to your hard disk. It's a good way to try out Linux before making any commitments and filling up your hard disk, and it is the wisest option if you're not totally sure about Linux. If you do want to install Ubuntu properly, select the Install Ubuntu option.

Next, you'll see the Ubuntu loading screen. It can take a while for Ubuntu to chug through

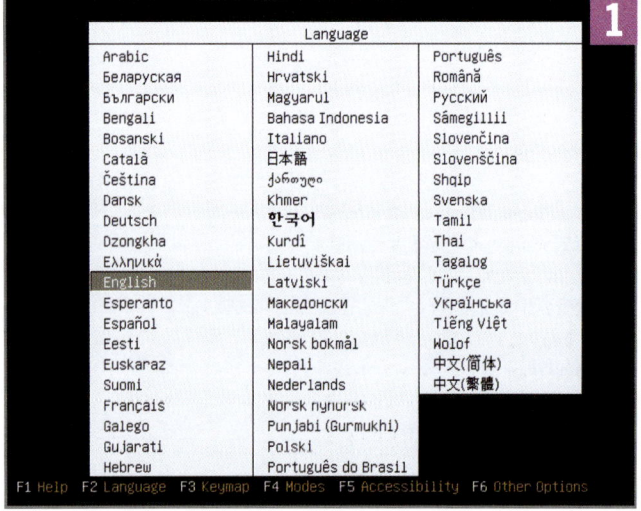
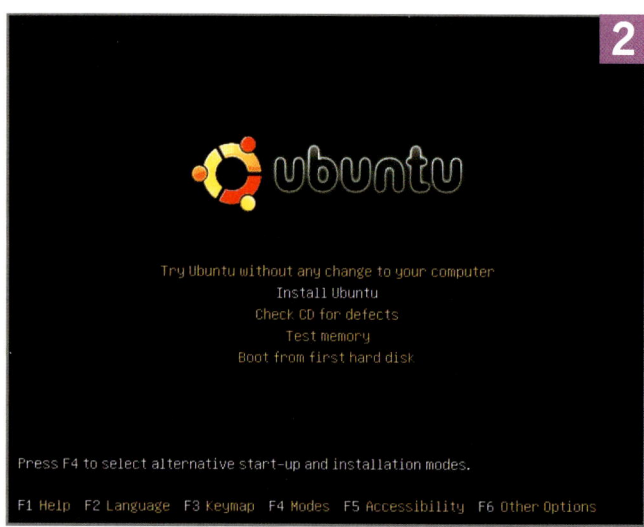

INSTALLING UBUNTU

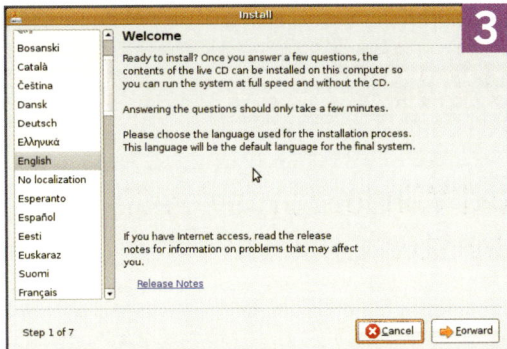
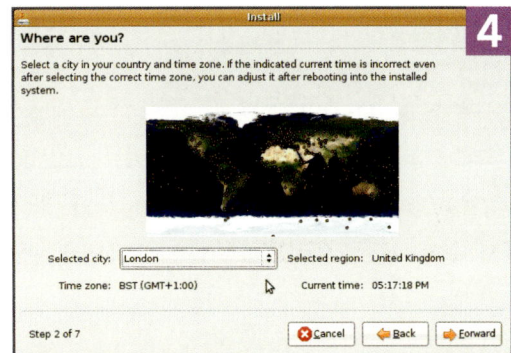
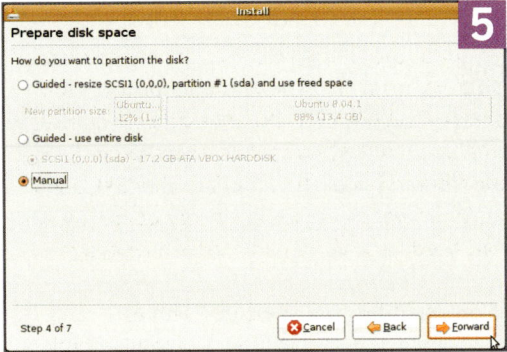
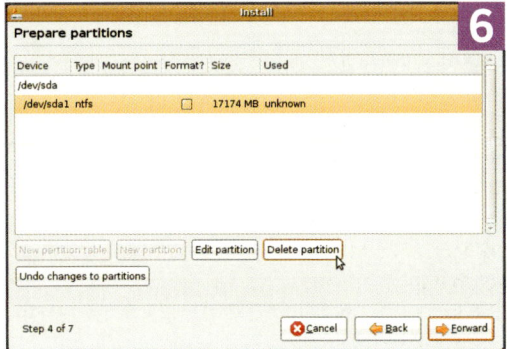

this part of the installation, so don't panic if the orange bar appears to freeze for a while.

3 Eventually, you'll see the Ubuntu wallpaper and a welcome screen. Hopefully, this is in a language you can understand; if it isn't, select English from the list on the left. If your PC is plugged into the internet via a wired connection, click the Release Notes link to find out about any problems that may affect you. When you've finished, click the Forward button to continue.

4 Select your location using the drop-down menu. UK cities are grouped under Europe towards the end of the list. Choosing a location in the UK should bring up the correct time zone. If it doesn't, select the right one using the drop-down menu.

When you've chosen the correct settings, click Forward to continue. Your keyboard layout should be set to United Kingdom; if it isn't, select this from the menu and click Forward.

5 Ubuntu uses a simple partitioning system on your PC's hard disk. Tweaking this will enable you to choose where your user files are kept and to create separate partitions for program files and virtual memory. Linux stores user files in the /home folder and moving this to its own partition is easy. However, if you opt to set up one partition manually, you'll have to set them all up this way.

If you just want to stick with Ubuntu's default partition scheme, leave the Guided option selected, click Forward and skip to Step 11.

6 Select the Manual option on the Prepare disk space screen and click Forward. The installer will scan your hard disk and display the disk partitioning tool. The first step is to delete all existing partitions on the hard disk, so select each one in the list and click the Delete partition button.

7 You should now have free space listed only under /dev/sda, which is Linux's name for the hard disk on the primary IDE channel. Since we're making partitions by hand, we need to create all the partitions that Linux requires, starting with the /boot partition. Select free space in the list of partitions and click New partition. Enter a size of 50 (we're working in megabytes) and then select /boot as the mount point. Click OK.

CHAPTER 2

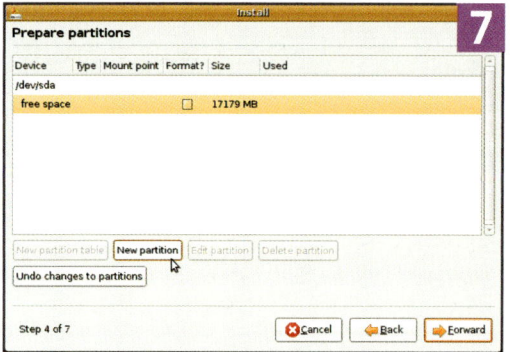
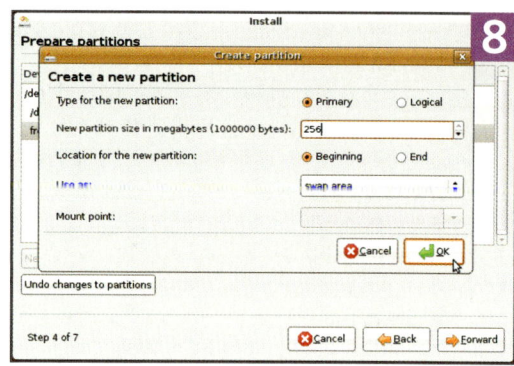
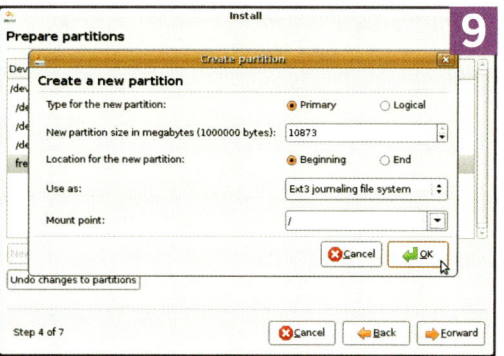
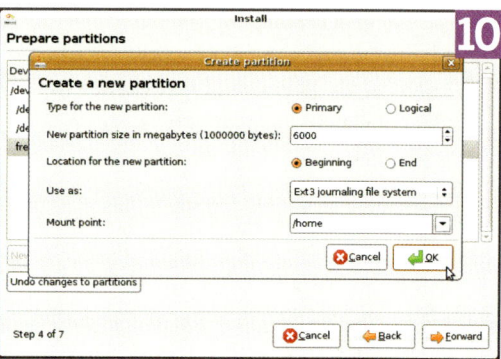

8 Linux also needs a /swap partition, which is the equivalent of the Windows swap file used for virtual memory. When your PC's real memory fills up, Ubuntu will swap bits of the memory that aren't currently being used – such as inactive applications, for example – to the hard disk. This gives the impression that your computer has more memory than it really does, so you can run more applications. Create another new partition in the free space and then enter a size (in megabytes) that is equal to the amount of RAM in the computer, remembering that one gigabyte is 1,024MB. Select Swap area from the 'Use as' drop-down list, leave the other settings at their defaults and click OK.

9 Next, you need to set the /home partition, which is where user files are kept. This is the equivalent of Windows' My Documents folder, but it is kept on a separate partition. The advantage of this method is that you can reinstall Linux and your documents won't be overwritten.

Make this partition as large as you like, remembering to leave a few gigabytes free for the final /root partition. Select /home as the mount point before clicking OK.

10 The final custom partitioning task you need to perform is to set the root or / partition. This is where Ubuntu is installed, and it will use all the remaining space. Set the mount point as / and click OK. You can see the final partition structure from the screen above. Click Forward when you're ready to continue.

[Install dialog screenshot labeled 11 — "Who are you?" form with fields: What is your name? "Steve Balmer"; What name do you want to use to log in? "steve"; Choose a password to keep your account safe; What is the name of this computer? "steve-desktop"; Step 5 of 7]

14 THE COMPLETE LINUX MANUAL

INSTALLING UBUNTU

11 You now need to tell Ubuntu who you are. Type your name into the 'What is your name?' box. This will generate a username for you in the 'What name do you want to use to log in?' box, but you can change this if you like. Then type in a password to protect your account and prevent unauthorised users logging on to your PC. Your computer will automatically have been given a name based on your name in the 'What is the name of this computer?' box, but you can change this to something else. Click Forward when you've finished.

12 So far, no files have been written to your hard disk – this is your last chance to back out of the installation. When you're ready to continue, click Install. Ubuntu will now copy the necessary files to the hard disk partitions you've created. This process will take a few minutes.

13 Once the installation is complete, the Gnome desktop will load. This is similar to the Windows desktop, and it's where most of your interaction with Linux is going to take place.
You'll find that a whole range of applications have already been installed. You can access these through the Applications menu at the top left of the screen. Ubuntu comes bundled with OpenOffice.org, which is a fully featured office suite, as well as the Firefox web browser and the Evolution email client.

14 Ubuntu simplifies the process of finding and installing new programs. Its Software Centre (available via the Applications menu) works in a similar way to the Windows Add/Remove Programs utility. However, Ubuntu has the added advantage of offering new applications to install, as well as old ones to remove. New programs are downloaded from the internet using an intuitive package manager. Any additional components (known as dependencies) are automatically downloaded, too, which goes a long way to making Linux more user-friendly.

15 Because of its rising popularity, Ubuntu Linux is attracting interest from malicious hackers, so you need to make sure the latest security patches are installed. Ubuntu has its own update manager and checks periodically for updates. When new updates become available, you'll see a warning on the application bar. Click the warning to bring up the list of updates and then click the Install Updates button.

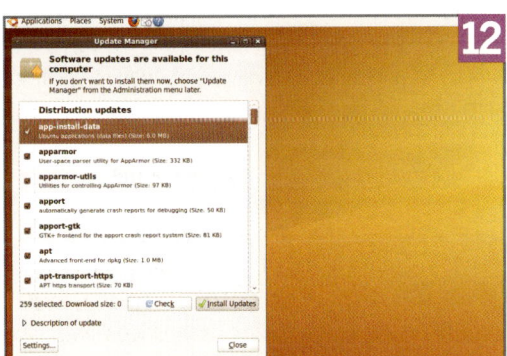
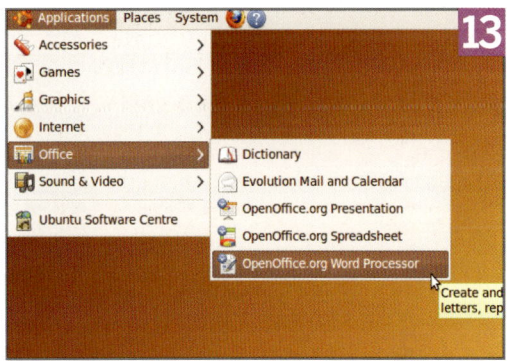
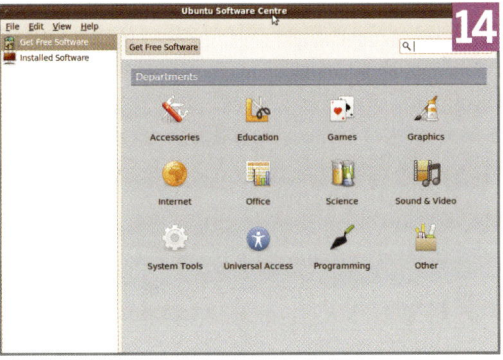
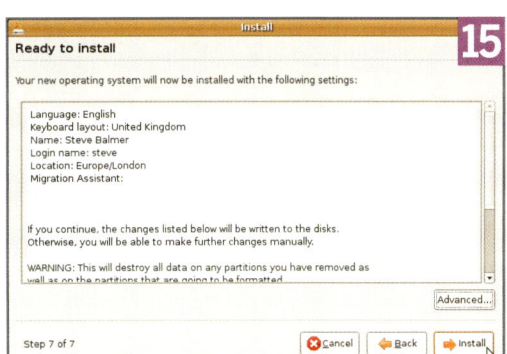

THE COMPLETE LINUX MANUAL

CHAPTER 2

Welcome to the Ubuntu desktop

You should have Ubuntu installed and running by now, so it's time for a whistle-stop tour of the desktop

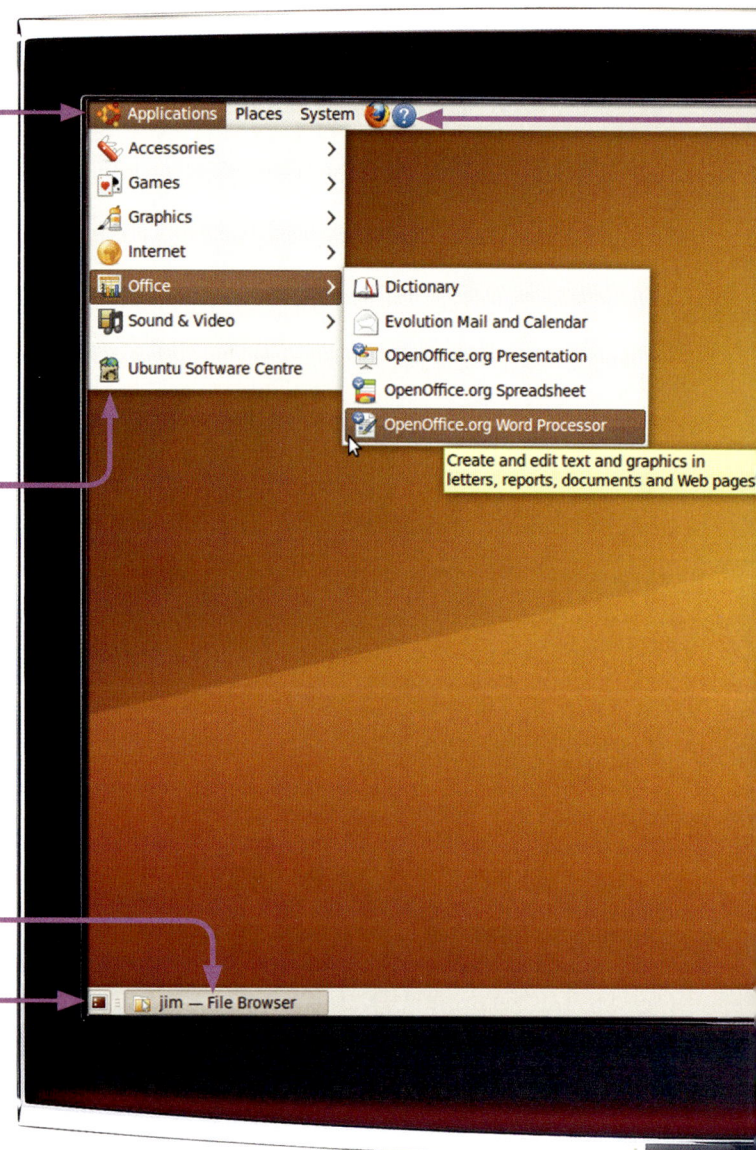

This is Ubuntu's 'start' menu, where you'll find all the preinstalled applications, such as OpenOffice. The Places menus gives you fast access to your documents and media folders, your computer's drives, network places and recently used files. The System menu, as you'd expect, is where you should head for changing preferences and running administration tasks.

A new feature in Ubuntu 9.10 is the Software Centre. This is like Apple's App Store for the iPhone, and is a much simpler way to add and remove applications than previously. A search box lets you quickly find free programs.

In a similar fashion to Windows, Ubuntu has a taskbar that shows icons for the applications you're currently running. Here we have a Firebox browser, two OpenOffice Writer windows and a File Browser window.

Click on this icon to minimise all your open windows and show the desktop. Click it again to restore all the windows that were open.

INSTALLING UBUNTU

These are quick-launch icons for loading frequently used applications. By default, these are Firefox 3 (web browser), Evolution (email) and Ubuntu's Help Center. It's simple to add more programs to this area; just click and drag them from the Applications menu.

This is the notification area, and looks just like Windows. Icons appear here to inform you of the status of various functions. For example, here you can see that the computer has a strong WiFi signal (the blue bars); the speaker icon lets you change or mute the volume, while clicking the envelope shows a menu listing all the messaging applications, including Empathy, which is Ubuntu 9.10's default instant-messaging program.

Clicking on your username brings up a menu similar to Windows' shut-down menu. This allows you to reboot the computer, put it into sleep mode, switch to a different user account or shut the computer down. The icon to the left of your username shows your current status for instant messaging.

Navigating your files and folders is simple with Ubuntu. If you can do it in Windows, you'll feel right at home here. Almost everything looks the same, from the menus to the navigation icons and folder listings. Just like Windows, there are pre-created folders for Documents, Music, Pictures and Videos.

This is where you control which workspace you're currently in. Clicking on the grey half takes you to a new blank desktop, while clicking on the orange half takes you back to your original desktop. The small icons within the orange half show which windows are currently open in that workspace.

This is Ubuntu's Wastebasket. It works in exactly the same way as Windows' Recycle Bin, and allows you to recover deleted files.

THE COMPLETE LINUX MANUAL 17

CHAPTER 2

Adding peripherals

If the thought of installing hardware has been putting you off Linux, think again: it's now easy to add peripherals in Ubuntu

There was a time when using the words 'Linux' and 'hardware' in the same sentence could make IT gurus cry, but not any more. Linux has grown up and works just as easily as Windows with peripherals.

Over the past few years, open-source developers have been busily writing drivers and applications for a wide range of peripherals. USB and Bluetooth have made their job far easier, but there are still a few issues to avoid, just as there are with any operating system.

Windows Vista often has problems with drivers for current hardware, whereas in Linux it tends to be obsolete hardware that causes problems. In Ubuntu, support for popular hardware is so good that the only problem you're likely to have is deciding which applications you want to use with your devices. Here we'll show you how to install a range of common peripherals using Ubuntu.

SOUND ADVICE

Getting sound hardware up and running should pose no problems in Linux, and any modern sound card should work straight away. Linux manages sound hardware in a different way to Windows, so it's worth taking a closer look at what's going on.

From Ubuntu's Desktop System menu, click Preferences and select the Sound option; if you can't hear anything when playing CDs, for example, this should be the first place you look. The resulting Sound Preferences dialog box lists the available sound devices on pull-down menus. In most circumstances, these will all be for the same sound card.

One common sound problem is caused by plugging speakers into a PC's analogue audio socket and leaving Linux set to use a digital output. This error should be obvious if you see the word 'Digital' in the name of the selected audio devices in the Sound Preferences dialog box. To correct this, use the pull-down menu to change it to 'Analog' and click the Test button. This should generate a steady tone. If not, try the Open Sound System (OSS) drop-down option for the device. If you still hear nothing, try the Autodetect option.

You can also use this dialog box to change the sounds played for specific system events. Click on the Sounds tab and you'll see a list of events, each with a status of Default or Disabled. If you click the status and select Custom, you'll be able to navigate to the sound file of your choice.

Once onboard sound is working in Linux, you can play music directly from just about any USB MP3 player. We used an old Tevion 512MB MP3

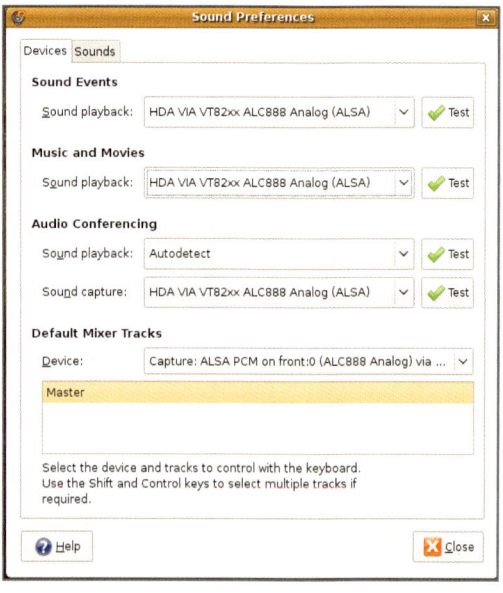

■ Checking the state of your sound output is really easy in Ubuntu Linux

INSTALLING UBUNTU

player to demonstrate. We've packed it with music ripped in Windows from CD by Windows Media Player.

Plug the player into a USB port on your Ubuntu PC. A dialog box will open to explain that the operating system has recognised the connection of an MP3 player. It will also ask if you'd like to open the RhythmBox Music Player. Click OK and the RhythmBox application will open.

When it first runs, RhythmBox will complain that codecs are required to play the contents of the connected MP3 player. Click OK to search for these online. After a few moments, a dialog box will open offering a choice of two codecs: one for audio file formats and one for video. When you click the tickbox by each codec, you'll be asked to confirm that you want to install it. Click the Confirm button each time. Finally, press Install. You'll need to enter your system password to confirm the changes, after which Ubuntu will download and install the necessary files.

Once installed, your MP3 player's track listing will appear in RhythmBox's main window. Try playing a song. The MP3 player also appears on your desktop and you can open it in RhythmBox by right-clicking it. Before disconnecting the MP3 player, right-click on its icon and select Unmount Volume. If you don't do this, you'll risk corrupting its contents. The same applies to any external storage device.

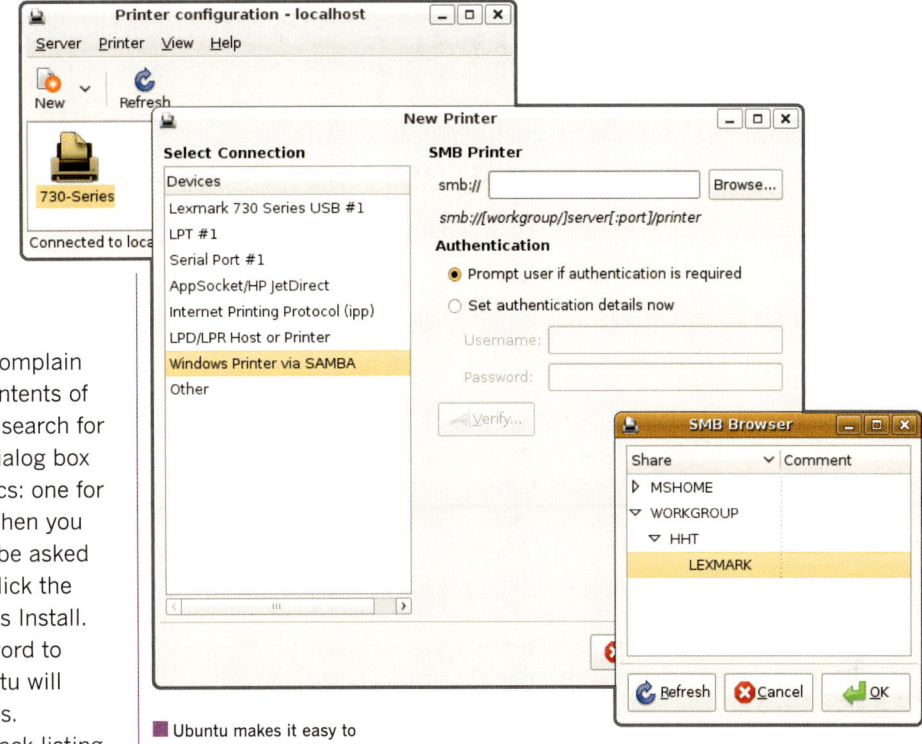

■ Ubuntu makes it easy to add a printer directly or use one shared by a Windows PC, but there are still driver issues for older models

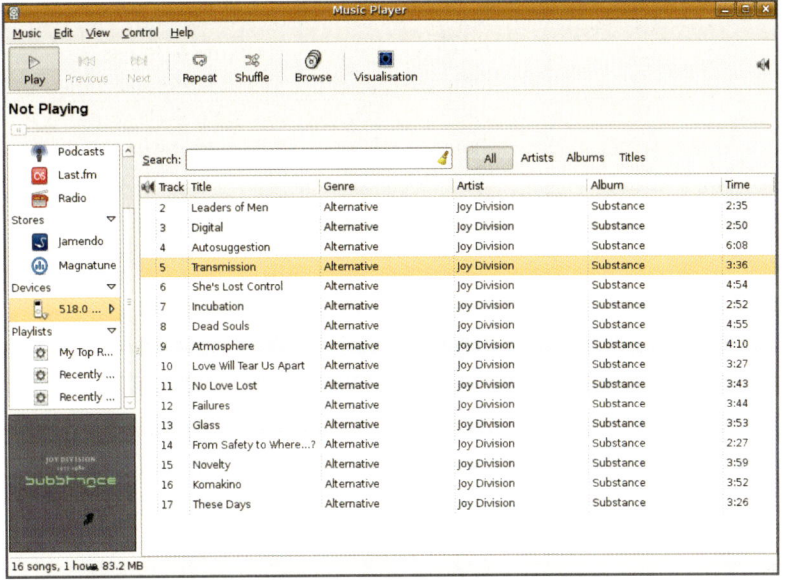

■ Connect an MP3 player and you can play its contents using RhythmBox

READ THE SMALL PRINT

Unfortunately, some printers – especially older or less popular models – aren't supported by Linux. Printers require proprietary drivers if an operating system is to access all their features, and Linux drivers don't exist for certain models. Fortunately, however, many printer manufacturers have made considerable efforts to provide drivers for current and some of the more popular older models.

It's wise to find out whether your printer is supported before you plug it into your Linux PC. You'll find an active database of supported printers at **www.linuxprinting.org**. Click on the Printers link on the left of the page and enter the make and model. The ranking system runs from three penguins for fully compatible to no penguins for incompatible or 'paperweight' printers, as the database calls them.

If your printer isn't listed, or it's listed as a paperweight but uses PostScript, you should find a PostScript Printer Definition (.ppd) file on your printer's original driver CD, which will tell Ubuntu all it needs to know. To load this file, plug in your printer, go to the Administration section of the desktop's System menu and select Printing. A dialog box should appear showing

THE COMPLETE LINUX MANUAL 19

CHAPTER 2

your printer; double-click the printer and another box will open giving its details.

Next to Make and Model, it should say that it's a generic printer. Click the associated Change button and another dialog box will open. Select Provide PPD file and insert your printer's driver CD. If you press the button marked None, a file browser window will open. Browse to and select the .ppd file on your CD and click OK.

If you'd prefer to use a printer shared by a Windows PC, you can, provided that there's a suitable Linux driver available. From the desktop's System menu, select Administration, Printers and click New in the dialog box that appears. Select 'Windows printer via SAMBA' and click Browse. This brings up a Windows Workgroup browser window. Browse to the PC with the shared printer and select it. Click OK followed by Forward, and you'll see the familiar printer driver installation window. Select the make and model of your printer and, when you finish the wizard, you should be able to print to the shared printer.

If your printer isn't a supported model, there isn't much else you can do short of writing your own driver. However, remember you can always save your documents to a Windows share and print them from a Windows PC. It's a cop-out, but printing is the last great stumbling block in Linux and it's getting easier all the time.

SCANNER TIME

Plug your USB scanner into your Ubuntu PC and run the XSane scanning application, which is installed by default in the Graphics section of the Applications desktop menu. When it runs, XSane will probe the USB ports for connected scanners. It may think that there are two instances of the same scanner, but it should be safe to select the default option and use that.

When the main XSane user interface opens, there are a few things to note. It may be set up to read binary data from the scan, which reduces the image from full colour to black and white. If it is, click the pull-down menu marked Binary on the XSane Control Panel and select Colour. This adds the controls for manipulating full-colour images to the interface. You may also find that scanned images appear grainy. If so, increase the points-per-inch setting from the default of 75.

GIMP, the standard Linux graphical manipulation program, can also access scanners via XSane. Run GIMP, which is also installed by default, and select File, Create, XSane. Then pick your scanner. The scanned image will open directly in GIMP, so close the XSane interface before you continue.

CAMERA ACTION

Webcams are ubiquitous these days, and Ubuntu has dedicated applications for shooting, editing and applying special effects to your images and video clips. We're using an old Logitech QuickCam Express camera. Because it's a USB device, using it should be as simple as plugging it in and installing a suitable application.

First, select Add/Remove from the desktop Applications menu. When the Application installer program runs, set the Show pull-down menu to All Available Programs and type 'webcam' into the search box. Press Enter and the program will bring up a list of webcam programs. Click the tickbox next to the Cheese Webcam Booth application and click Apply Changes.

After the program downloads and installs Cheese, select the graphics section of the desktop's Applications menu. When Cheese runs, it will display a live image. It can record a video or take a still snapshot from the webcam. You can also apply several trippy effects to the video stream by clicking the Effects button. Vertigo, for

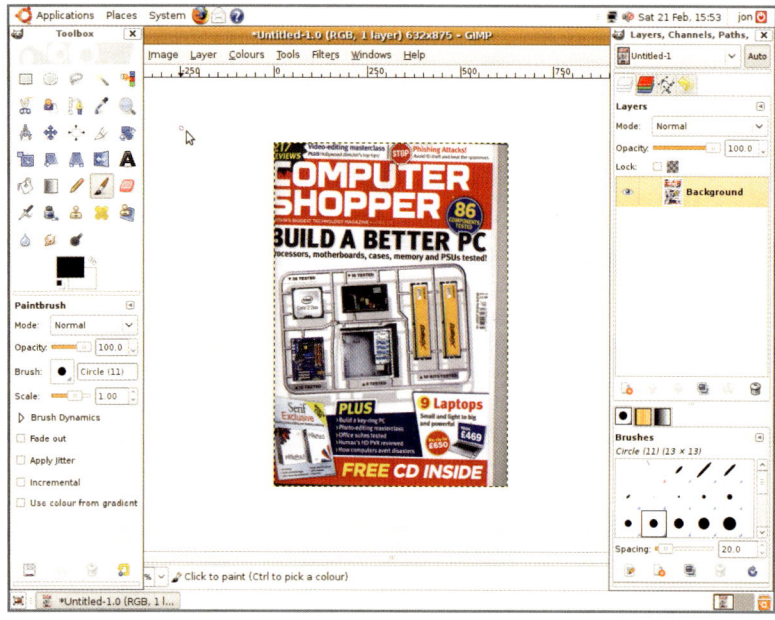

■ You can scan images directly into GIMP, the standard Linux image-manipulation program

INSTALLING UBUNTU

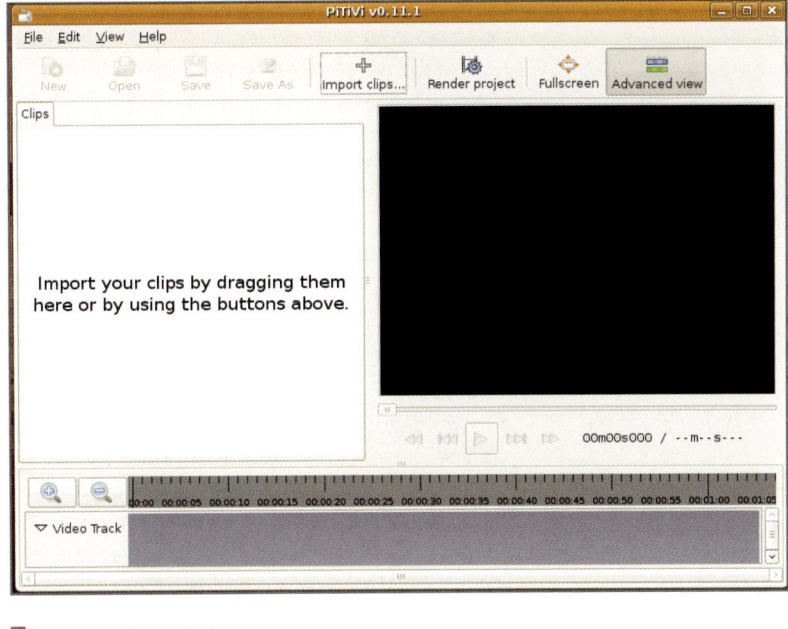

■ Ubuntu has plenty of video-editing software, including PiTiVi, which is similar to Windows Movie Maker

example, produces an effect that wouldn't look out of place on *Top of the Pops* circa 1973.

Ubuntu also has access to plenty of video-editing applications. PiTiVi is a good substitute for Windows Movie Maker and contains everything you need to edit your movies. It also renders the final cut ready to be burnt to DVD with a program such as DeVeDe, which is also bundled with Ubuntu.

WIDE BLUE YONDER

Ubuntu has excellent Bluetooth support. If your PC lacks the necessary adaptor, connect a cheap USB Bluetooth dongle and the Bluetooth icon will appear on the desktop's launcher bar. When you want to connect to a Bluetooth device, click this icon and a dialog box appears with options for setting the visibility of your PC. The options are hidden, visible or visible for a short while after being plugged in. For now, make it visible.

After making sure your Bluetooth phone is turned on and its Bluetooth service is enabled and visible to other devices, press the button on the dialog box marked with a plus sign. A wizard pops up to add the phone. Click Forward and the Bluetooth device should appear in the list. Select the phone and click Forward again. The wizard will connect to the device and ask you to enter a security PIN to establish that it has the correct device. On the phone, add the Ubuntu machine to its list of devices and enter the same PIN. Your phone is now ready to take advantage of any Bluetooth management software you install.

Linux's support for all kinds of popular gadgets is becoming so good as to be virtually transparent. If you've been frustrated using older Linux distributions, now's a great time to try again. Just remember that if you want to add a printer to your Linux PC, you'll need to make sure it's supported first.

Close call Working with the BlueProximity utility

BlueProximity is a useful utility that locks Ubuntu when you (or a Bluetooth phone paired with your PC) move away from it, and unlocks it again when you return. You can install it from the Add/Remove option on the desktop's Applications menu. It runs automatically when you boot the PC, placing a small icon on the desktop's launcher bar.

Click on the icon to open the Preferences window, then click Scan For Devices to detect your Bluetooth phone. Click Use Selected Device, then select the Proximity Details tab. Use the sliders to choose how far away you must be from your PC before the screensaver kicks in (go for three metres or thereabouts), and how near you need be to turn it off. Walk away with your phone to test it.

■ BlueProximity allows your Bluetooth phone to lock your screen automatically when you move away from it

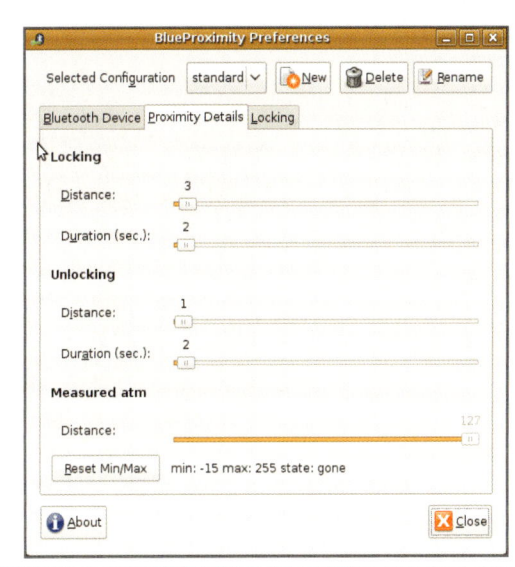

CHAPTER 2

Installing software

Although Ubuntu is packed with programs, you can easily add more. Here we'll show you how to bring your system to life

Everyone knows how to install software in Windows: just double-click the setup program and answer a few questions. If that sounds simple, you'll be amazed to discover that adding programs to a Linux system is even easier.

In many cases, you won't even need to download the software yourself, because Linux's software-management system knows where to download it from. In other words, Linux does the hard work for you.

One of Linux's major advantages is that it grants you easy access to a huge library of free applications, ranging from astronomy tools to virtualisation programs that let you run Windows or other operating systems inside Linux. These programs are pre-built and ready to install. Here we'll show you how to do this, and also explain how to keep your system up to date and upgrade your version of Ubuntu without losing any data.

DECISION TIME

Click Software Centre at the bottom of the desktop's Applications pull-down menu. This allows you to browse a large archive of software. Across the top of the interface, you'll see the View pull-down menu, which enables you to filter the programs lists. Select 'All applications' (some of which are closed source) to show everything, or choose to see Canonical Maintained Applications to see programs certified for Ubuntu.

You can also search the names and descriptions of applications for keywords. This means you can find a program that does a particular job even if you don't know its actual name. In fact, you can sometimes generate a long list of programs that deal with a certain subject. For example, entering 'graphics' and hitting Enter brings up a long list in the right-hand pane. You can sort the list by clicking on the column headers.

Sometimes you know the type of application you're looking for in broad terms. Look in the left-hand pane and you'll see several categories. When you click on one, the right-hand pane will fill with the software available in that category. If you click on the first ('All'), you'll see a full list of all available applications.

To install an application, simply click the tickbox to the left of its name. If the software is closed source, a pop up will ask you to confirm that you want to install it. When you install software in Ubuntu, you can click on as many applications as you like. When you click the Apply Changes button at the bottom right, you'll be asked to confirm the list of programs and to

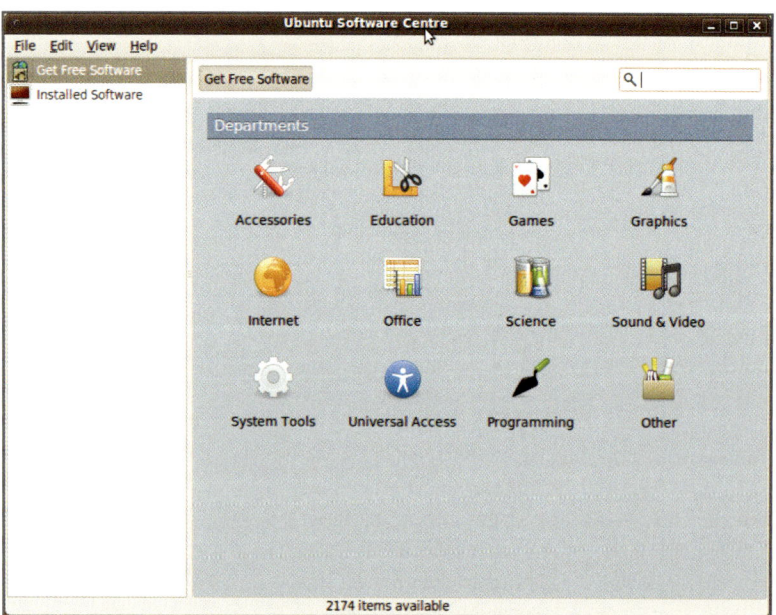

■ Installing software into Ubuntu has never been easier – all you need to do is point at the application and click

INSTALLING UBUNTU

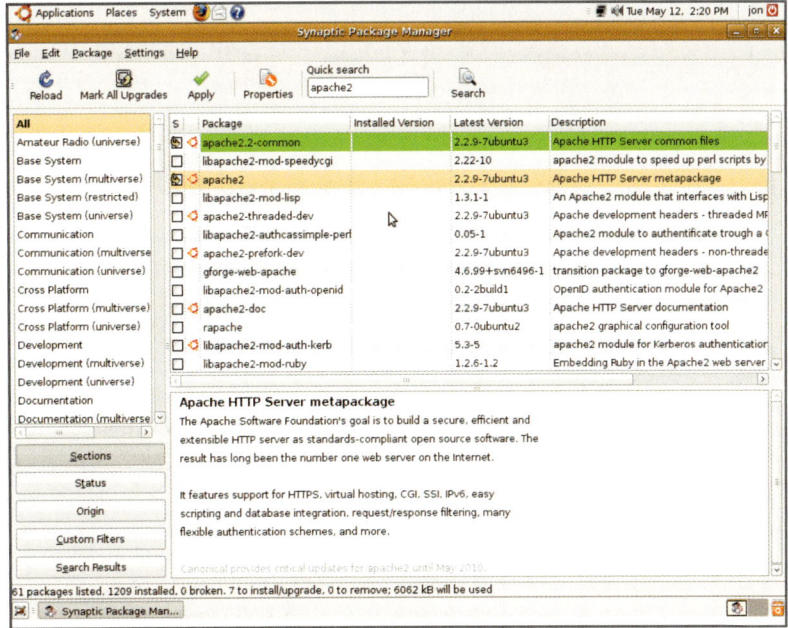

■ Synoptic Package Manager provides access to a wealth of other software, but it's still easy to use

enter the system password, which is the one you use to log in. The applications are then added to the system one after the other.

PACKAGE HANDLING

The list of applications available may seem extensive to some people and restricting to others. If you're in the latter group, don't despair. There's a galaxy of software available with the Synoptic Package Manager. This is the main choice for experienced Ubuntu users, because it gives access to individual packages. It also provides direct access to server software for advanced Linux users. The package manager software does a lot of work in the background to ensure that everything installs properly.

You can find The Synoptic Package Manager by clicking on the launch bar's System button and selecting Administration. The Package Manager is near the bottom of the resulting menu. Run it and click the Reload button. This contacts Ubuntu's website and re-reads the list of available packages. The number of categories that appear in the left-hand panel are larger than those listed by the Add/Remove applications utility. However, using Synoptic Package Manager is just as simple. To demonstrate it in action, we're going to show you how to install the Apache 2 web server, after which we'll show you how to uninstall it.

First, select All in the left-hand categories pane, type 'apache2' into the search box and press Enter. The full list of Apache 2 packages will appear in the main pane. Tick the box next to the 'apache2' entry. This 'metapackage' brings together all the packages upon which the main application will rely. If any other packages are required, a dialog box will appear asking you to confirm that they should also be installed.

The tickboxes on all the packages to be installed change to show an arrow wrapped around them. To begin installing Apache 2, click the Apply button. A dialog box will ask you to confirm the actions to be taken. Click the Apply button again and Synoptic Package Manager will begin downloading the latest versions of all the packages and install them. This should take around a minute or so. If you now point your web browser at **http://localhost**, you should see a web page served from the newly installed Apache 2 web server exclaiming, "It Works!"

MOVING ON UP

Once you've installed a package, the Synoptic Package Manager will be able to help you when it's time to remove or upgrade it. The tickboxes next to the installed packages should be green, indicating that they're installed properly. If you click one, a context menu will give you the option of re-installing it (which is useful if you

CHAPTER 2

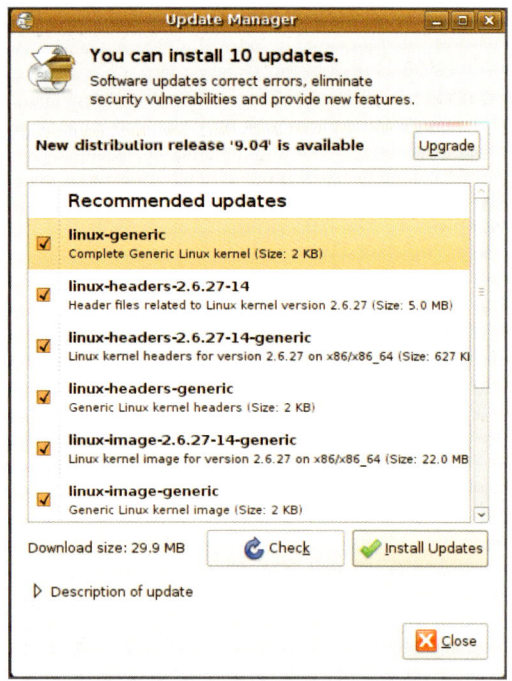

■ The Update Manager allows you to apply patches to Ubuntu quickly and easily

make a mess of things while configuring it) or uninstalling the package completely.

You can also upgrade packages. When an upgrade becomes available for one of your packages or applications, open the Synoptic Package Manager and hit the reload button. Find the package you want to upgrade and click its tickbox. Click the upgrade option and hit the Apply button, just as you did when installing it.

The procedure for removing a package is much the same as for installing it. In Synoptic Package Manager, simply select the package you want to remove from the system by clicking on its tickbox. Hit the Apply button and a dialog box pops up asking you to confirm your actions. Choose Apply on this box and the package will be removed from the system.

UPDATING UBUNTU

From time to time, Ubuntu publishes updates that fix bugs, improve functionality and fill security holes in the operating system and its installed packages. When this happens, you'll see a red arrow or orange star on the launch bar at the top of the Gnome desktop. Click this and Ubuntu's Update Manager will open. This lists all the available updates. Click the Apply button and enter your system password. The Update Manager will download the relevant updates for your system, which can take a few minutes. Occasionally, you'll need to reboot the system after updating certain packages – notably, those to do with the Linux kernel.

You have several options for upgrading to a new version of Ubuntu. You can download a disc image (ISO) from a peer-to-peer service or from Ubuntu's own website, and then burn the ISO file to a DVD and boot this to begin the installation process. However, you can also upgrade Ubuntu from within the Gnome desktop itself, thereby saving you time and the cost of a DVD.

Before deciding to upgrade, make sure your favourite third-party applications will work with the new version of Ubuntu. If not, you could be left waiting until someone builds them for the new version. Check the software maintainer's download page for the latest version.

When a new version of Ubuntu is released and you're ready to upgrade, run the Update Manager. Its icon is near the bottom of the Administration menu, found using the launch bar's System menu. You may recognise the Update Manager as being the same window that pops up when you opt to apply system updates.

At the top of the Update Manager, you'll see a message announcing that a new version of Ubuntu is available. Click the Upgrade button and a window will open, displaying release notes that explain the features of the new distribution. Click the Upgrade button on this window and Ubuntu will download its upgrade tool and work out which packages to install.

After completing this process, you'll be told how much data will be downloaded; when we tried this, we had to download about 559MB to

■ Upgrading Ubuntu is a pain-free process, but it take about an hour to complete

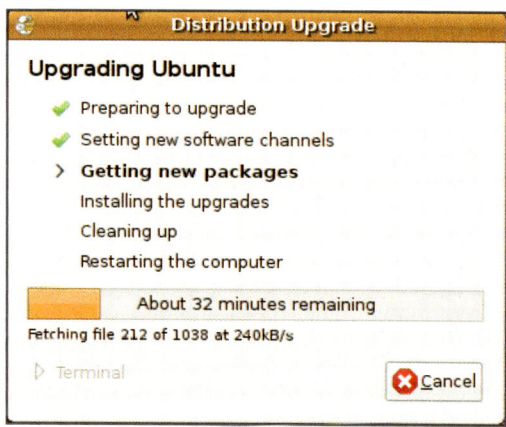

INSTALLING UBUNTU

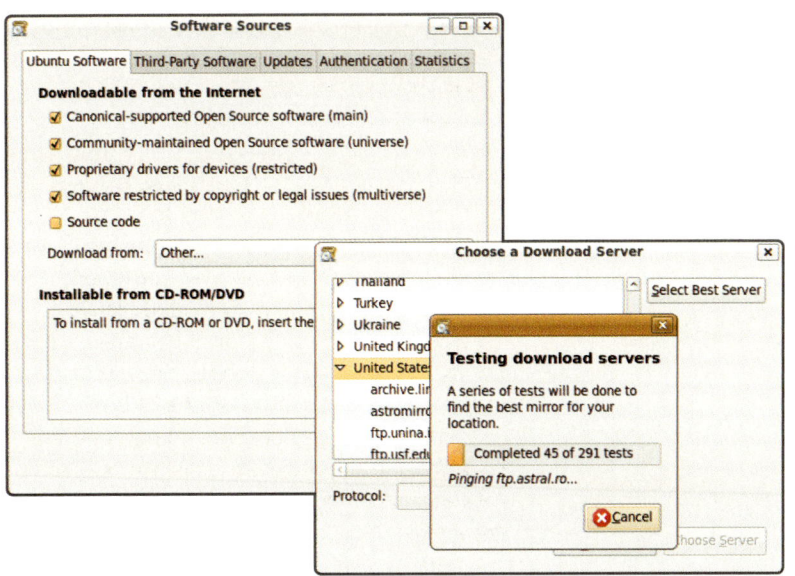

■ You can exert some control over the system update and package installation process, such as finding the fastest download server

upgrade from version 8.10 to 9.04. You'll also be told how many packages will be installed and how long it will take to download everything given the speed of your broadband connection. When you're ready, close all other applications and click Start Upgrade.

A progress bar will keep you informed of the amount of time left and how many packages have been downloaded. Once downloaded, the upgrade tool performs all the tasks required to install the new packages and to reconfigure the system so that they work properly. There's nothing to do now but wait until the process completes, which can take up to an hour.

After the installation process is complete, the upgrade tool will ask if you want to delete all obsolete packages from the system. Select Remove to free up some disk space.

BEST OF THE REST

Finally, you can take some control over system updates and package installation. From the Administration menu on the launch bar's System menu, select Software Sources. This brings up a box with several tabs. The first is for installing Ubuntu software.

On this tab, click the Download from pull-down menu and select Other.... This brings up a dialog box that enables you to select a new download server. However, you can have Ubuntu find the fastest server automatically by pressing the Select Best Server button. Ubuntu contacts each update server in turn and selects the one with the best response time. When it's finished, press Choose Server to finish the procedure.

You can also define when to check for updates using the Updates tab. Use the pull-down menu in the Automatic Updates section of the tab to decide how frequently to check for updates. It's usually fine to leave it on every day.

Pack it in Installing Debian packages

It used to be a nightmare to install packages in Linux, but that's all changed thanks to a raft of excellent graphical desktop tools. Ubuntu is based on the Debian distribution of Linux, so it can easily install any .deb packages you download from the internet. By default, this process is handled automatically by the GDebi package manager.

Take Sun's free VirtualBox virtualisation software (**www.virtualbox.org/wiki/Downloads**). There are different versions available, and the one you need depends on the processor in your PC and the version of Linux you're running. There are versions for five different kinds of Ubuntu, in fact.

If you visit the VirtualBox website and try to download it, Firefox will ask which package manager to use to open the file. It will default

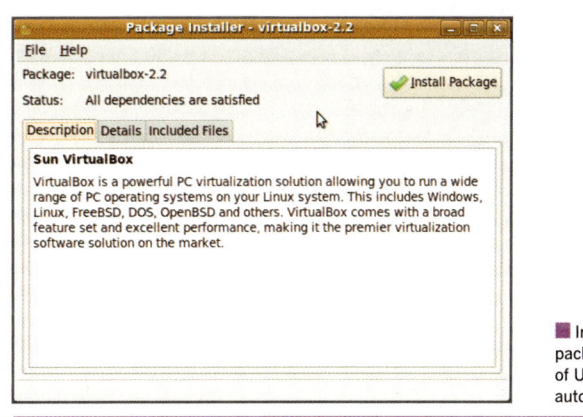

■ Installing Debian packages for your version of Ubuntu is handled automatically by GDebi

to using GDebi. Once the file is downloaded, GDebi will run. Hit Install Package and enter your system password, and the installation process begins. Who said installing software in Linux was difficult?

CHAPTER 3

Getting to know Linux

If you've been following the previous chapters and have already installed Ubuntu, you should have a fully working computer and be familiar with the desktop. In this chapter, we'll dig a little deeper into the operating system and show you how to use the desktop, copy files and customise the look and feel to suit your own tastes.

You'll also learn how to transfer files to Ubuntu from your old computer, both over a network and by using removable storage devices such as memory cards and USB flash drives.

Finally, we'll show you how to create new user accounts so that several people can share one computer, and explain how to change your logon options, allowing you to choose whether to enter a password or not.

Getting started	28
Transferring files to your new computer	32
Configuring Ubuntu	36
Installing a dock	38
Creating user accounts	39

CHAPTER 3

Getting started

Allow us to guide you through your first steps with this powerful, free operating system

Now that you've installed Ubuntu Linux, the next step is to explore the interface and find out how to perform tasks that were second nature to you in Windows. Here, we'll give you a whistle-stop tour of the default Gnome desktop, which is what you'll be looking at if you installed Ubuntu using the default options. We'll explain how to perform common tasks as easily as you did in Windows, if not more so.

Using a new operating system can be a scary business. To start with, you don't know where anything is, so even just running a simple program can be tricky. Tasks such as customising the look and feel of the interface, searching for files or writing data to a DVD may seem distant goals. Over the next few pages, we'll show you how to get started with Ubuntu Linux. Within minutes, you'll be doing the same things you were doing in Windows, and hopefully finding that life's even smoother.

Many of the options you'll need are available via the launch bar, which is similar to Windows' taskbar. This is a narrow area that runs across the top of the screen. It displays a number of clickable icons and text links. The left-most option is the Ubuntu logo along with a text label that reads Applications. This is the equivalent of the Windows Start menu. If you click it, a drop-down menu appears showing a list of programs you can run. Click on the System menu, which appears further to the right of the launch bar, and you'll see the sort of options you find in Windows' Control Panel.

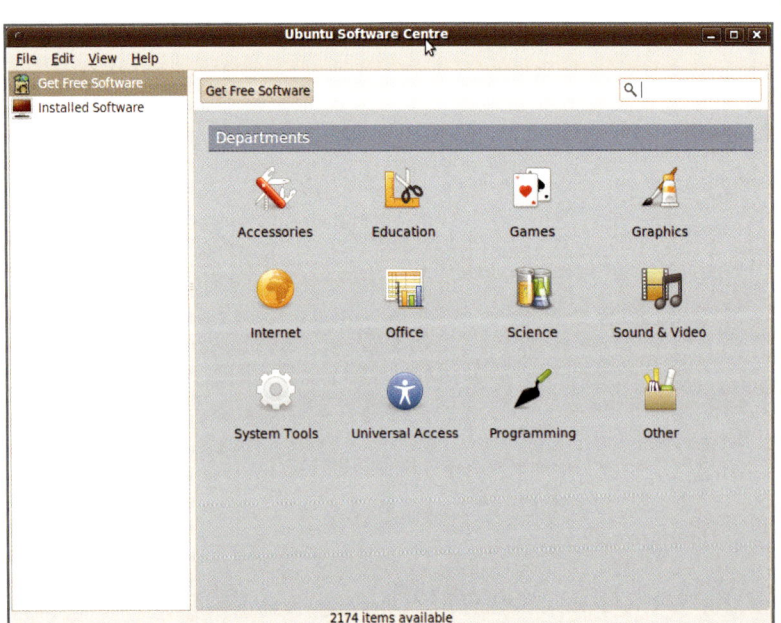

■ There's a wealth of free, well-supported open-source software for you to install, and it's easy to do so

INSTALLING AND RUNNING APPLICATIONS

Click Applications on the launch bar to access the programs that were installed when you first set up Linux. These will be listed in a number of different categories. Move the mouse over a category to open it, and left-click on an application once and it will run.

To add a new application, click Software Centre on the Applications menu. A three-paned window appears. In the left-hand pane, you'll see the categories available. Select one, and a list of applications appears in the main pane. Pick one, and its description appears in the lower pane. You can select one or more programs to install by clicking the tickboxes. Then press Apply Changes. After you've been given a final chance to change your mind, you'll be asked to enter your password. Ubuntu will download the latest relevant packages and install them. Your new programs will now be available from the Applications menu.

GETTING TO KNOW LINUX

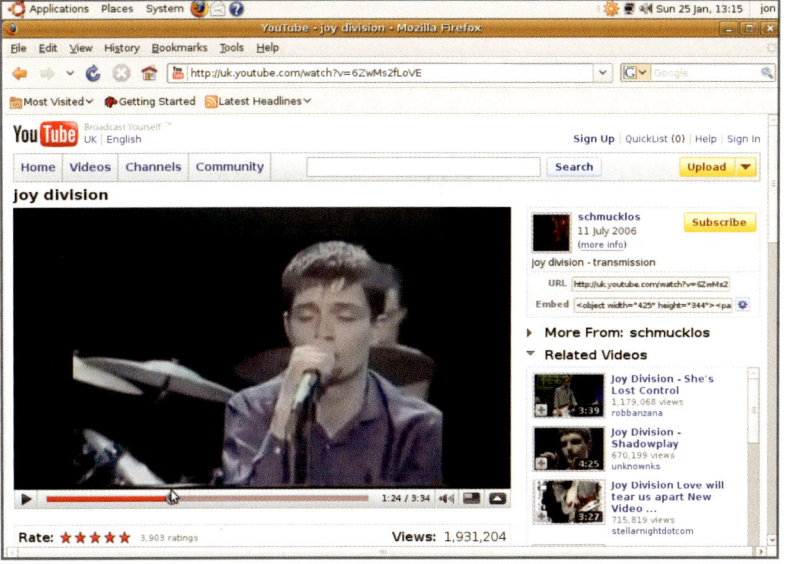

■ Many popular sites such as YouTube rely on Adobe's Flash Player to work properly

INSTALLING FLASH PLAYER
To view YouTube videos and get the most out of many other sites, you need Adobe Flash Player. If you visit YouTube using your web browser, you'll see a link to Adobe's site. Follow this and select .deb for Ubuntu 8.04+ as the software type. Then click Agree and Install Now. In the pop-up, click OK. This opens the file using the package installer. Press Install Package. After a short wait, you'll be able to view video footage on YouTube.

CHANGING SCREEN RESOLUTION
Changing the screen resolution is simple. On the System menu, select Preferences. Near the bottom of the menu, you'll see the Screen Resolution option. When you select this, a window will open displaying a pull-down menu of resolutions and monitor frequencies that your hardware supports. Simply select one and press Apply, and the resolution will change.

A slight glitch affects certain machines when changing from a lower resolution to a higher one. It may seem to have no effect, but logging out and back in again automatically picks up the correct resolution. In other cases, you may be unable to use a resolution higher than 800x600. If you see a small green icon at the top-right, hover over it. If you see a 'Restricted drivers available' message, click it and choose the recommended graphics driver. Click the Activate button and the driver will be installed, thereby enabling higher display resolutions.

CUSTOMISING THE DESKTOP
To change the desktop wallpaper, right-click on the desktop and select Change Desktop Background. A window will pop up showing a

---

Changing your passwords Tough to crack, easy to remember

It's important to use secure passwords and change them regularly. This is especially true if you use Ubuntu on a laptop. This method will help you create easily remembered passwords that are very tough to crack.

Think of a song or poem you know well. Take the initial letter of each word in the first two lines. Turn each vowel (except 'u') into the number that physically resembles it, so A=4, E=3, I=1 and O=0. So the first two lines of All Things Bright and Beautiful gives you 4tb4b4cg4s. There's no way a hacker could guess this, and it's also easily remembered.

To change your password, select About Me from the Preferences menu. Press Change Password, enter the current password and press Authenticate. Enter and re-enter your new password and press Close.

■ Make sure you change your password regularly

THE COMPLETE LINUX MANUAL 29

CHAPTER 3

selection of pictures. Press the Add button to bring up a file selector that gives you the chance to add your own pictures to the list. Select one from your collection and press OK, and it will become your new wallpaper.

You can open this window another way if you prefer. Click on the System menu and choose Preferences and Appearance. You'll see a number of tabs. Click the Theme tab, and you'll be able to change the overall theme Gnome uses, just as you can in Windows. By selecting a theme and pressing the Customise button, you can change the shape of the borders, colours and so on. If you click on the Fonts tab, you can set up the look and feel of these, too.

You can also install downloaded themes. The Gnome website has a theme area (http://art.gnome.org/themes) that contains an ever-growing list of free themes. Select a category, browse until you find one you like and then click the download link. Save the file (it's saved to the desktop by default) and press Install Theme. In the subsequent file selector, navigate to the desktop (stored in your home folder) and select the theme file, and it should install.

CUSTOMISING THE TASKBAR
You can customise the Gnome launch bar in more ways than you can the Windows taskbar.

Right-click it and select Properties. You can set its height in pixels and whether it appears as a centralised bar or stretches the width of the screen, as well as if it should be hidden automatically. You can also choose to display manual hide and show buttons (which is useful if you don't use the auto-hide feature). Click the Background tab and you can set the launch bar's transparency.

You can also add gadgets and applications to the launch bar. Right-click it and select Add to Panel. Choose from the list of available options. For example, you can add the Network Monitor to see your IP address and the amount of network traffic processed. Select Application Launcher... and click the Forward button. Choose a category, click the triangle button to expand the list and select a program. Press Add. Finally, you can move gadgets and applications around the launch bar by right-clicking and pressing Move, or delete them by choosing Remove.

USING THE HOME FOLDER
Click the Places menu on the launch bar. The first few entries are standard folders set up during installation. These are in your Home Folder, the equivalent of My Documents in Windows. Left-click once on your Home Folder to open the file browser window.

As in Windows, right-clicking allows you to create a new folder, rename it and delete it. You can also increase and decrease the size of the icons. Furthermore, Gnome remembers the various zoom levels that you set for different folders. Across the top of the folder window, you'll see several icons that represent steps in the path from your home folder down to the current subfolder. This enables you to navigate and move files quickly. Simply drag and drop the file on to one of these icons. To delete a file, right-click it and select 'Move to the Deleted Items folder'. You can find this on the right end of the launch bar. If you click it, you can get rid of all deleted files, delete individual items and restore them, just as you can in Windows.

FINDING THINGS
To find a file or folder, click Places and select 'Search for files'. Enter a snippet of the filename into the field called 'Name contains'. There are more options available if you click on the triangle next to 'Select more options'.

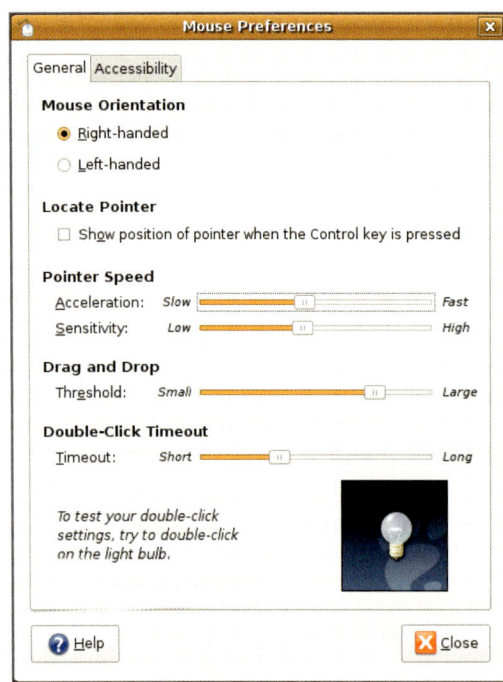
■ Get your mouse responding the way you like and your Ubuntu experience will be more positive

GETTING TO KNOW LINUX

You can add extra search criteria, such as the number of days since modification, the owner or the file size. You can also search the content of files. Use the Available Options list to select a criterion and press Add. The list builds as you add and remove options. Press Find, and a list of files matching your requirements should appear. Right-click on a result to open it, open its location or delete it.

EXPLORING THE NETWORK NEIGHBOURHOOD
Ubuntu has excellent support for Windows shared folders. Make sure you have at least one folder shared on a Windows PC on your network. Click Places and select Network. The window that appears will show an icon called Windows Network. Double-click this to see its contents; you should see the Windows workgroup. Double-click this to display a list of PCs with shared folders. If you double-click one, you'll see the shared folders themselves. Click on one of these and you'll see the shared files.

MAKING MOUSE ADJUSTMENTS
If you're used to slow mouse movements in Windows, the speed at which Ubuntu initially moves the pointer may be too fast. You can easily slow it down. Click on the System menu in the launch bar and select Preferences. Then click on the Mouse category. In the subsequent window, pull the acceleration slider to the left and test the mouse until it moves the way you'd like. Finally, click the Close button.

CHANGING BETWEEN DESKTOPS
Ubuntu supports multiple desktops called workspaces. These let you switch between virtual monitors, which is an excellent way to jump between lots of programs. On the second launch bar at the bottom right of the screen, you'll see two small boxes: one brown and one grey. These represent the default two workspaces.

Right-click on them and select Preferences. You can then select the number of workspaces you want, rename them (by double-clicking on a name in the list) and stack them rather than displaying them in a line. If you select 'Show workspace names in switcher', the names will appear on the toolbar; by default, you use Desk 1. If you click Desk 2, Gnome displays a second view of your desktop.

You can switch quickly between workspaces by holding down Ctrl-Alt while pressing the left or right cursor key. The icon at the top left of all windows gives you the same options as in Windows (Restore, Minimize and so on), but also allows you to move the window between workspaces, as well as allowing you to display it in front of all other windows each time.

■ Gnome supports multiple desktops, which is very useful for organising your work

WRITING FILES TO DVD
Trying to save files to optical media in Windows can be a deeply frustrating experience. In Ubuntu, it's easy. Simply insert a blank DVD or CD and wait for the system to open a window asking which application you'd like to use. Leave the selection on Open CD/DVD Creator and press OK. Drag and drop the files you want to save into the subsequent file browser window. Then enter a name for the disc and press Write. That's all there is to it.

KEEPING UP TO DATE
Each time you log in, the system contacts Ubuntu's servers for updates to its installed packages. If there are any, it displays a small speech bubble on the launch bar that you click to start the update. Press Install Updates on the pop-up window and enter your password. Ubuntu asks for your password this way whenever you're about to change the system. Enter it, and the system downloads and installs the updated packages. You may be asked to reboot.

CHAPTER 3

Transferring files to your new computer

Now your new Ubuntu computer is up and running, you'll want to transfer your documents and media to it. Here's how

Hopefully, your computer is now set up just the way you want it, and hopefully you can already tell that Linux feels considerably quicker than Windows. It should shut down faster, and boot up in just a few seconds.

However, you probably have lots of files from your old Windows PC that you want to transfer to your new one, such as documents, music, photos and videos. Alternatively, you may need to copy files from an external hard disk or USB flash drive that you've backed up files to. If your computer has a memory card reader, you'll also want to be able to transfer files from the card to your hard disk. Over the next few pages, we'll show you how it's done.

CONNECTING OVER A NETWORK

In most cases, your Ubuntu computer will be connected to your home network by a network

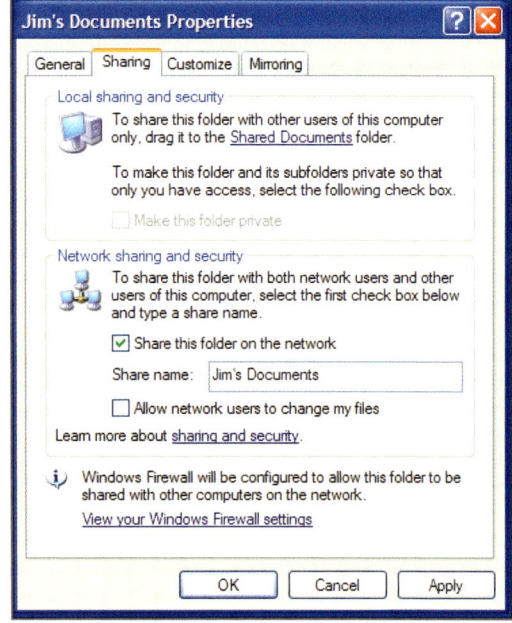

■ You need to share folders in Windows before they'll be visible on the network

■ Your WiFi network should provide the correct connection settings, but you can alter these easily

cable or WiFi. Somewhere on your network is likely to be a broadband router that allows you to share internet access between all the computers on the network. This router will also allow PCs to share files with each other, and this is one way to transfer files to your Ubuntu computer.

Before you can do this, you have to share the folders that contain the files you want to transfer on the other computers on your network, otherwise Ubuntu won't be able to access the files. In Windows XP, use Windows Explorer to navigate to the folder you want to share, but don't open the folder itself. For most people, it

GETTING TO KNOW LINUX

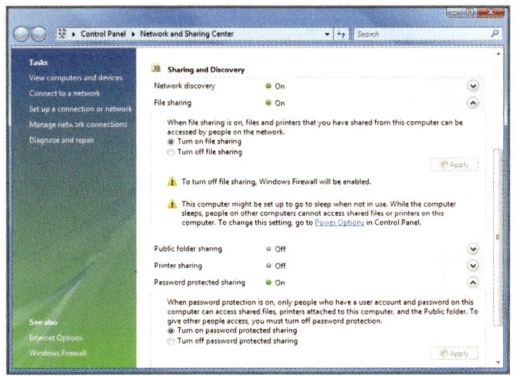

■ Vista's folder-sharing options are a little different to Windows XP's, but it's still simple to share files on the network

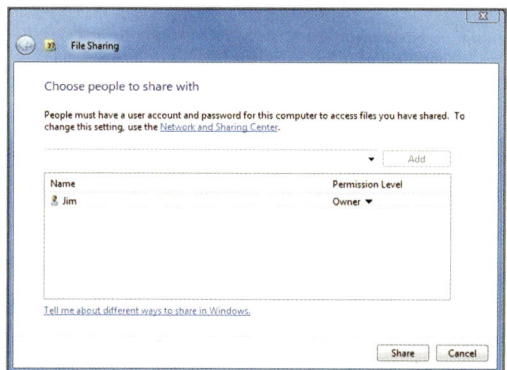

■ In Vista, you need to enable several options in the Networking and Sharing Center before folders can be shared

makes sense to share the My Documents folder. Right-click on the folder and click Sharing and Security. If you want to share a whole hard disk, you'll need to tick the box next to the warning that says "If you understand the risk but still want to share the root of the drive, click here".

On the Sharing tab, which should be visible, tick the box next to Share this folder on the network. You can change the name of the folder so you can easily identify it on your Ubuntu computer. For example, you might change 'My Documents' to 'Jim's Documents' if you need to share the My Documents folders for multiple users on the PC. Click OK, and Windows will apply the changes. This could take several minutes if you have a lot of files within the folder.

HASTA LA VISTA

For computers running Windows 7 and Vista, go to the Control Panel and click on the Networking and Sharing Center. Under the Sharing and Discovery heading (in Windows 7, click Change advanced sharing settings), click the downward-pointing arrow next to both Network discovery and File sharing. Set both so they are turned on. If password-protected sharing is enabled, you'll need to know the user account name and password of the Vista account in order to access files over the network.

Next, as in Windows XP, head to the folder you want to share. Right-click on it, choose Share... and a window will open asking who you want to share the folder with. Simply click the Share button at the bottom, and you'll see a progress bar until all the files are shared.

If you want to share your Windows 7 or Vista user folder, you'll have to browse to it through Windows Explorer, as clicking on it from

the Start menu will open it and show all the folders within it. From the Start menu, click on Computer, then the hard disk on which Windows is installed (usually drive C:).. Click on the Users folder and you should see a folder with the name of the user account you want to share. Now you can right-click on it and share it as normal.

Head back to your Ubuntu computer and click Network on the Places menu. You should see a Windows Network icon. Double-click on it and you'll see icons for each PC on the network. Double-click on the one you want, and you may see a password window open. Enter the correct username and password for the account in which the shared folder is, and check the Remember forever option before clicking Connect.

If you find that this doesn't work, and you get a message saying, "Unable to mount location", there may be a firewall on the

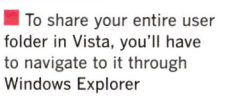

■ To share your entire user folder in Vista, you'll have to navigate to it through Windows Explorer

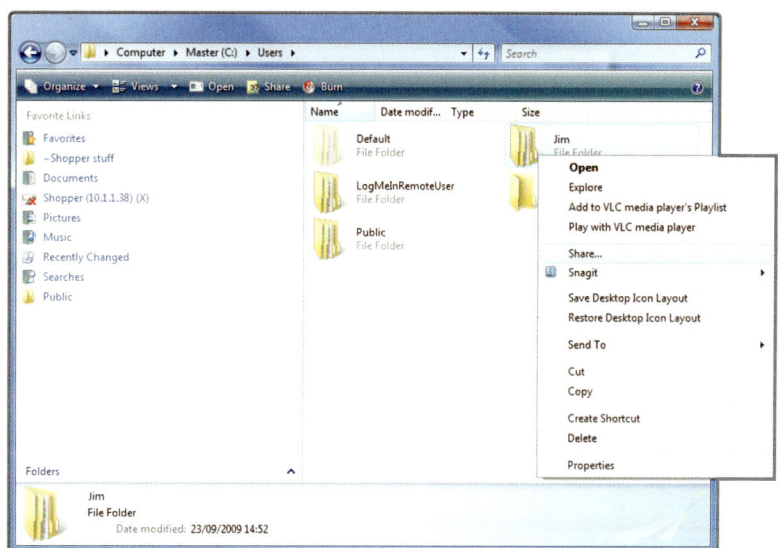

THE COMPLETE LINUX MANUAL 33

CHAPTER 3

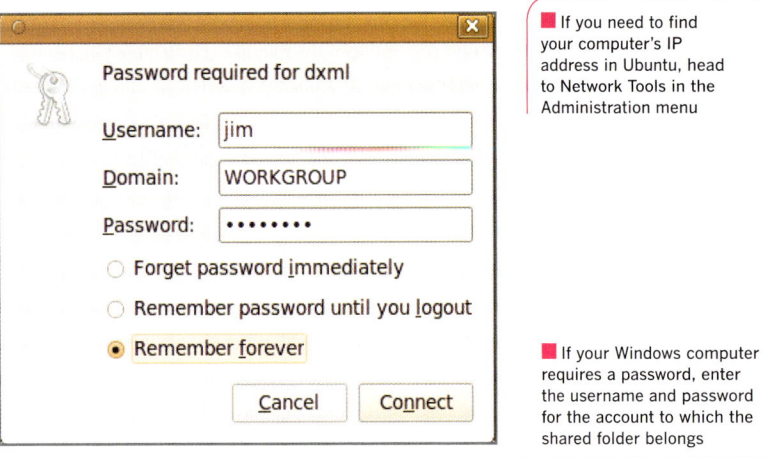

If you need to find your computer's IP address in Ubuntu, head to Network Tools in the Administration menu

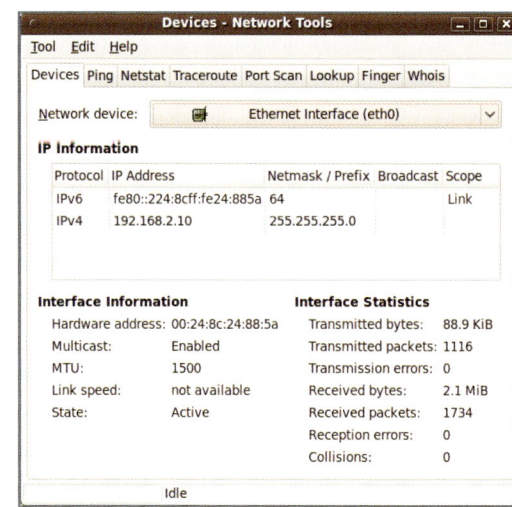

If your Windows computer requires a password, enter the username and password for the account to which the shared folder belongs

Windows PC blocking access. This commonly happens if you've installed a third-party firewall such as ZoneAlarm, which blocks incoming connections from computers on the local network by default. You'll either need to disable the firewall temporarily or add your Ubuntu computer to the list of 'trusted' IP addresses.

You can find the IP address by clicking on the System menu, then Administration, then Network tools. Select the correct network adaptor from the drop-down box next to Network device. If you're connected by WiFi, this will usually be wlan0, but if you're using a network cable, it will usually be eth0. Next to the IPv4 protocol, you'll see your computer's IP address, which you'll need to enter into your firewall software. Now, you should be able to connect to the Windows computer without any problems.

VIEWING SHARED FOLDERS

When you've successfully managed to connect to the remote folder over the network, you should see all the files, just as you would if you were sitting at the Windows computer. Ubuntu has three views: Icon, List and Compact. You can switch between these using the drop-down menu near the top-right corner of the File Browser window. You can select the files you want to copy in a number of ways:

1 Click and drag your mouse to select a block of files. Don't click on a file, though, as this will simply move it around in the window. Instead, click on an area of white space and make your selection cover the block of files you want.

2 If you want to select all the files in a folder, click Edit, then Select All. You'll notice that, just as in Windows, keyboard short cuts are shown on the right-hand side of the menu. For Select All, the shortcut is Ctrl-A, which means that instead of clicking on the Edit menu and clicking Select All, you simply press and hold the Ctrl key and tap the A key.

3 To select some files but not others, hold down the Ctrl key and click on each file that you want to select. Alternatively, if the files you want are in a block, click on the first file, then hold down the Shift key and click on the last file you want. Only the files between the first file clicked and

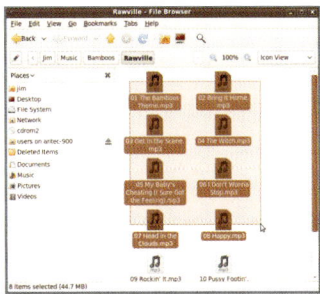
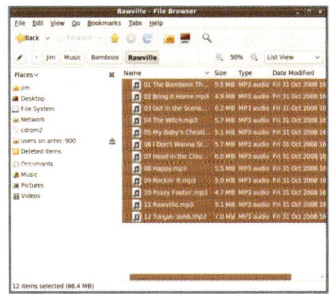
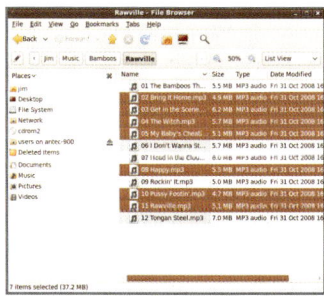

There are several ways to select the files you want: making a selection with your mouse, selecting everything, or selecting just some files

GETTING TO KNOW LINUX

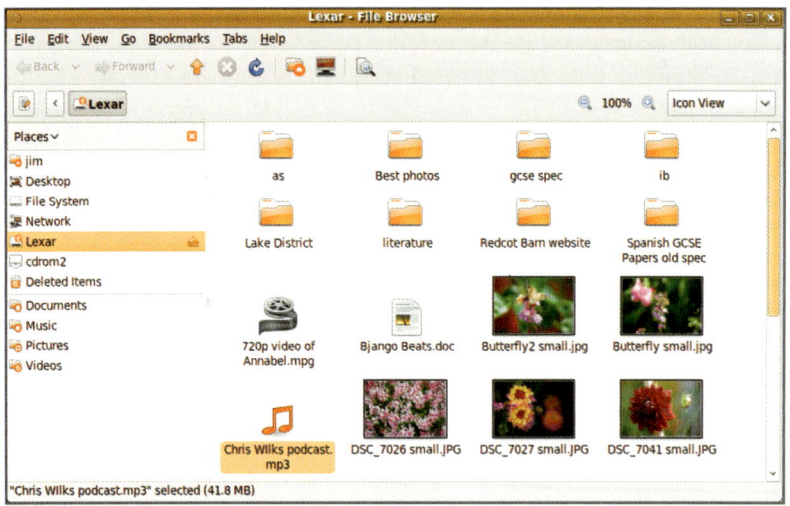

■ When you plug in a USB storage device, its contents should automatically appear in a File Browser window, and a short cut icon will appear on the desktop

last file clicked will be selected. You can use a mixture of the Shift and Ctrl keys to select several blocks of files.

When you've selected the files you want, either press Ctrl-C to copy them or choose Copy from the Edit menu. Navigate to the folder on your Ubuntu computer to which you want to transfer the files (you can open a new File Browser window; just head to the Places menu and choose one of the folders there). Then choose Paste from the Edit menu or press Ctrl+V if you prefer to use keyboard shortcuts.

If you want to move the files rather than copy them, choose Cut from the Edit menu when you've selected them. However, this will work only if you ticked the 'Allow network users to change my files' box when sharing folders in Windows XP. This shouldn't be a problem with shared folders on Windows Vista computers, as the default permission level is 'Owner'.

WHAT A DRAG
Another way to transfer files, which may be the easiest way for some people, is to have two File Browser windows open on your desktop. One window will show the files stored on the remote computer, while the other will show the folder on your local hard disk that you want to copy the files to. To resize the File Browser windows so they sit neatly side by side, simply hover your mouse over the bottom-right corner of each window until the cursor changes, then click and drag until the window is the right size; it's exactly the same process as in Windows.

Now you can simply select the files you want from the remote computer using one of the methods we've already described, then click and hold on one of them and drag it to the right-hand pane in the other File Browser. The mouse pointer will turn into a hand, and you'll see outlines of the other files being taken with it.

Look out for the extra icon that appears to the bottom-right of the hand before you let go to drop the files. If it's an arrow pointing to the hand, the files will be moved rather than copied. If you want to make copies of the files and leave the originals in place, hold down the Ctrl key before you let go of the mouse button.

EXTERNAL DRIVES
The process of transferring files from a USB hard disk, flash drive or memory card is almost identical to the process we've just described for networks. The only difference is that when you plug one of these storage devices into your computer, a File Browser should automatically appear showing the contents of the drive. A neat feature of Ubuntu is that a shortcut to the drive will appear on the desktop so you can quickly access the drive while it remains connected.

You can now select files and copy them to your hard disk using the same methods as for transferring files over the network. Before unplugging USB flash drives, hard disks or memory cards, it's a good idea to hit the eject icon, which appears to the right of the drive in the Places pane of the File Browser window. This helps to prevent files from becoming corrupted.

■ Ubuntu will recognise a USB drive or memory card, just like Windows

CHAPTER 3

Configuring Ubuntu

Everyone likes to customise their PC to their liking. Here we'll show you how to tweak Ubuntu's themes and enable its special effects

In the same way that you can set Windows' wallpaper to an image of your choice, you can do the same in Ubuntu. You can also change the theme so that the colour scheme, icons and windows are personalised to your taste.

1 To see Ubuntu's default themes, go to the System menu at the top of the screen, click Preferences, then Appearance. You'll find there are 11 themes to choose from, and that Human is already selected. Click on any theme and it will be applied immediately so you can see how it affects not only the window you have open, but the whole desktop, including the top and bottom bars. Some are more subtle than others. Clearlooks, for example, makes very minor changes to the icons and switches the default orange/brown colour to a light blue. However, click High Contrast Inverse and the changes are much more noticeable. If you like a particular theme, simply click the Close button and the theme will remain applied.

The default themes are a little limited, so it's worth installing some new ones. Leave the Appearance Preferences window open and head to the System menu again, but this time click Administration, then Synaptic Package Manager. Enter your password, and the Package Manager will open and update the list of packages. In the Quick Search box type 'gnome themes'. You should see the package list update and show gnome-themes-extras at the top of the list. Click on the grey square to the left of it, and then Mark for Installation in the menu that appears.

2 Click on the green Apply button near the top of the window, and you'll be asked if you want to mark additional required changes. This is simply saying that additional packages need to be installed or other packages need to be updated, so click on the Mark button. You should now see a progress bar showing three files being downloaded. Once this is complete, click OK on the box that appears.

3 You should see the new themes in the Appearance Preferences window, so click on them to find one you like. We've chosen Nuvola here. Of course, if you don't like any of them, you can install more theme packages

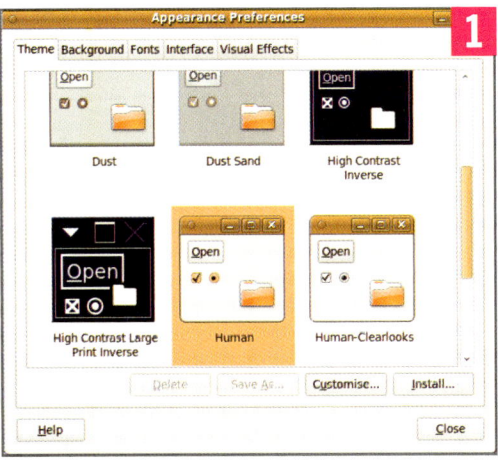

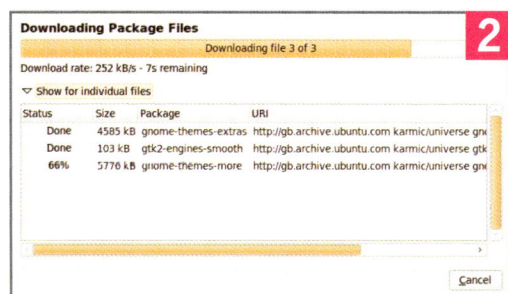

GETTING TO KNOW LINUX

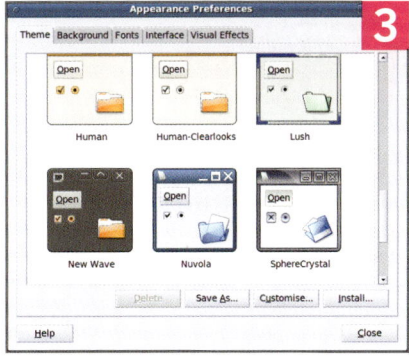
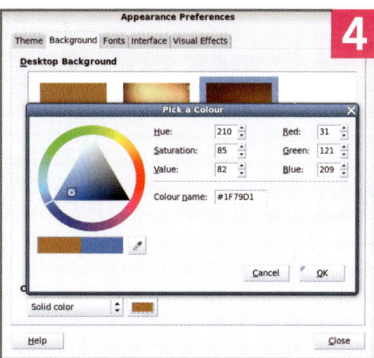
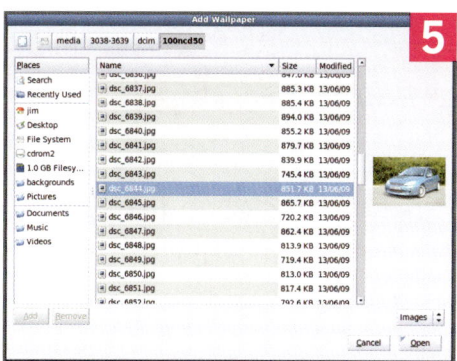

from the package installer. You can also click the Customise button at the bottom of the Appearance Preferences window and modify a theme. You can change the look of the controls, the colours, icons, window border and pointer. You can pick from the lists under each tab.

4 Even though you've now changed the theme, you still need to set a wallpaper, or background as it's called in Ubuntu. In the Appearance Preferences window, click on the Background tab and you'll see Ubuntu's default backgrounds, plus the option of no desktop background (the top-left thumbnail).

If you don't like any of the images, you can try a solid colour by clicking on the 'no background' thumbnail. You can choose the colour by clicking on the colour swatch at the bottom of the window. This opens another window with a colour wheel on it. Click on the eyedropper tool to pick a colour from somewhere on the screen – we've clicked on the title bar of the dialog box to choose its blue shade. You can click anywhere on the colour wheel or inside the triangle to pick your own colour.

5 If you'd prefer to use a photo or other image, click the Add... button and browse to where your image is stored. If you don't yet have any pictures on your computer, see page 32 to find out how to transfer all your documents from your old computer to the one running Ubuntu. Alternatively you could download a photo from the internet, or plug in a USB flash drive or memory card from your camera. Here we've chosen a photo from an SD memory card.

If you have more than one monitor, it's worth noting that Ubuntu doesn't deal with the screens separately, so the image will appear stretched across both screens. Resizing an image so it fits properly on your screen using the Gimp image-editing application (see page 48) is simple.

6 You'll see three more tabs in Appearance Preferences. Fonts allows you to change the system fonts, while Interface lets you tweak menus and toolbars, so you can decide whether to show text labels under icons, beside them or not at all, for example.

If you have a PC with a relatively modern graphics card – virtually all computers made in the past three or four years will – then you're more likely to want to skip straight to the Visual Effects tab. The default setting is Normal, but we recommend selecting the Extra setting. This turns on lots of nifty effects that you'll notice when doing mundane tasks such as dragging a window to another position or maximising a small window. It's effects like this that make Ubuntu a lot of fun to use.

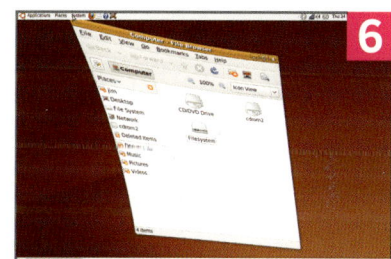

7 One final tweak you may want to make is to adjust the sensitivity of your mouse. Head to System, Preferences, Mouse. This will open a window that lets you adjust the pointer speed, double-click speed and more.

If you have a laptop with a touchpad, there's another tab with touchpad-specific options, such as disabling it when typing – this prevents the cursor jumping around the screen when you brush the touchpad while typing.

THE COMPLETE LINUX MANUAL 37

CHAPTER 3

Installing a dock

A dock is a great way to keep all your favourite programs and gadgets easily accessible. Here we show you how to install it

A dock is essentially an animated application launcher, and one of the neat features of Mac OS X. You can have one in Ubuntu too, thanks to Cairo-Dock. It comes with a number of themes, so you can choose whichever one you prefer.

Download the dock using Synaptic Package Manager, under Administration in the System menu. Use the Quick search box to look for cairo-dock. Right-click the box next to cairo-dock in the list and choose Mark for installation. Click Apply, accept the other packages that need to be downloaded and close the Package Manager.

1 You'll find two entries for Cairo-Dock under Accessories in the Applications menu. The OpenGL version needs a better graphics card, so try the 'without OpenGL' program if you have graphical glitches. The default dock is quite basic, but has a nice fire effect when you move your cursor over the icons. However, it sits awkwardly over the bottom taskbar.

2 Right-click anywhere on the dock and hover over Cairo-Dock, then click Manage themes in the menu that appears. Use the drop-down box to choose between the installed themes; a preview should appear after a few seconds. The Mac OS X theme is a good choice, but here we've chosen the one called Ubuntu. The two boxes below the preview let you select whether to use the theme's launchers and behaviour. Make sure that they're ticked and click Apply.

3 You might think the theme hasn't been applied, but that's because Ubuntu is a hidden dock. Hover your mouse at the top of the screen and the dock should magically appear. If you don't like it at the top, right-click and choose Configure from the Cairo-Dock menu. Click the Position icon, choose Bottom from the drop-down menu and click OK. Now when you hover your mouse at the bottom of the screen the dock will appear. Hold down Alt and you can click and drag the dock so it sits above the taskbar.

You can now click on the icons to launch applications. If you want to add extra programs – or launchers – to the dock, right-click on one in the Applications menu and click Add this launcher to desktop. Then drag the icon from the desktop to the dock. You can delete the icon from the desktop if you don't want it there.

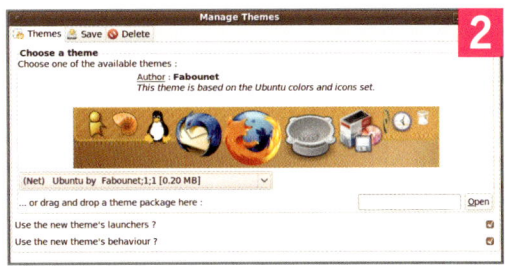

GETTING TO KNOW LINUX

Creating user accounts

Creating separate user accounts for all the people who use your computer has many benefits. Here's how to do it

If you share your PC with several family members, it makes sense to create a user account for each person. Creating separate accounts means that each user will have their own set of folders to store documents and media.

Separate accounts also allow each person to customise the theme and background to their liking. They can also put whichever shortcuts and files they like on the desktop, which can otherwise become cluttered with everyone's junk.

In Windows you can create multiple accounts when you first install it, but in Ubuntu you have to do it via the Administration menu.

1 Go to the System menu, Administration, then Users and Groups (the final entry in the list). This will open the Users Settings window, but you'll notice that the Add User button is greyed out. You won't be able to make any changes until you click on the key at the bottom of the window and enter your user password and click Authenticate.

2 The buttons for adding and deleting users are now active. Click Add User and the New user account window will open. Here you can enter a username, real name and password.

You can also set the type of account using the Profile menu. Ubuntu gives you three choices: Administrator, Unprivileged and Desktop user. You should only choose between the latter two, as Administrator accounts give more access to the operating system than is necessary for a normal user, and can be a security risk, as the user could delete crucial system files. Desktop user is the best choice in most cases, as this allows users to access external storage devices, connect to the internet, use CD or DVD drives and use the computer's audio system. Unprivileged users can do none of these things.

3 You can change the privileges manually by clicking on the User Privileges tab. This lists the various tasks that the user can or can't do, but the only items you might want to change from the default Desktop user profile is to allow a user to configure printers and share files with the local network.

You can fill in the user's address and phone numbers on the Contact Information tab, but this won't usually be necessary. Settings on the Advanced tab will be greyed out and should be ignored. Click OK to close the window and add the new account. You may have to enter your password and click Authenticate to complete the process. The new user will appear in the list, and you can repeat the process for additional users.

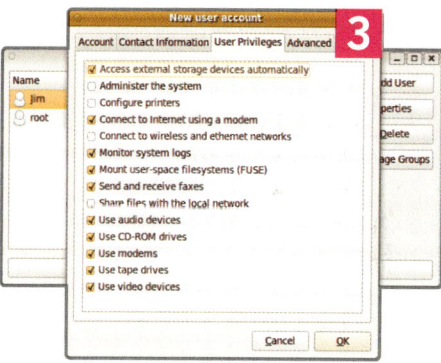

CHAPTER 4

Basic desktop tasks

Once you've installed and configured Linux, you'll want to start using it. This chapter is devoted to showing you how to do all the common tasks in Ubuntu that you can do in Windows.

Ubuntu comes with a wide range of preinstalled applications, from the excellent OpenOffice suite to the comprehensive image-editing program, Gimp. We'll show you how to use these useful tools, as well as how to achieve a host of other tasks, such as burning CDs and DVDs, watching movies and playing MP3s.

Using OpenOffice	42
Burning CDs and DVDs	44
Connecting a digital camera	46
Getting started with Gimp	48
Improving your photos using Gimp	50
Organising your photos with Picasa	52
Connecting a video camera to your PC	54
Editing video	56
Playing DVDs	58
Playing music files with Rhythmbox	60
Connecting an MP3 player	62
Connecting an iPod	64
Synchronising a mobile with Linux	66
Using Google Desktop	68

CHAPTER 4

Using OpenOffice

Ubuntu comes with a complete office suite that caters for your word processing, spreadsheet, presentation and business graphics needs

I f you've ever used an office suite such as Microsoft Office or Works, you'll be right at home with OpenOffice. In fact, you'll be hard pushed to tell the differences between Word, Excel or PowerPoint and Writer, Calc or Impress, their OpenOffice equivalents.

OpenOffice wouldn't be much use if you couldn't save documents in a format that Microsoft Office users could open. Fortunately, OpenOffice can save documents in many formats, so you can pick one that's compatible with the people you'll be sharing it with.

WRITER

Writer is almost indistinguishable from Microsoft Word and has a very similar set of features. Even the menus are organised in the same way, so you should be able to find all the commonly used function in seconds.

Since Ubuntu comes with the latest version of OpenOffice (currently 3.1), you'll always get updates when they're released. However, few people will need more features than Writer provides. In addition to the usual text-formatting controls, you can insert pictures, tables, videos, audio, headers and footers.

As you'd expect, Writer includes spelling and grammar-checkers, and you can also add notes to a document; these appear in the margin with the author's name and a date. The Format Paintbrush works just like Word's: highlight some text, click the Paintbrush icon and everything you subsequently highlight adopts the formatting of the text you originally selected.

By default, Writer's word completion is turned on. This predicts which commonly used word you're typing and automatically displays it onscreen. If you don't like it, you can easily disable it by going to Tools, AutoCorrect Options... and unticking Enable word completion on the Word Completion tab.

Another change you'll probably want to make is to prevent Writer from saving every file using the .ODT format. Head to Tools, Options... and then click on Load/Save in the left pane. This will expand to show the General tab; click on this and change the format in the Always save as box. A good choice is Word 97/2000/XP, but the latest 2007 XML format is also there.

CALC

Calc is the application to use if you need a spreadsheet, and is happy to open most Excel spreadsheets without fuss. Whether you just want to create a basic sheet to keep track of a project's costs or you need more complex

■ Writer mimics Microsoft Word so closely that you may not even realise you're not using Word

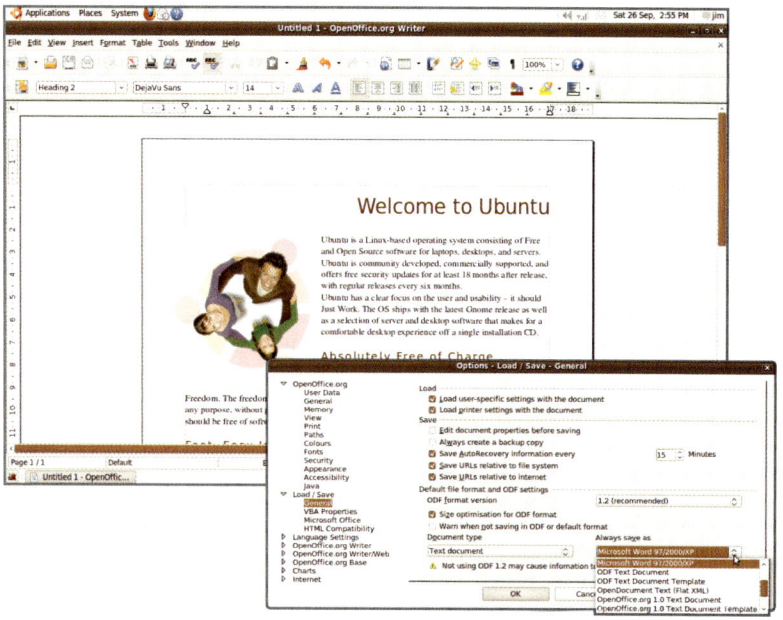

42 THE COMPLETE LINUX MANUAL

BASIC DESKTOP TASKS

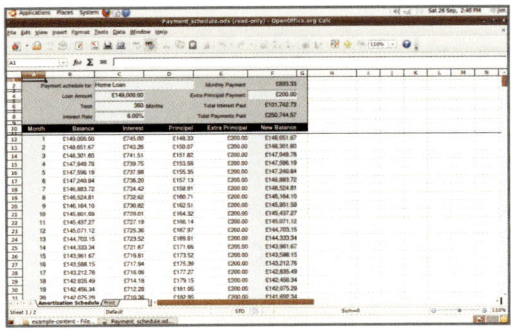

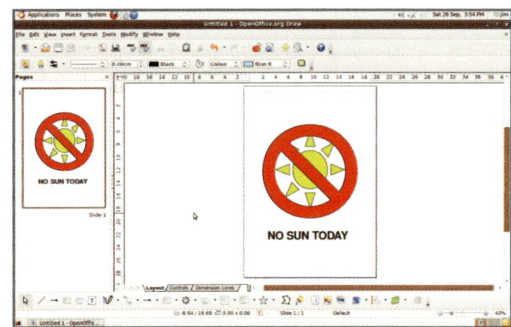

■ Not too many people will need Draw's vector drawing capabilities, but it's there if you need it

■ Calc deals with all your spreadsheet needs, whether it's a basic table of information or complex formulae that you need

formulae, Calc will be up to the job. There's a Function Wizard that helps you to build formulae, a Chart Wizard for graphs and a neat Navigator pop-out window that helps you set and return to specific areas on large sheets.

As with Writer, there's spelling and grammar-checking built in, and it's easy to alter the page settings before printing to fit a whole sheet on a single page of A4, for instance. Also common across the suite of applications is a zoom control in the bottom right-hand corner. There's also a PDF button in the toolbar at the top so you can export spreadsheets directly as PDF files, which just about every computer can read.

Calc will save in .ODS format by default, so make sure you select a format that's compatible with anyone that needs to see the spreadsheet. Microsoft .XLS formats are supported.

IMPRESS

If you need to create a presentation, Impress is just as flexible as Microsoft's PowerPoint. Built-in templates mean you can follow the wizard to choose a background you like, the transition effects between slides – there are lots to choose from – and whether you want slides to advance automatically after a preset time.

Once your basic presentation is created, there are lots of slide layouts from which to choose, and you can add text just as you would in PowerPoint, by typing directly on to the slide. You can also easily insert charts, images, movies and audio clips into slides.

Impress has several different views of each slide, one of which lets you add notes below a slide for printing it out on A4 paper. There's also a Handout tab so you can print nine slides per sheet to give to your audience.

Impress saves files in .ODP format unless you change the default settings. We recommend

■ If you're familiar with PowerPoint, Impress will be easy to use. It doesn't mirror every single feature of its rival, but still lets you create clean, attractive slides

saving in .PPT format for the best compatibility. You can also export files as PDF files.

DRAW

Draw is most similar to Microsoft's Publisher or Adobe's Illustrator graphics packages. It won't be useful for everyone, but it could come in handy if you need to create a logo or any other vector-based image.

Vector images can be resized without losing quality. When you enlarge a JPG image, for example, it can become blocky and lack detail. With a vector drawing, the quality remains the same no matter what size you scale it to.

Draw has lots of tools for drawing shapes, lines and speech bubbles, and its interface shares the same design as Writer, Calc and Impress, so it's fairly easy to find where things are. If you need to draw a chart, you're better off using Calc, but Draw can do it if you have the patience. As with the other applications, you can export files as PDFs and preview before printing.

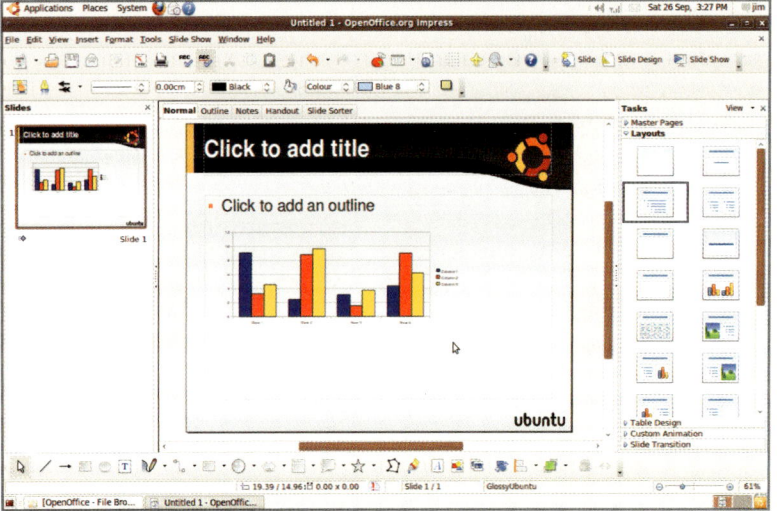

CHAPTER 4

Burning CDs and DVDs

Brasero is Ubuntu's built-in disc-burning application and it offers a range of easy-to-use options. Here's how to use it

Creating data discs and audio CDs is easy with Brasero. The friendly interface has a selection of large buttons that allow you to burn audio CDs and data discs, create video DVDs, make direct copies of CDs and DVDs and burn ISO images of a CD or DVD. It can also erase rewritable CDs and DVDs.

HOW TO... BURN AN AUDIO CD

1 Insert a blank CD-R into your CD writer and launch Brasero Disc Burner, which you'll find under Sound & Video in the Applications menu. Click the Audio project button under the Create a new project: heading.

2 Add some audio files by clicking the green + button and browsing to your music. Brasero supports any format for which you have the codecs installed. Fire it up immediately after you install Ubuntu and you'll find it won't even support MP3s. To install a codec, simply search for the formats you need in Synaptic Package Manager and mark them for installation. When this is done, choose the files you want to burn. Ctrl-A selects all files in the folder, or click on the first one you want, hold Shift and click on the last to select a block of files.

3 Click Add and the files will be added to the project. You can type a title for the CD in the box at the bottom, and double-click on each track to edit the information; useful if you have a CD player that displays text. You can split tracks using the knife icon in the toolbar, while the pause icon adds a two-second pause after a track.

4 Click the Burn button in the bottom-right corner. The only option you may want to change if you have problems burning discs is to reduce the burning speed to a setting lower than the default Maximum. Once you've clicked Burn, Brasero will make all the tracks the same volume (normalisation), write the CD text information and then burn the tracks. When the process is complete, the disc should eject and will be ready to play.

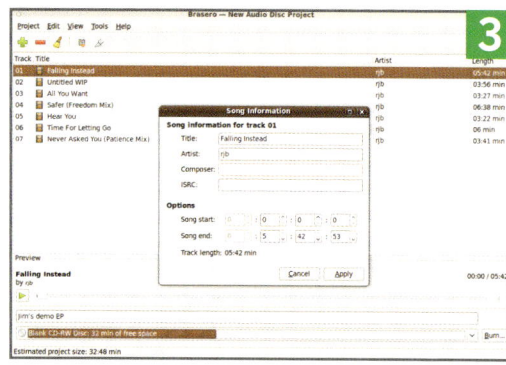

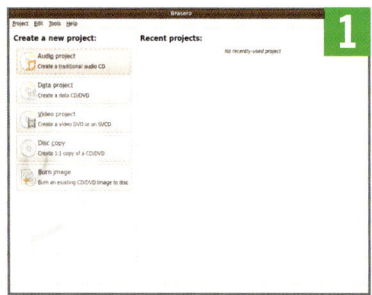

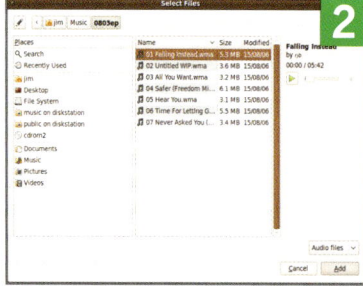

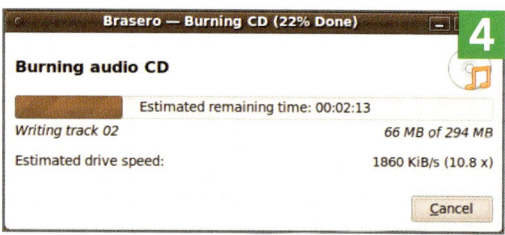

BASIC DESKTOP TASKS

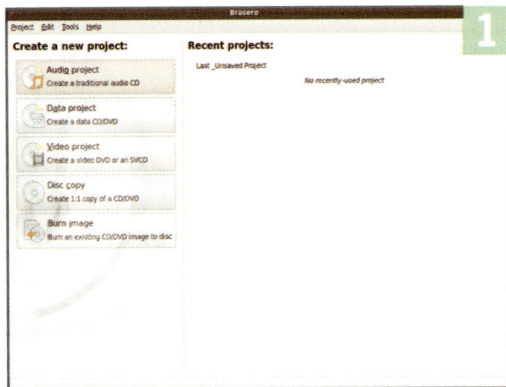
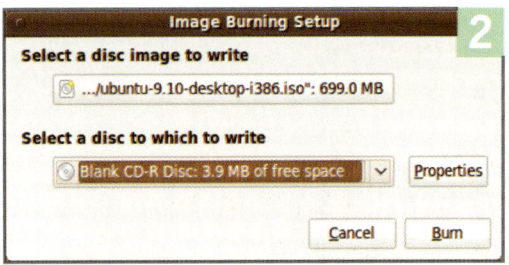
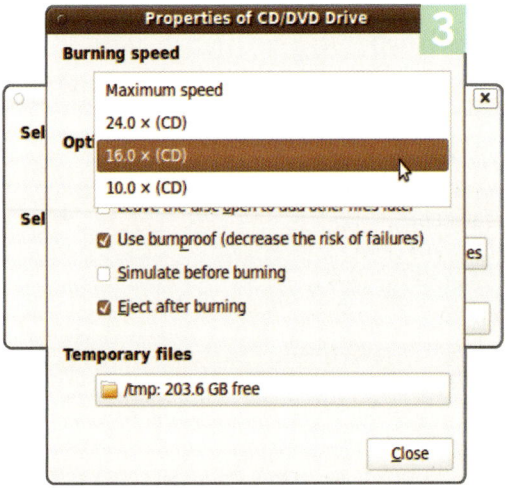

HOW TO... BURN AN ISO IMAGE

There are often times when you'll want to burn a CD or DVD from an ISO image you've downloaded, perhaps when a newer version of Ubuntu becomes available or you want to install another Linux distribution. Brasero can handle this with the minimum of hassle.

1 An ISO image is like a ZIP archive of all the files on a CD or DVD. When you burn an ISO image, the files contained within it are written to the disc in the correct folder structure. Download the ISO image that you want to burn, then launch Brasero and click the bottom-most button, Burn image.

2 Insert a suitable disc for the size of the image to be burned into your CD or DVD writer. Usually, the size of the ISO file is the size of the disc you'll need. As we're burning a Ubuntu 9.10 disc, we'll need a CD-R or CD-RW, as the ISO file is 698MB.

The Image Burning Setup window will appear. You'll need to select the ISO image, so browse to the folder or drive where it's located.

3 Now, click the Properties button. You can alter the burning speed here, but it's advisable to choose a speed less than the maximum rated speed of your disc only if you find there are errors when you burn the disc. You can choose to leave the disc open – so that more files can be added later – but as we're leaving just 3.9MB of free space, there's no point in this example. If your CD or DVD writer supports a 'burnproof' mode (which most do), ensure that this checkbox is ticked. Finally, click the Close button.

4 All that's left to do is click the Burn button. Brasero will display a progress bar telling you long is left and what is being written to the disc. When the disc is burned, it should automatically eject from the drive, unless you unchecked that option.

It's a good idea to write on the disc so you remember what's on it, but it's now ready to use. In this case, the disc is bootable, so it can be popped into the drive of the computer on which we want to install Ubuntu. If you do the same but find the computer doesn't boot from the CD, you may need to enter your PC's BIOS to change the order of boot devices, making sure the CD or DVD drive is the first, or at least comes before the hard disk.

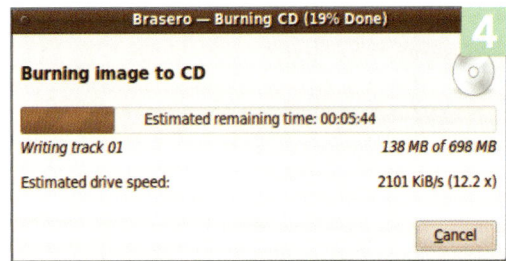

THE COMPLETE LINUX MANUAL **45**

CHAPTER 4

Connecting a digital camera

Before you can edit your photos, you need to transfer them from your digital camera. This is as easy in Linux as it is in Windows

Linux has come a long way since it was first created. It's now just as friendly towards multimedia devices such as digital cameras as Windows is. In this guide we'll show you how to connect your digital camera to your computer and download your photographs.

USING A CARD READER
One of the easiest ways to download pictures to your PC is to use a USB card reader, just as you would in Windows. These simple devices cost around £10 for a reader that will work with pretty much every camera format in the world. Make sure that your format is supported before you buy, remembering that you need a device that will support SDHC if you use SD cards larger than 2GB in size.

Other than that, it couldn't be easier. You simply plug in the card reader into your computer and Ubuntu will recognise it immediately. When you plug in a card, it will be recognised in a similar way to a USB disk, allowing you to copy files from it using the File Browser; the memory card will be listed on the left where all your other drives are listed.

IMPORTING FROM YOUR CAMERA
The alternative method is to download pictures directly from your digital camera. This, too, is very easy to do, but there are some things you need to look out for first. To start with you should check the modes that your camera supports. Many modern digital cameras can be set to be recognised as either a mass storage or a Picture Transfer Protocol (PTP) device.

When set to mass storage, the camera is recognised by your computer as a standard USB storage device. PTP mode lets the computer know that it's a camera that's been connected. We tested both modes and found that Ubuntu supports them both, so you probably won't need to change anything; however, if you're having problems, we recommend changing your camera's mode. We typically set our cameras to use PTP, as this is slightly easier to use with a computer.

■ You may need to change your camera's mode for your computer to recognise it

■ A USB card reader is an easy and convenient way to transfer pictures from your digital camera

BASIC DESKTOP TASKS

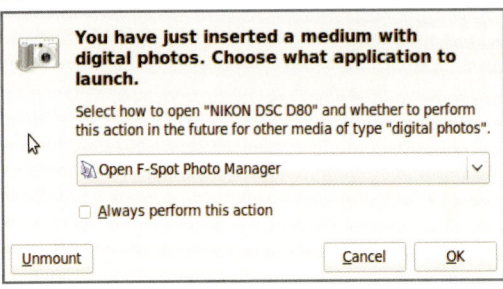

■ You can choose how you deal with image files when you connect a digital camera to your PC

■ The thumbnail previews help you manage which pictures you want to copy from your camera

GETTING CONNECTED
Plugging your camera in is as simple as connecting the provided USB cable to your computer and camera, and then turning your camera on. Depending on the make and model of your camera, you can also select the PC mode, so that the camera knows it will be transferring images to a computer.

Once connected, a window will pop up onscreen telling you that you've just inserted a medium with digital photos. You then need to choose what application to launch.

Here you have two options: the F-Spot Photo Manager or Open Folder. The latter option lets you access the camera directly and manually copy files from it. We prefer the F-Spot Photo Manager option; select this and click OK.

F-SPOT PHOTO MANAGER
F-Spot Photo Manager will start and display a window with a list of photos on your camera, complete with a thumbnail preview. The software supports pretty much every major image format and could even display RAW images from our

■ Once you've imported your photos, you can edit them in F-Spot Photo Manager

Nikon D80 DSLR. All you have to do is select the images that you want to copy. Pressing Ctrl-left-click lets you select individual images; using Shift-left-click selects a range of images.

When you're happy with your selection, you can choose where you'd like to copy them. The default location is the Pictures/Photos folder, but you can select Other from the drop-down menu and create a new folder. In fact, we recommend that you create a new folder every time you import pictures, as this will help you organise your photos better.

When you're ready, click Copy to start copying the images from your camera to your hard disk. Depending on the size of your memory card, the size of the images and the number of photos, this process can take anything from a few seconds to a good few minutes to complete.

IMPORTING PICTURES
When you've completed copying files from your digital camera, the photos will be stored on your computer. You can then edit them and organise them using Gimp (see page 48 for more information). Alternatively, if you'd like to view them in F-Spot, you'll need to import them.

Click Import from the Photo menu, select the drop-down menu and click Select Folder. Navigate to the folder where your new photos have been copied and click Open. Remove the tick from the Copy files to the Photos folder and Detect duplicates boxes and click Import. The process will take a few minutes to process.

You'll now be able to see thumbnails of all your photos. Double-click on an image to open it up in the Photo Editor. Here you can view the image full-screen, adjust its colour, straighten and crop it and remove red-eye. The tools are fairly simplistic, though; we prefer Picasa (see page 52) and Gimp (see page 48).

CHAPTER 4

Getting started with Gimp

It may have a funny name, but Gimp is a powerful photo-editing application, and it comes free with Ubuntu

If you can look past the unusual name, Gimp is an excellent image-editing package. Its interface isn't quite as easy to use as Adobe's Photoshop Elements, but it has improved hugely over the past few years. In fact, the three-separate-window approach makes it much more like the full-blown Photoshop, and there are lots of features that will keep even enthusiastic photographers happy.

This is the main window and shows the photo you're editing.

Click this button to show the undo history.

This is where you'll find the bulk of the tools, including selection, scaling and perspective, cloning, blur, sharpen and smudge. There's even a Healing Tool, which can automatically fix blemishes.

Layers let you work on different parts of an image without affecting the rest of it, a little like transparencies on a projector; placing several on top of each other will result in an image being projected on the wall. In this case, the final image is the one in the main window. You can show or hide a layer by clicking the eye icon.

The brush options let you choose the shape of the brush, its size and opacity, and a number of other advanced settings.

The zoom control lets you zoom in and out of the image. Selecting 100% shows you the actual pixels that make up the image.

The brushes palette can be switched for patterns or gradients by clicking the respective icon at the top.

THE COMPLETE LINUX MANUAL

BASIC DESKTOP TASKS

■ You can undo changes by using the Undo History and clicking on the point just before you made a mistake

You can find Gimp in the Applications menu, under Graphics. It loads quickly, but doesn't automatically ask if you want to open a photo. You can either drag a photo from a File Browser window or use the File, Open... menu.

Be careful when dragging images into Gimp if another image is already open as, by default, Gimp will add a new layer to the existing image and plant the new photo on top of the old one.

The quickest way to zoom in and out of a photo is to hold down Ctrl and roll your middle mouse wheel up or down. You can also use the magnification box at the bottom, or click on the magnifying glass icon in the tool palette and click and drag on the area you want to zoom to.

ROLLING BACK THE YEARS

If you think you've made a mistake and want to go back to a previous version of your photo, click on the yellow arrow near the top of the Layers palette on the right. This switches the view from Layers to Undo History; to switch back, click on the stack of white frames, or press Ctrl+L.

In the Undo History, you'll see all the changes you've made to the photo. Each time you make a change, the list is updated with a small icon showing the change and a description of the tool or effect used. Just click on any entry in the list to revert the image back to that point in time.

LAYING IT ON THICK

Layers are a powerful way to edit photos. You can load multiple photos as different layers of the same image, but you're unlikely to want to do this. Only the photo in the top-most layer will be visible unless you make it more transparent. This will then let the layer behind show through, creating an effect likely to be ghastly.

There are many uses for layers, one of which is to create high dynamic range photos. This is where you load the same photo shot at different exposures: one underexposed, one correctly exposed and one overexposed. By blending the three together and erasing portions of each layer, you can create some striking results.

Each new layer uses up more of your PC's memory, so if you find that Gimp feels sluggish as you have lots of layers in your image, you may need to upgrade your computer's RAM.

TOUCH-UP JOB

Layers may be interesting, but for the most part, you'll probably want to improve photos in order to print them, send them to friends and family or post them on the internet after a party, for example. On the next two pages, we'll show you how to use Gimp's tools to turn a rather flat-looking photo into something that looks as if you've got real photographic flair.

CHAPTER 4

Improving your photos using Gimp

For the first-time user, Gimp's interface can be a little overwhelming. These brief tutorials will guide you through using the main tools

Gimp may not be the easiest photo editor to use, but it is one of the most powerful. It gives you much more control over your photos than programs such as Picasa.

DEALING WITH RED EYE

There are bound to be photos in your collection in which the subjects are suffering from red eye. Otherwise great photos can be ruined by laser-red eyes staring out at you. It's caused by the light of the camera's flash reflecting off the subject's retinas, and you'll almost always see the effect in photos taken indoors at night. Fortunately, red eye is easy to remove using Gimp, and should take only minutes.

1 Start Gimp and open the photo you want to edit. Our shot was taken in a restaurant at night, and we used a compact camera with its flash turned on. Both subjects' eyes have that devilish look, which we'll need to address.

2 Zoom into the first eye you want to tackle, to around 400 per cent magnification. Use the lasso tool (third from the left on the top row of tools) to draw a circle around the offending area. If necessary hit Enter to complete the selection. Then hold the Ctrl key and select the white highlight in the middle of the eye, as we don't want to adjust this portion.

3 In the Tools menu, click Colour Tools, then Hue-Saturation. Drag the Saturation slider to the left, and also the Lightness slider, until the shade is darker than the outside of the eye. You can adjust the hue if necessary to match the actual colour of the subject's eyes, but once zoomed back out, it's unlikely anyone will notice.

4 Press Ctrl-Shift-A to deselect the eye and you'll see that it's looking reasonably good. Now repeat steps 2 and 3 for the other eyes in the image. Finally, change the zoom level to 100% using the drop-down box at the bottom of the window, and you can admire your skilful work. Don't forget to save the image before moving on to the next one.

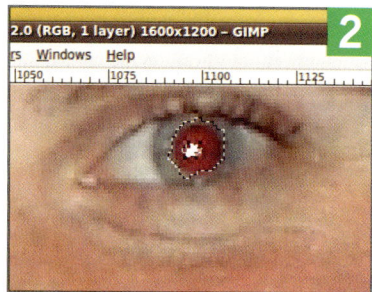
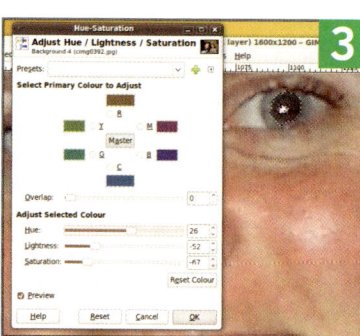

BASIC DESKTOP TASKS

ENHANCING YOUR SHOTS

This shot, which we took in the Lake District, almost didn't make it into our 'Best images' folder after sorting out the good ones from the not so good. However, despite its flat appearance, we could see it had the potential to be great. Gimp came to the rescue and allowed us to enhance it. Here we'll show you how to use Gimp's main retouching tools.

1 Open the image in Gimp and head straight for the Levels tool, which you'll find in the Colours menu. This opens a window that may look daunting, but it's worth getting to know as it's one of the most effective tools in Gimp's arsenal, especially for injecting contrast into lifeless shots such as this one. The histogram shows a representation of the intensity of pixels in the image. At the left are very dark pixels, which become progressively lighter as you move to the right. Drag the left-hand arrow inward until it's in line with the start of the rising curve. This deepens shadows. On the right, grab the white arrow and drag it left to the point the graph trails off. This brightens highlights.

2 Now we need a little saturation boost, so open the Hue-Saturation tool from the Colours menu. Drag the Saturation slider a little to the right – depending on your camera's processing you may need more or less than the +15 we've applied here.

If you want to increase the saturation of individual colours – say, green for grass or blue for skies – just click the white circle next to the colour you want and adjust the slider for each one you want to modify. If you make a mistake, just hit the Reset button.

3 If the Levels adjustment hasn't given you quite enough contrast, you can add it easily with the Brightness-Contrast tool, which again you'll find in the Colours menu. Simply adjust the Contrast slider until you see the desired result.

4 Sharpening your photos is always a good idea, as digital cameras tend to err on the side of caution and leave images a little soft. Gimp's Unsharp Mask tool is excellent for doing this. You'll find it in the Enhance section of the Filters menu. Move the preview window to an area of the image that shows fine detail and toggle the Preview tick box on and off to see the difference the default settings make. Don't oversharpen an image, or you'll cause unwanted artefacts to appear.

Now the image is looking good, and we're finished with the retouching. It's a good idea to save a copy rather than saving over the top of the original photo. This means you can start again from scratch if you decide you don't like the changes you've made.

CHAPTER 4

Organising your photos with Picasa

Google's photo-management software is hard to beat, and it works well in Linux. Here we'll show you how to use it

Sometimes, there are better applications for a job than Ubuntu provides. F-Spot Photo Manager isn't bad, but Google's Picasa can do a whole lot more, and it has a slicker interface.

If you already know the Windows version of Picasa, you'll be pleased to hear that it's identical in Linux, since it uses Windows Emulator (or WinE). To download Picasa, go to http://picasa.google.com/Linux and click on the large download button. We've chosen the beta version 3, but you can install 2.7 if you prefer a more stable program. Make sure you download the .deb file for Debian/Ubuntu, and choose the appropriate version for your operating system: i386 for 32-bit or AMD64 for 64-bit.

There are various ways of installing Picasa, but the easiest is to double-click the file on your desktop and see if it installs. If it fails, copy the file to the /tmp folder and hit Alt-F2 to open a command prompt. Type in this command:

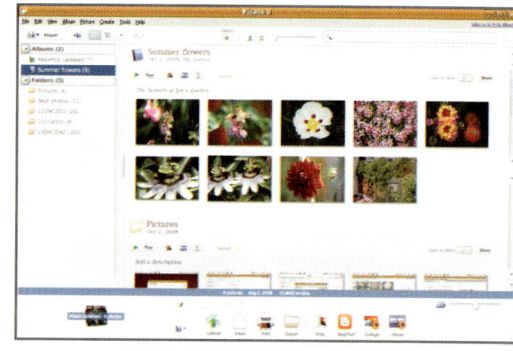

■ Picasa has a friendly interface that's easy to get to grips with

```
sudo dpkg -i /tmp/picasa_2.7.3736-15_i386.deb
```

Picasa should now install, and you'll find it under Graphics in the Applications menu. Load it, and it will automatically scan your disks for photos. You should then see something similar to the screenshot (above). If it hasn't found your photos, you can import them using the Add Folder to Picasa... option in the File menu.

Picasa can monitor folders and add new photos when they're copied to those folders. To choose which folders Picasa monitors, use the Folder Manager, which is under the Tools menu.

STARTING TO USE PICASA
As you'll see, Picasa is split into two main panes: a folder list and thumbnails of the images in each folder. In the bottom-right corner is a zoom slider that lets you change the size of the thumbnails. The shuttle control on the right doesn't work like a normal scroll bar: the more

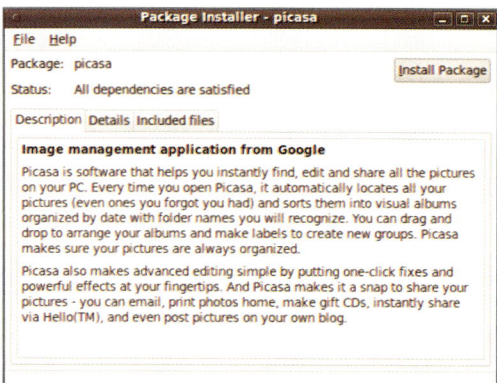

■ There are several ways to install Picasa. Downloading and double-clicking the .deb file is the easiest method

BASIC DESKTOP TASKS

■ You can enhance your photos with ease in Picasa. There are tools for cropping, straightening, removing red eye and adding effects

you move it higher or lower, the faster Picasa scrolls up or down through your photos. This is handy when you want to scan through a folder slowly to find the image you're looking for.

Just above the Folders list is an Albums list. These are collections of pictures that can be stored in multiple folders on the disk. Albums make it easy to view your favourite photos from an occasion, without having to copy them to a separate folder. To create an Album, click New Album… in the File menu. Type a name for it, and you can then drag and drop photos into it from the thumbnails you see on the right.

IMPROVING YOUR PHOTOS

Picasa doesn't just allow you to organise your photos; it lets you enhance them, too. Picasa is what's called a non-destructive photo editing application, which means that it doesn't touch the photos stored on your hard disk. Instead it saves the changes you apply to the photo and combines these with the original photo to display your edited version.

Double-click on a photo to open it in the viewer/editor. You'll see three tabs on the left: Basic Fixes, Tuning and Effects. These allow you to crop and straighten photos quickly. It's very easy to remove red eye or apply auto contrast and colour. Under the Effects tab you can turn colour photos to black and white, increase saturation, or apply effects such as soft focus. There's none of the fine control offered by Gimp (see page 50); everything here is a quick fix.

Above the photo you're tweaking are thumbnails of other images in the Album or Folder, along with left and right arrows to move between them. To return to the library view, just click Back to Library on the left.

SHARING PHOTOS

You'll probably want to show others your photos at some point, and one way is a slideshow. If you're in the Library view, you'll see a little green play arrow at the top-left corner of each Album or Folder. Clicking it will display a full-screen slideshow. Move your mouse to display the hidden menu at the bottom of the screen. This lets you pause the slideshow, set the interval and transition between photos, and even rotate them. Hit Esc or click Exit to return to the Library view.

Picasa also lets you share photos with distant friends and family using Web Albums. There's a link to Web Albums in the top-right corner. You'll need to create a free Google account if you don't already have one. Once you're signed up and logged in, you'll be able to use the Sync to Web toggle button at the top-right of each Folder or Album to upload the photos to the web.

When you click the button, Picasa will ask you what size you want the photos to appear, and whether to make them public, unlisted (hidden) or require a password to view them. Click the Change Settings… button to make your choices.

When the photos are uploaded, you can click on the View online link to see how your photos look in your web browser. Alternatively, you can click the Share button to invite people to view the photos. This will open a window where ou can enter email addresses. These will auto-complete if the person is one of your Google Mail contacts.

■ Full-screen slideshows make the most of your photos, and Picasa lets you decide the interval and transition between images

THE COMPLETE LINUX MANUAL

CHAPTER 4

Connecting a video camera to your PC

Linux is perfectly capable of editing your video files. Here we'll show you how to transfer your files from your camcorder to your PC

Connecting your digital video camera to Ubuntu should be pretty easy, as the operating system has built-in support for camcorders. However, there are some areas that could give you problems. Before we start, we'll talk you through the difficulties that you might face.

There are two types of video camera that you're likely to want to connect to your computer: MiniDV and modern flash storage models. In short, MiniDV models will be very tricky to install. Many require a FireWire port to connect to and a specific driver to be installed. It's not impossible to work around the problem, but you're likely to run in to a number of difficulties when doing so. Our advice is to keep a PC running Windows handy for connecting this kind of camera.

If you have a flash-based or hard-disk-based camcorder, things are a lot easier. In this section we'll show you how to connect this type of camera and copy files from it to your Ubuntu computer.

■ Modern flash-memory or hard-disk-based camcorders are easy to connect to Ubuntu

CONNECTING YOUR CAMERA

Depending on the type of camera that you own, you'll have a choice of connection methods. If your camera uses removable storage, such as an SD card, you can use a USB card reader. Ubuntu recognises these devices in the same way as Windows does. All you have to do with a card reader is take the memory card out of your camcorder and plug it in to your card reader. The card will become available in Computer from the Places menu. All you have to do is copy the files that you require from it.

If your camcorder uses internal memory or a hard disk, or you don't have a memory card reader, your only option is to plug in your camcorder using USB. In our experience, camcorders can use a weird and wonderful collection of USB cables, so remember to use the one that came in the box with your camera.

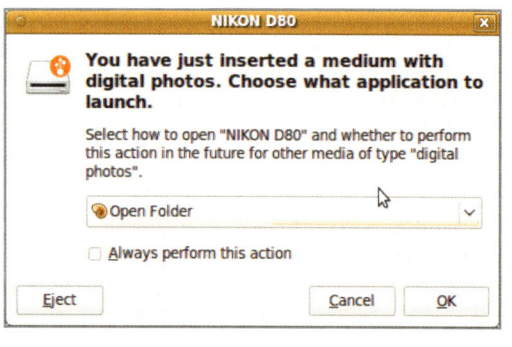

■ Select Open Folder to view your camcorder's files

BASIC DESKTOP TASKS

Digital cameras may offer multiple connection modes, such as the Picture Transfer Protocol (PTP), but video cameras only have one: mass storage. All you have to do is plug your camera in via USB and it will be recognised as a flash storage device. If you have photos stored on your camera, using its stills mode, as well as videos, you'll see a dialog box telling you that "You have just inserted a medium with digital photos. Choose what application to launch."

The default option will be F-Spot Photo Manager. Don't select this option; instead select Open Folder and click OK.

Alternatively, you can view your camcorder's files by clicking on Computer from the Places menu. You can then browse your camcorder as though it were any other folder or storage device. Any videos that you find can simply be copied from the device to your hard disk by dragging and dropping.

VIEWING FILES

Before you start editing your videos (see page 56), you may want to check the files first and delete any that you don't want to use. Ubuntu can play back most file types, and we had no problems with 1080p HD video files from our Samsung camcorder. However, some HD cameras have been known to use strange formats, so you may need to search the Ubuntu forums for help.

To view a file, simply double-click it and the Totem Movie Player will start. By default this player doesn't have a lot of video codecs (the software used to display a video file) installed, but it can detect automatically what it needs to install. When you first try to play a file you'll see an option to install additional plugins, such as

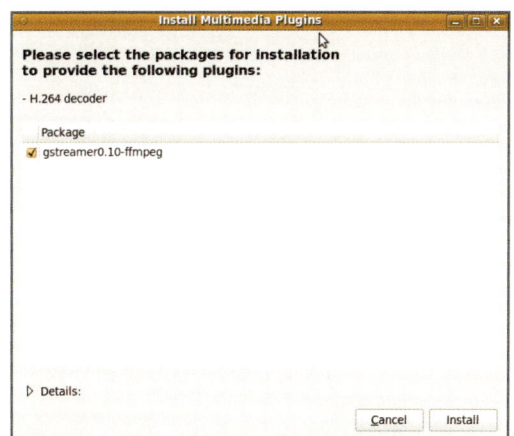
■ Before you can play a video file, you may have to install an additional codec

■ You can preview your video files and just keep the ones worthy of being edited

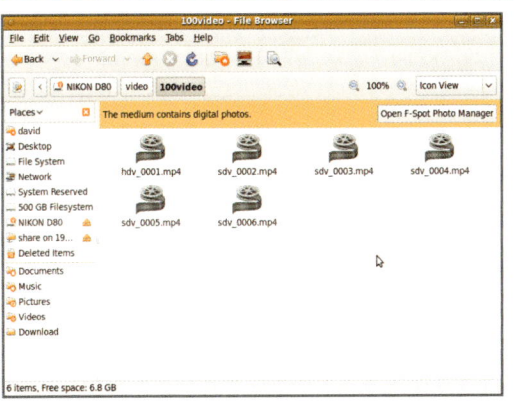
■ You can browser your camcorder's files just like any other folder or storage device

the gstreamer0.10-ffmpeg H.264 codec. Select the default option and click Install.

Once the codec has been installed, you'll be able to preview your video. The software doesn't always get it right, so if the picture looks squashed, select 16:9 from the View, Aspect Ratio menu. This should fix the video and make it look right. Once you've previewed your clips, you can simply delete the ones you don't want and save the others to be edited.

Installing the codec also means that supported videos will automatically have a thumbnail image generated in the file browser. This is similar to the way in which Windows handles video files. It makes it easy to see quickly what you've got and always select the right clip without having to preview it first.

Once you're happy with the files that you've copied from your camcorder, you can edit them in the package of your choice. We've got more details on how to do this in our guide to video editing with Kdenlive on the following page.

CHAPTER 4

Editing video

Want to cut out the chaff from your video footage before uploading it to YouTube? We'll show you how using Kdenlive

You may have noticed that Ubuntu doesn't come with an application to edit video. That's because it's only recently that developers have started work on programs for this purpose. Currently, the best choice is Kdenlive, but as it's still an unfinished project, you may experience a few bugs and crashes. However, as long as you

The render button. Click this when you're ready to export your finished movie in a format that your player is compatible with.

Click the Add Clip button to import video clips from your hard disk, memory card or directly from your video camera.

These are the video clips in your project. They can be added to the timeline as many times as you like.

These two waveforms represent the left and right audio channels in each video clip.

The playback marker shows the current position in the movie.

There are two clips on the timeline. The tracks work like layers in photo-editing software. Video on top will obscure clips below unless the top video is transparent or occupies part of the frame.

Drag an effect from the list on to a clip to add that effect. You can add multiple effects to each clip and adjust their properties with the Effect Stack tab on the left.

The project monitor shows the whole movie, but you can switch it for a view of the current clip by clicking on the Clip Monitor tab below.

If you make a mistake, you can use the Undo History to jump back to the point you want to restart from.

The zoom control lets you see more detail when you need to adjust and edit clips more precisely.

The Razor tool lets you split video clips into multiple chunks while on the timeline.

The selection tool is used for dragging and trimming clips on the timeline.

56 THE COMPLETE LINUX MANUAL

BASIC DESKTOP TASKS

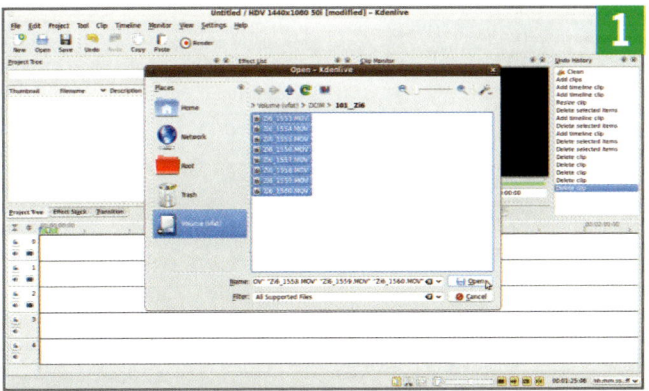
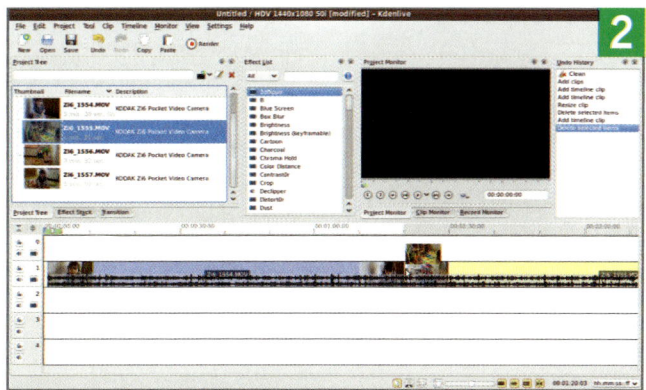
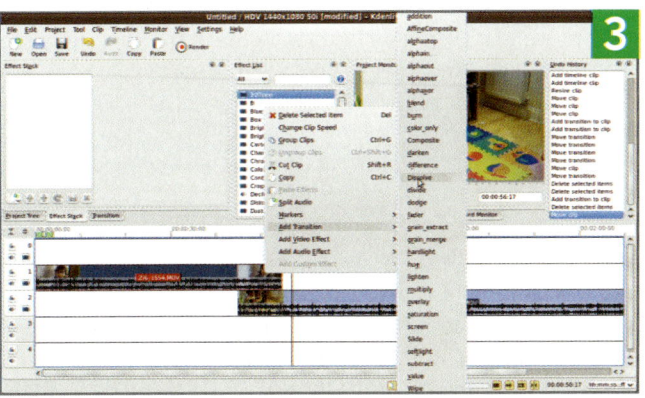
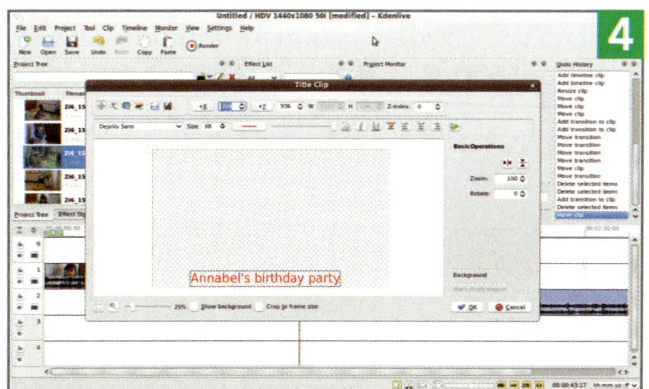

regularly save your work, you can just reload the application and carry on.

As Kdenlive's interface is relatively complex, it's worth spending a few moments acquainting yourself with the various elements and controls.

To install Kdenlive, use the Synaptic Package Manager, under Administration in the System menu. Search for kdenlive in the Quick search box, and mark it for installation. Accept the extra packages needed when asked, and allow the installation to complete. You'll find Kdenlive under Sound & Video in the Applications menu.

1 Copy any video clips from your camcorder to your hard disk. You can't work with clips stored on the camera itself or on a memory card, as they are too slow. Start up Kdenlive and click the Add Clip button. Browse to the folder where you've stored your clips, select the ones you want and hit the Open button.

2 Clips may take a few minutes to be indexed, and until they are they'll be greyed out. Once this is done, drag clips one by one on to the timeline into track 1. Order the clips as you like.

3 Trim clips by hovering your mouse over the left or right edge of it and, when the cursor changes, drag the clip to the desired point. If you want to add transitions, you'll need to overlap clips in adjacent video tracks. Right-click on one of the clips, hover over Add Transition and then choose Dissolve from the menu that appears.

4 You can add a title to the start of your movie by clicking the down arrow next to the Add Clip button and choosing Add Title Clip. Using the text tool (the icon with the letter T on it), type in the title you want, changing the font, size and colour as appropriate. You can move it around using the X and Y controls at the top. Click OK and then drag the title from your clip list to the beginning of track 0.

You can now click the Render button to save your movie in whatever format is most appropriate. You'll find lots of presets in the Destination drop-down menu. To save to a DVD, choose DVD, then PAL 16:9 VOB (assuming your video camera is widescreen). Tick 'Open DVD wizard after rendering' and you'll be able to burn a DVD with the resulting MPEG file.

CHAPTER 4

Playing DVDs

Using your computer to watch movies and videos is easy with Ubuntu. All you need to do is download and install VLC

Ubuntu comes with Totem Movie Player, but due to licensing laws in certain countries, it can't play commercial, encrypted DVD movies. Don't worry, though, as it's simple to install the excellent VLC media player.

You can install the MPEG2 codec required to play DVDs, but installing VLC is an easier way to watch movies. You may already be familiar with it as it's also available for Windows and Mac OS X, and it looks and works identically under Linux.

It supports more than just DVDs, however. In fact, it can play MPEG2, MPEG4, H.264, DivX and MPEG1 video formats, as well as MP3, OGG, AAC and other audio files. You can even use it as a media converter or for streaming video across a network.

Menus are self-explanatory, and many functions can be accessed quickly by right-clicking on the video itself.

Double-click on the video to make it full screen. Another double-click will return it to a window.

Drag the bar to jump to a point in the movie. Hover your mouse over the handle to display the time.

Click and drag on the volume control to increase or lower the volume.

Controls let you play and pause the move, jump to the menu or go to the next or previous chapter.

The extended settings button lets you tweak audio and video effects.

BASIC DESKTOP TASKS

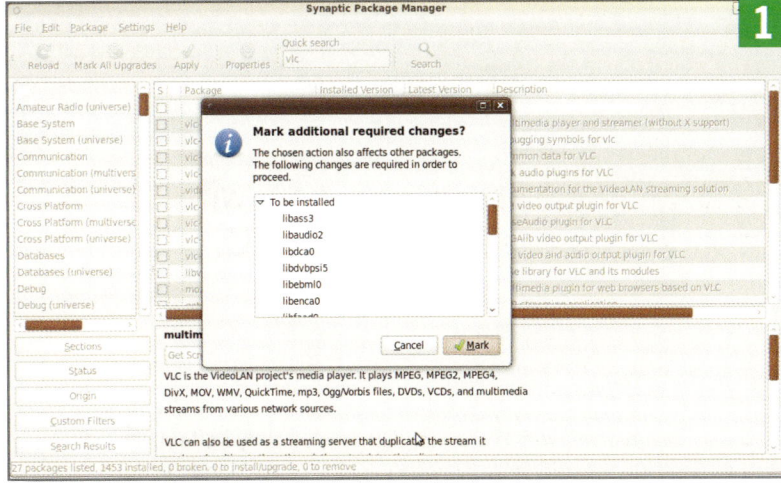
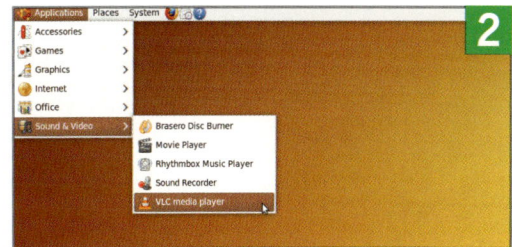
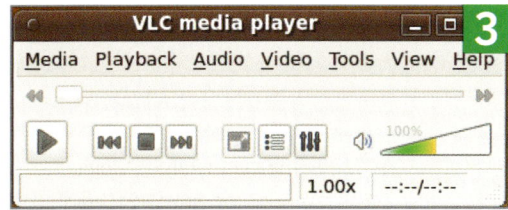

HOW TO... INSTALL AND USE VLC MEDIA PLAYER

1 Open the Synaptic Package Manger, which is in the System menu under Administration. Enter your password and then type vlc into the Quick search box. The top-most result should simply say vlc. Right-click on the grey square on the left of it and choose Mark for installation. A window will appear asking you to approve additional downloads, so just click the Mark button.

2 The package files will be downloaded and then installed. Once this is complete, you can close the Package Manager. You'll find VLC media player has been added to the Applications menu under Sound & Video.

3 A warning will appear, asking for your authorisation to download CD covers, track information and check for updates. Choose your preferred option from the menu and click OK. The minimal VLC player will open.

4 To play a DVD, insert the disc into your drive and wait until it is recognised. A pop-up window may appear asking you to select how to open the Video DVD. We recommend choosing Open VLC media player and ticking the Always perform this action box, before clicking OK.

5 The DVD should play automatically, but if it doesn't, choose Open Disc... from the File menu. A slightly bewildering window will open, but you can simply click the Play button.

6 You can now use the menus with your mouse, selecting scenes or playing the movie from the beginning. To play video files stored on your hard disk or an external USB device, simply browse to the file using a File Browser window and drag it on to VLC's interface. As VLC supports most video formats, it should play your file. To play high-definition files, you'll need a reasonably powerful computer. If yours isn't up to the job, you may see stuttering video or no video at all.

THE COMPLETE LINUX MANUAL 59

CHAPTER 4

Playing music files with Rhythmbox

Ubuntu's built-in music player lets you organise your music, create playlists and listen to podcasts and internet radio stations

Rhythmbox Music Player can be found in the Sound & Video section of the Applications menu. It was originally inspired by iTunes, and although it doesn't look quite as slick as Apple's player, it's still a powerful music-management application. You can use it to rip your CDs to MP3 format, just as you can with iTunes.

Before you start, you need to install the necessary audio codecs. Click on Software Centre from the Applications menu and type Restricted into the search bar. Double-click Ubuntu restricted extras and click Install. You can now start Rhythmbox.

On the left, you'll find a pane with your library short cuts, music stores and playlists. On the right, when Music is selected under Library, you'll see three panes: artist, album and a track listing. These will be blank, of course, until you import your music collection.

To import tracks from a CD, you need to set your import preferences. Click on Preferences from the Edit menu, then click on the Music tab.

Select CD Quality, MP3 (.mp3 type) from the Preferred format (select a different format if you use something other than MP3).

To rip an audio CD, simply insert it into your computer's optical drive. The disc will appear in the left-hand panel of Rhythmbox, and its name and track title will be automatically downloaded from the internet. Simply right-click the CD and select Extract to Library to convert the tracks to MP3. A status bar at the bottom shows you how far through the process it is. When it's finished, you can remove your CD.

IMPORTING OLD MUSIC

The best place to store tracks that you already have in MP3 format is in the Music folder, which you can access in Ubuntu's Places menu. To import your existing MP3 tracks, head to the Music menu in Rhythmbox and choose Import Folder. Click on the Music folder in the left pane of the window that opens and click Open. All your music will now be added to Rhythmbox's library.

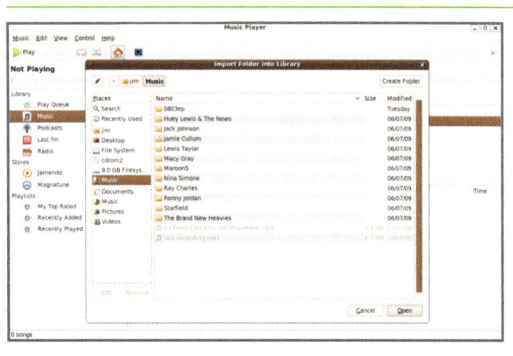

■ The first job you need to do in Rhythmbox is import your music collection

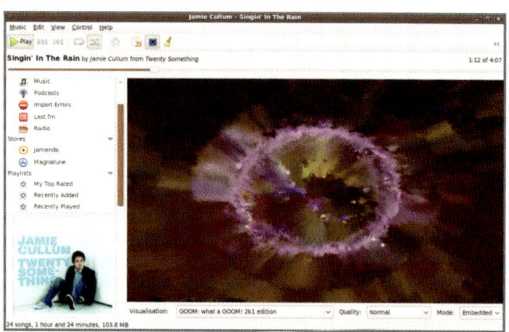

■ Rhythmbox supports album art and will show garish visualisations when playing tracks if you so desire

BASIC DESKTOP TASKS

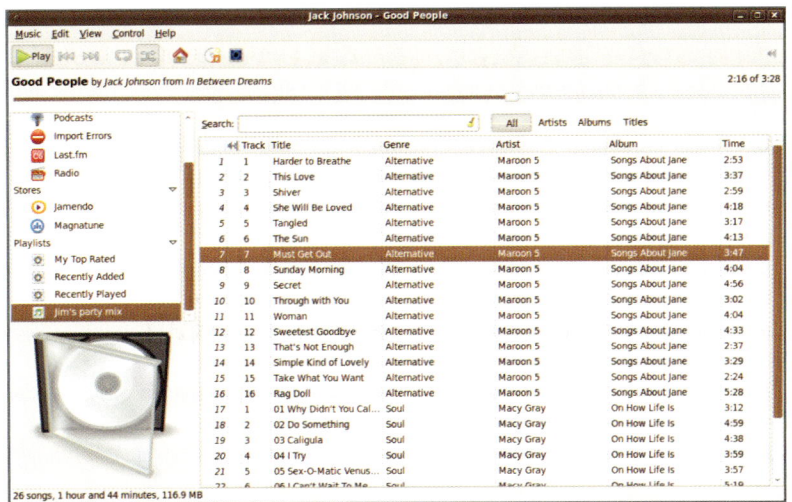

■ Playlists are easy to create and are useful for listening to a variety of music

You may have music in several formats (MP3, WMA and AAC, for example), and the codecs for some of these formats may not be installed. If they're not, Rhythmbox will ask if you want to search for the appropriate codec using Ubuntu's Package Manager. Follow the instructions to download any required codecs.

PLAY TIME

Once the importing process has finished, you can browse the library and play tracks by double-clicking on them. Unless you want to listen to a single track, you'll want to use playlists. The simplest way to do this is to drag an entry from the Artist or Album panes to the Play Queue on the left. Now click on Play Queue to start the first track. Rhythmbox will play all the tracks in order unless you click the Shuffle button at the top of the window.

A separate section called Playlists in the left pane has three pre-defined lists: My Top Rated, Recently Added and Recently Played. To add a new custom playlist, go to Music, Playlist then New Playlist. A new playlist will appear in the list. Once you've entered a name, drag tracks to it from the Artist, Album or Track panes.

LISTENING TO PODCASTS

To listen to a podcast in Rhythmbox, you'll first need its URL. Usually, the best place to find this is at the website that hosts the podcast. For example, navigate to the Friday Night Comedy podcast on Radio 4's website and you'll see an RSS link. Click on this and copy the URL from

the address bar in your browser. Now, back in Rhythmbox, click on Podcasts and then right-click somewhere in the right-hand pane. Choose New Podcast Feed... and paste the URL you just copied into the box and click Add. Rhythmbox should download the most recent episode automatically. You can download other episodes simply by double-clicking on them.

BLAST FROM THE LAST

Last.fm is a website (www.last.fm) that lets you listen to music you choose for free, like a personalised radio station. Visit the website and sign up for a free account. Return to Rhythmbox and click on Last.fm. Enter your username and password and you'll see Neighbour radio and Personal radio. The latter sticks with artists you like, while the former also includes tracks from similar artists. Type an artist into the box at the top to build a new station, which will be added to your list in the pane below.

RADIO STAR

Rhythmbox comes with a small selection of preset stations, but you're bound to want to add your own. As with podcasts, you'll need to get the URL of your chosen station before you can add it. To add BBC Radio 2, for example, we searched on www.radiofeeds.co.uk and found Radio 2's address of www.bbc.co.uk/radio/listen/live/r2.ram. Right-click on Radio in Rhythmbox and then New Internet Radio Station. Paste or type in the URL and click Add. It should now appear in the Radio list.

■ Adding podcasts can be tricky as you'll need to know the URL of the feed

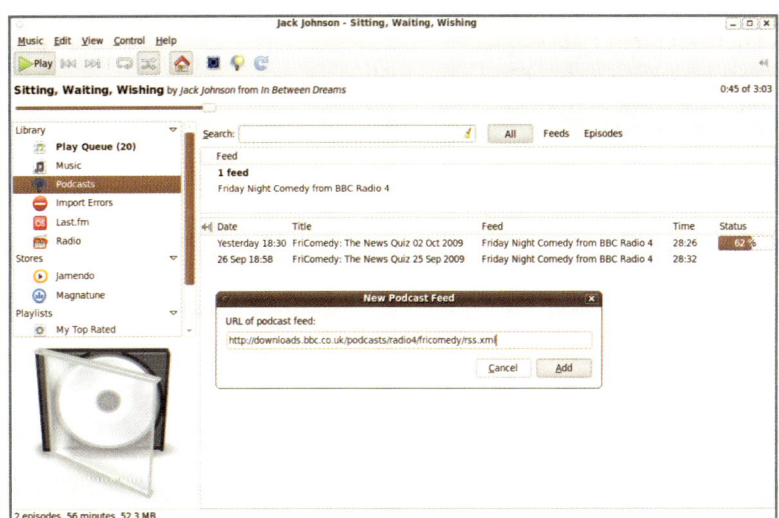

THE COMPLETE LINUX MANUAL 61

CHAPTER 4

Connecting an MP3 player

Transferring music, videos and podcasts to your MP3 player is simple in Ubuntu. Here we'll show you how

We've already looked at Rhythmbox on page 60, and seen that it's extremely easy to use. It's also great for MP3 players, as it autodetects most portable players that use the MSC standard and shows them in the left-hand pane under the Devices heading.

MSC stands for Mass Storage Class, and is essentially the standard used by most USB devices that have storage capabilities. Ubuntu (and Linux in general) is able to recognise when these devices are plugged in, just as Windows does. A window should pop up asking which program you'd like to open, and an icon should appear on the desktop. You can then access the device just like any hard disk.

MSC OR MTP?

Some MP3 players support both MSC and MTP standards. MTP – the Media Transfer Protocol – is closely linked with Windows Media Player and allows DRM-protected audio files (usually those that have been purchased from an online music store) to be transferred to authorised audio players.

If you find that Ubuntu doesn't automatically detect your MP3 player, check its settings menu to see whether you can switch its USB mode from MTP to MSC. Some players, such as certain models in SanDisk's Sansa range, require a combination of buttons to be pressed to switch

■ Most MP3 players should be recognised by Ubuntu without any problems

■ If you prefer to transfer files manually, just use a File Browser window to copy music – and video if your player supports it – straight to its internal memory

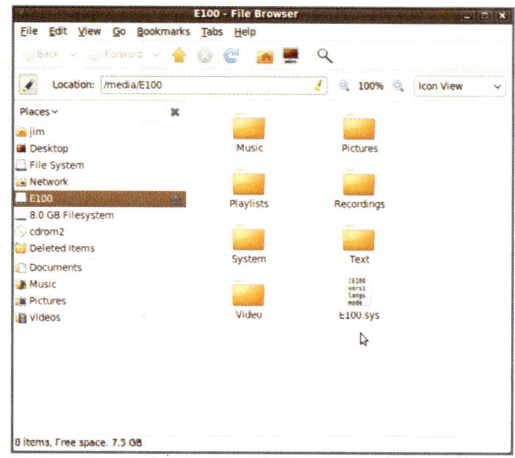

BASIC DESKTOP TASKS

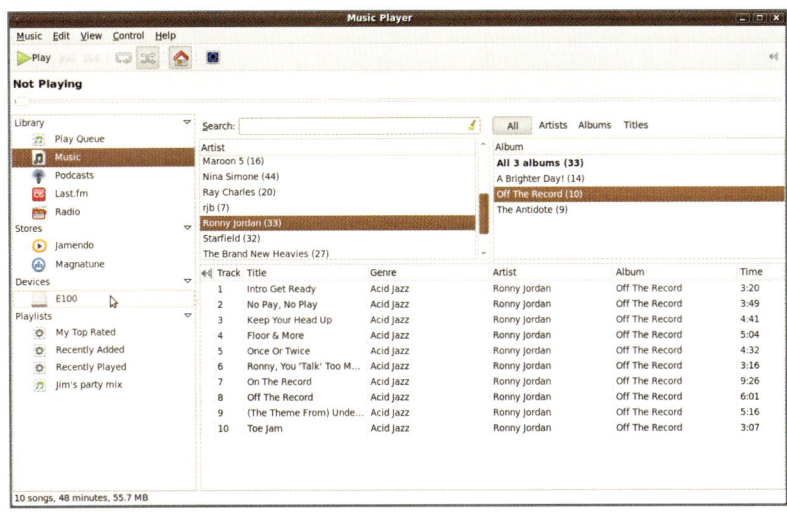

MP3 players that support MSC should work fine with Rhythmbox

modes, rather than having a menu setting. If in doubt, check with the manufacturer.

While it's possible to install programs that allow MTP devices to be detected by Rhythmbox, it's usually easier to use a File Browser to copy music and other files to MTP-only players manually. It's also best, if possible, to avoid any DRM-protected music, as you're likely to run into problems getting Rhythmbox to play it or transfer it to a player.

MANAGING MUSIC IN RHYTHMBOX

Rhythmbox makes it easy to get music on to your player. Once you see your MP3 player listed under the Devices heading, all you need to do is drag and drop tracks on to it. You can select a range of tracks, artists or albums to transfer, or you can drag the All artists or All albums list entries on to your player if it has enough room for your entire library.

When you drop tracks on to your player, you'll see a progress bar appear in the bottom-right corner of the window. This shows you how many tracks have been transferred in the current queue.

The same goes for podcasts. Just drag and drop them on to your player, and they'll be transferred. Unfortunately, Rhythmbox doesn't have any synchronisation capabilities, so it can't fill your player automatically with a random selection of music in the same way as Windows Media Player. If you want an application that can sync music, you'll have to install Amarok using the Synaptic Package Manager.

MANUALLY MANAGING MEDIA

Rhythmbox has no support for videos, so it may not meet your needs if you have an MP3 player that can also play video. In this case, the best method may be to copy files to it manually, just as if it were an external hard disk.

If you browse your player's contents in a File Browser window, you'll probably find it has several folders on it, perhaps Music, Videos, Podcasts and Voice Recordings.

While a File Browser will let you transfer any files you like into any folder, your player will support only certain formats. If you need a program to convert tracks from one format to another, try searching in Synaptic Package Manager for soundconvert; this will install Sound Converter, which you'll find in the Applications menu under Sound & Video.

Any videos you download will almost certainly need to be converted. WinFF can also be installed via the Package Manager, and supports most formats. As with audio files, you'll need to know the specific format your player can handle, including both the video and audio codecs, the resolution, plus the maximum bit rates for audio and video. A process of trial and error should help you find the best settings, and once you've done that, you can carry on using them for batches of other files. As we've already said, check the manufacturer's website for these details, or contact its technical support.

Amarok is an alternative music player that can synchronise tracks with MP3 players

THE COMPLETE LINUX MANUAL 63

CHAPTER 4

Connecting an iPod

iPods can be a little trickier to use with Ubuntu than other MP3 players. Here are some tips on how to synchronise music and video

If there's one area in which Ubuntu might prove frustrating, it's compatibility with iPods. This is mainly Apple's fault, not Ubuntu's. Most iPods don't show up as generic mass storage devices, which means you can't copy music and videos to them using Ubuntu's file manager as you can with most MP3 players. The portion of storage that does appear when you connect a modern iPod to Ubuntu is the part that stores photos and possibly contacts, calendars, notes and recordings.

The internal database is in a proprietary format, which Apple created to prevent music and videos being illegally copied from an iPod to another computer. However, there are ways to use your iPod with Ubuntu, and plenty of models can be successfully synchronised, just as you would in Windows or on Mac OS.

The only models that are likely to cause problems are the iPod Touch, iPhone and the latest generation of Nano, Classic and Video, which may not yet be supported by Ubuntu applications. Don't hold your breath for support to be added quickly after a new generation is released, as Linux applications can sometimes take an age to catch up.

■ Most iPods, such as this Classic, will work fine with Ubuntu

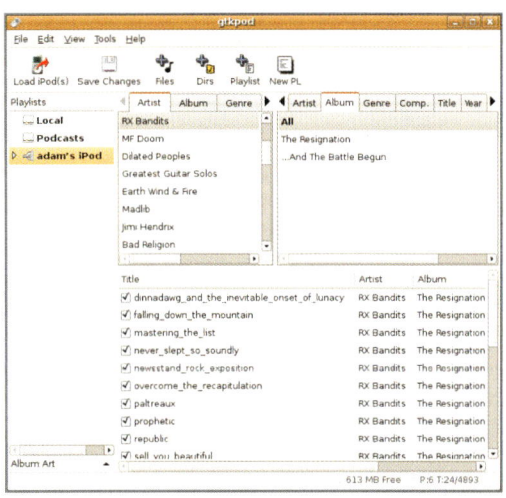

■ Amarok is great for music, but it doesn't support video

VIRTUAL WINDOWS
As you'll see, it isn't just different applications that support iPods; you can also run iTunes in Ubuntu using VirtualBox, which is an application through which you can install and run a virtual copy of Windows, and subsequently, iTunes.

A word of warning, however. Don't try using WinE (Windows Emulator) to run iTunes in Ubuntu. It supports only old versions of iTunes, and many iPods require newer versions, so won't work at all. In addition, previously purchased music won't play, and the Apple Store won't work.

The bottom line with iPods in Ubuntu is that there's no guarantee that it will be easy to get your particular model working. Some programs require your iPod to be 'jailbroken'. If that's

BASIC DESKTOP TASKS

meaningless to you, suffice to say that they won't work with your iPod. Another point to note is that you'll need to format (or initialise) your iPod on a Windows PC if it's previously been formatted on a computer running Mac OS, otherwise Ubuntu won't be able to recognise it.

If you have another computer running Windows or Mac OS, or you're running both Windows and Ubuntu on the same computer, it's likely to cause far fewer headaches if you stick to the 'real' iTunes. However, if you own an older iPod and are made of sterner stuff, read on.

USING GTKPOD

Gtkpod is a lightweight application that's solely designed to synchronise media with iPods. Search for it in Synaptic Package Manager and it will appear immediately. When it's installed, you'll find it under Sound & Video in the Applications menu. It supports first-generation iPods through to fifth-generation models, including the Mini, Photo, Shuffle, Nano and Video, but not the iPod Touch or iPhone.

It's capable of transferring MP3, WAV, M4A, audiobooks and various video files to your iPod, but you'll additionally need to install bashpodder or gpodder if you want podcasts. The interface is basic, but it gets the job done.

AMORAK

Amarok is a music player that has a Linux version and looks a lot like iTunes. It works

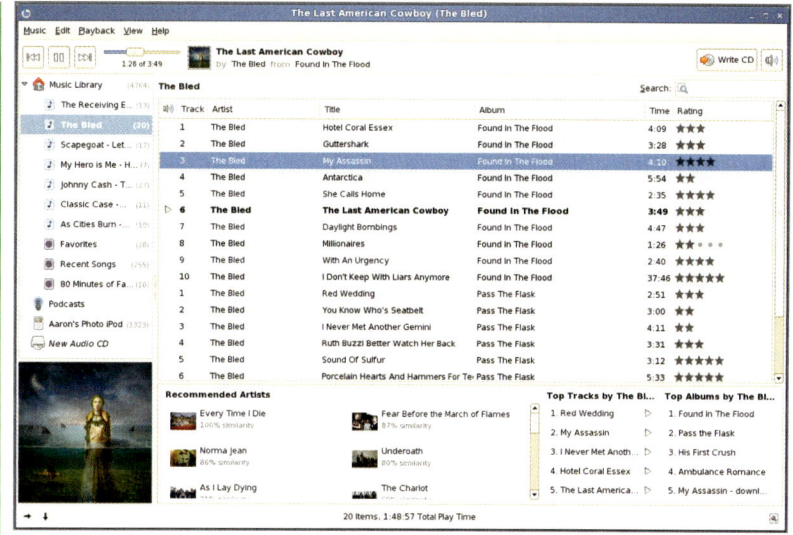

■ Banshee is a slick-looking iTunes alternative, but even the latest version lacks support for the iPod Touch and the iPhone

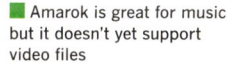

■ Amarok is great for music, but it doesn't yet support video files

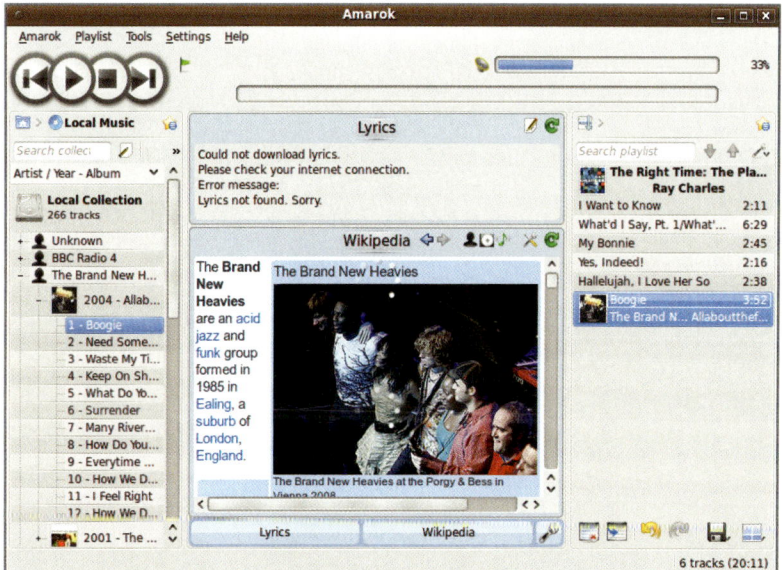

well with most iPods and can synchronise your music. The only snag is that music is all it does – forget synchronising any videos you may have. As a music management application, though, it's well worth trying out as it's an improvement over Ubuntu's built-in Rhythmbox.

Banshee is the default music manager in several Linux distributions, but not Ubuntu. The latest version of Banshee is 1.4, and it now supports videos. It can sync both music and video to your iPod, and also supports podcasts. Unfortunately, although it has the polish that gtkpod lacks, it still doesn't support the iPod Touch or iPhone.

VIRTUALBOX

Virtualbox can run whole operating systems in a Ubuntu window. As long as you have a legitimate Windows disc and product key, you can use it to install, say, Windows XP in Linux. You can then install any Windows programs you like, including the latest version of iTunes.

Virtualbox doesn't provide direct access to your computer's hardware so Windows may not run particularly quickly, but it should allow you to synchronise your iPod properly. For many people, though, this is a cop-out, and almost pointless as you could just as easily install Windows on a separate hard disk partition to Ubuntu, and use it independently.

If you do decide to install Virtualbox and give it a try, you'll find it, as ever, if you use the Quick search box in Synaptic Package Manager.

THE COMPLETE LINUX MANUAL

CHAPTER 4

Synchronising a mobile with Linux

Backing up your phone to a PC is a great way to save your settings and make sure you have the same contacts wherever you are

With Windows PCs, all the phone manufacturers provide software that lets you synchronise your phone with your computer. With Linux, this isn't the case. Fortunately, that doesn't mean you're stuck, as there's third-party software that should work with most phones so that you can back up your messages.

There's no simple way to synchronise your phone directly with Ubuntu's email client, Evolution, so think first about what you want to do. If your phone can synchronise its settings with an email service over its data connection, such as Google Mail, this might be the best option, as you can simply synchronise Evolution with the same source.

Even if you decide to use a different method, connecting your phone to Ubuntu can be useful for other reasons, such as downloading pictures. First you need to work out how you want to synchronise: Bluetooth or USB. USB is the easiest way as you just have to plug in a compatible phone; Bluetooth is arguably more convenient, as you never have to physically connect your phone to your PC.

If you're using USB, you'll probably see several connection options when you plug in your phone. A Mass Storage, or similar, option will make your phone appear as a normal flash storage device; a native

■ When Bluetooth is installed on your computer, you'll see a new icon to show it's working

■ You can easily synchronise mobile phones with Ubuntu

mode, such as Nokia, will make your handset appear as a phone, and you'll need other software to connect to it.

CONNECTING WITH BLUETOOTH

To use a Bluetooth connection, you need a Bluetooth adaptor on your PC. If you're using a laptop this may be built in, but for a PC you'll need to buy a Bluetooth dongle. These cost just a few pounds and should be recognised by Ubuntu when you plug one in. Once you've connected your adaptor you should see a Bluetooth icon at the top-right of the desktop. If you don't, restart your computer.

When you click this icon you'll see a list of options, including Setup new device, which lets you search for a new Bluetooth device. However, this doesn't always work, so it may be easier to manage the connection from your phone. First, click the Bluetooth icon and select Preferences. Click the Make computer discoverable box and type in a name for your computer, which will appear on the phone you're searching from.

Go to the Bluetooth menu on your phone and

BASIC DESKTOP TASKS

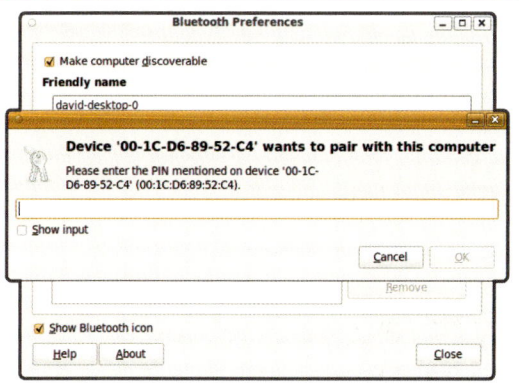

■ Type in your passcode to connect your phone to your computer

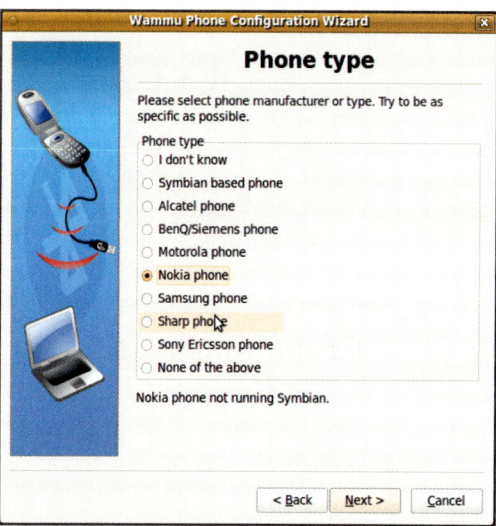

■ Wammu makes it simple to connect to most mobile phones

make sure it's turned on. Next, look for an option for Paired devices. Follow the instructions to start a search and your Ubuntu computer should be discovered. Select to pair and then type in a numeric code of your choice and select OK. A dialog box will appear on your PC asking you to type in the same code. Do this and click OK.

Once your devices are paired, your phone will appear in the list of devices, along with the type of device it is (Phone). On your phone you may get an option to connect to your PC automatically. Select Yes, and your phone will connect to your computer every time it's in range. This prevents you having to make a physical connection each time.

BROWSING YOUR PHONE

When you click on the Bluetooth icon, your phone will appear under the Devices entry. Select it and you'll see an option to browse files. Choose this and you'll be able to copy files to and from the phone's internal memory.

BACKING UP YOUR PHONE

To back up your mobile phone, you'll need to install the Wammu application. Select Software Centre from the Applications menu, and type 'wammu' into the search box. Double-click on Wammu in the search results and then click on the Install button.

Once Wammu has downloaded, run it from the Applications, Accessories menu. Follow the wizard through using the Guided configuration to select your connection type and the type of phone you're using. The default options are usually the best. If you're using Bluetooth, you'll need to make your phone temporarily visible, otherwise Wammu won't find it.

To connect to your phone, select Connect from the Phone menu. If there's an error, try running the wizard again and selecting different connection options. To view contacts, phone messages, calls made and calendar entries from your phone, select the appropriate option from the Retrieve menu. You can edit existing data, and create new calendar entries, contacts and messages using the Create menu. All changes are automatically written to the phone.

To back up your data, select Save from the Backups menu. You can either save all data or use the drop-down menu to save only contacts (vCard and LDIF formats) and calendar (vCalendar and iCalendar) entries. If you save contact and calendar information separately you can import them into another application, such as Evolution mail. If you export your calendar and contacts from Evolution, you can import them into Wammu and save them on your phone.

■ You can export just your calendar or contacts and import them into another application

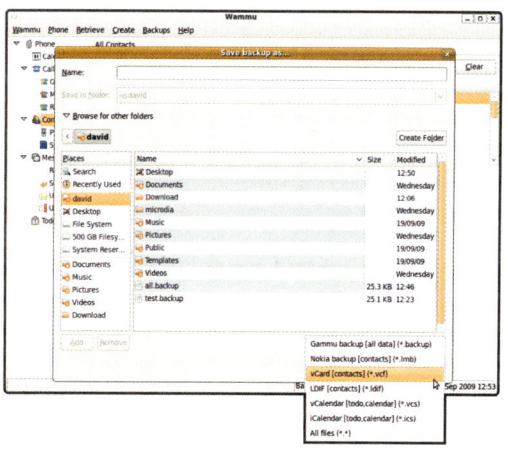

THE COMPLETE LINUX MANUAL 67

CHAPTER 4

Using Google Desktop

Just as Google makes searching the web easy, it can do the same for your PC. We show you how to make finding files and emails simple

The fact that Ubuntu does everything slightly differently to Windows can make it a bit confusing at first. In particular, locating your files can be tricky, as they're stored in different places.

Even when you get used to your new operating system, keeping track of and locating specific files can be difficult. Fortunately, it doesn't have to be this way. With Google Desktop you can search your PC for files and emails (including those stored in Ubuntu's email client, Evolution) as quickly as you can search the internet.

Google Desktop is available for Windows and Linux and works in the same way on both. If you've already used the Windows version, you'll be right at home with the Linux version. However, the installation steps differ for the Linux version, so here's how to get started.

DOWNLOAD AND INSTALLATION
Google Desktop isn't available from Ubuntu's Software Centre utility, so you have to download it manually. Go to **http://desktop.google.com/linux/index.html** and click on the Download Google Desktop button.

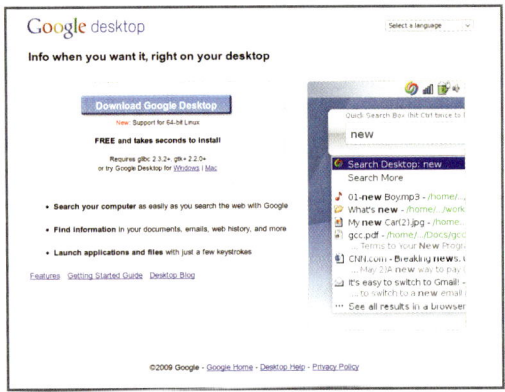

Google Desktop has to be downloaded manually

On the next page you'll be presented with a choice of applications. Choose the .deb version, which is for Ubuntu. Make sure you get the right version for your operating system (32-bit or 64-bit). After clicking the correct link, select Accept and Install on the next page.

You'll be prompted to install the file to your hard disk. Once the download has completed, double-click the file in Firefox's Downloads window. This will launch the Package Installer.

Click the Install Package button, type in your password and click OK. The necessary files and any other required components are downloaded automatically and installed on your computer. The whole process should take only a few minutes to complete. Once it's done, click Close and shut down the Package Installer.

RUNNING GOOGLE DESKTOP
Google Desktop is accessed through the Applications menu. The first time you run it you'll be prompted to set your homepage to Google. You should leave this option selected as it makes it easier to search your computer. You can also choose to send Google crash reports, which can be used to improve the software in the future. When you've selected all the options that you want, click I agree.

Before it becomes useful, Google Desktop has to index your computer. Depending on the number of files you have, this can take anything up to a few hours to complete. Until the process has finished, Google Desktop won't be able to present you with accurate search results.

SETTING PREFERENCES
While you're waiting for your computer to index your files, it makes sense to configure Google Desktop to work the way you want it to. At the

BASIC DESKTOP TASKS

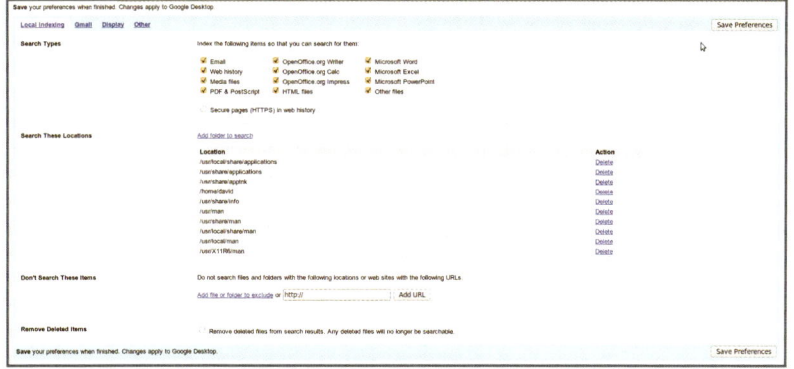

■ You can tell Google Desktop the types of files it should index and where they're located

top-right of the desktop you'll see a coloured swirly icon. This is the short cut to access Google Desktop, and it loads automatically every time you start your computer. Right-click it and select Preferences.

The first page shows you which folders and files are indexed. You can select which file types you want to index using the tickboxes, and add new folders to search, too. You may want to select 'Remove deleted files from search results', otherwise you'll find that performing a search also returns results from files and emails that have long since disappeared.

By default Google Desktop will index only the contents of your email client, but you can click on the Gmail tab if you'd like it to index your Google Mail inbox, too. Just select Index and search email in my Gmail account and type in your username and password. The software will automatically scan your online inbox, too.

Finally, Google Desktop will by default search the internet first, rather than your computer. To change this, click on the Display tab. Change the 'Default search type for the quick search' box to Search Desktop. You can use the other options here to select how many search results you want to see. Click Save Preferences when you're done.

SEARCHING YOUR COMPUTER

The easiest way to search your computer is to tap Ctrl twice. This will bring up a search box. Type what you're looking for into this and results will appear in the drop-down list. The icons next to each result tell you if it's an image, file or email. If one of the options listed is what you're after, select it and it will be opened directly.

Alternatively, if you can't see what you're looking for in the short list, you can select 'See all results in a browser'. This will start Firefox and display the standard Google page, only it's searching your computer not the internet. You can either change the search term by entering something different in the search box, or you can filter the results using the links at the top of the page. These let you refine your searches to view only emails, media files and websites you've visited recently, and all other types of file.

Where available, search results will be accompanied by a thumbnail of the file and a text extract. Both help you narrow down the search results to find the file that you're after.

Once you've chosen a type of search result, you can use further options to find a specific file. For example, if you select Media, you can then specify from the drop-down menu that you only want to look at JPEG files; for email, you can specify that you only want to look at emails from a particular person.

Finally, the search results pages will also tell you how complete the index of your computer is. If you see a red warning message, you should wait until the index has been completely built and then search again; searching too soon means there's a good chance that the file you're looking for hasn't been indexed yet.

■ You can quickly search your computer using the pop-up search box

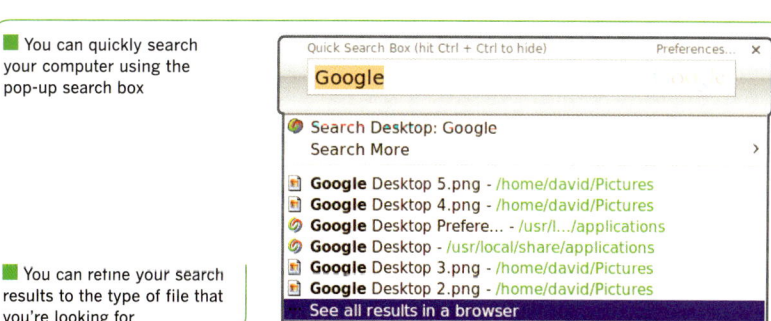

■ You can refine your search results to the type of file that you're looking for

THE COMPLETE LINUX MANUAL **69**

CHAPTER 5

Internet on Linux

Ubuntu has been designed from the ground up to use the internet. In fact, it's more tightly integrated into the online world than Windows, and most of the applications you install are automatically downloaded from the web.

However, there are some tricky online jobs that you'll want to do in Linux that are easy in Windows, such as viewing videos online, uploading files to your website and more. In this chapter we'll take you through all these options and show you how to turn your Ubuntu computer into the ultimate internet PC.

Getting connected	72	Connecting a webcam	88
Controlling the web	76	Firewalls and internet security	91
Configuring email	80	Storing files online	96
Using VoIP	84	Uploading files with FTP	98
Using instant messaging	86		

CHAPTER 5

Getting connected

Here we'll show you how to connect your Linux PC to a local network and take advantage of the mobile internet

What use is a computer that isn't on a network? A few years ago, that would have been an odd question to ask. Times have changed, however, and connectivity is now as much a part of computing as USB flash drives and flat-screen monitors. Over the next few pages, we'll outline the different options for connecting your Linux computer to your home network. We'll also help you set up wireless networking and 3G so you can use your laptop on the move.

The internet has revolutionised the way we use computers. Once, PCs were standalone devices that communicated with the outside world through the medium of floppy disks, but now almost every home PC in the UK is connected to a global network. Not only that, but the connection is probably provided by a high-speed broadband service. The idea that you would forgo an internet connection is almost inconceivable, so we've explored all the issues you'll encounter when connecting your Linux PC, whether you're at home or on the move.

The good news is that if you have a working home network with an internet connection, you can simply attach an Ethernet cable to your Linux PC and connect it to your broadband router. Turn on the computer and it will connect to the internet automatically. However, if you want to customise your setup, or if you experience problems, read the Using an Ethernet connection section below. To connect on the move, skip to Going Wireless opposite.

USING AN ETHERNET CONNECTION

The typical way to connect a PC to a network is to use a standard Ethernet network card and cable, which plugs into a simple router or hub. This is arguably the most secure way of networking your computer. There's no likelihood of data leakage, as there is with WiFi, and Ethernet has a considerably higher data throughput. Ubuntu should have no trouble recognising any network card built into today's PCs and laptops.

As long as the rest of your network is connected to the internet, several things should happen automatically when you boot Ubuntu. First, it will try to obtain an IP address automatically using a service called DHCP. There's usually only one DHCP server on a network, which is probably your broadband router. If you use an Ethernet modem, the DHCP server is run by your ISP.

Ubuntu usually refers to your Ethernet card as eth0. If you have two cards, the other will be known as eth1. You can add more cards and these will be labelled in a similar way, with a higher number. Finding the IP address that's assigned to your card or cards is easy.

From the Applications menu, select Accessories and then Terminal. This brings up a command line. Type ifconfig, and some information will appear. Part of the information

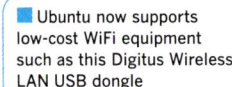
■ Ubuntu now supports low-cost WiFi equipment such as this Digitus Wireless LAN USB dongle

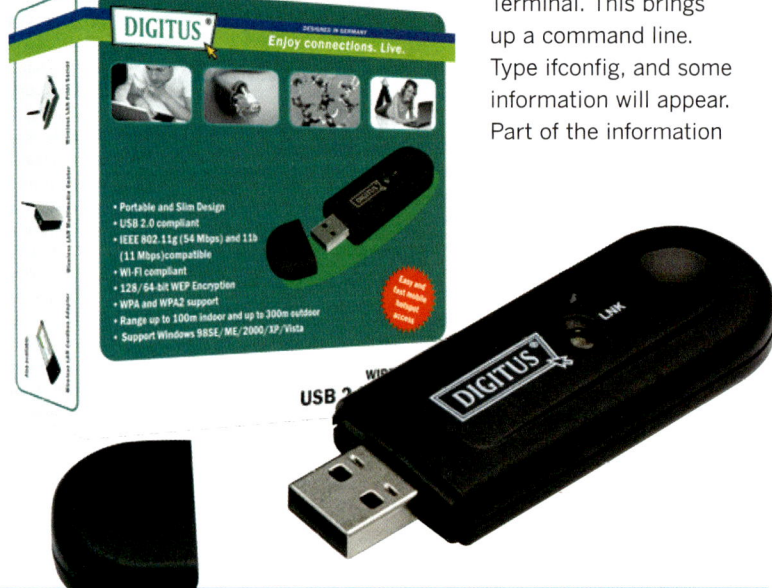

INTERNET ON LINUX

associated with eth0 contains a line that starts 'inet addr:' The address that follows is the IP address for that network interface.

The first three numbers in the address are called the network address. This sequence of numbers will depend on how your router is configured, but on a home local network the default is usually 192.168.0. You'll need to know this address if you want to assign a permanent or 'static' IP address to your Ubuntu computer, rather than using an ever-changing DHCP address. This is easy to achieve.

ADDRESSING THE SITUATION

First, before you close the terminal window, enter the command 'route -n'. The last line of the output that appears will contain an address something like 192.168.0.1, which is the address of your network's default gateway. This is your broadband router, through which all non-local traffic flows – in other words, it handles all traffic destined for the internet. Next, enter the command 'more /etc/resolv.conf'. The last line here contains the name of the DNS server that machines on your network use to turn domain names into IP addresses. Note down these two pieces of information.

Select Network Connections from the Preferences option under the System menu. This will cause a small box to appear. Next select your hardwired network adaptor from the list and click Edit. A second box will then pop up, displaying the network card's configuration options.

Click the IPv4 Settings tab. By default, this will show that the method of assigning an IP address is set to Automatic (DHCP). Use this pull-down menu to select Manual. When you do, the other options on the window become active. Click the Add button and enter the same network address noted above, but append a number between two and 254 for the fourth number in the address. For example, you could choose 192.168.0.50. Enter a Netmask value of 255.255.255.0 and, in the Gateway field, enter the IP address of the default gateway (for example, 192.168.0.1).

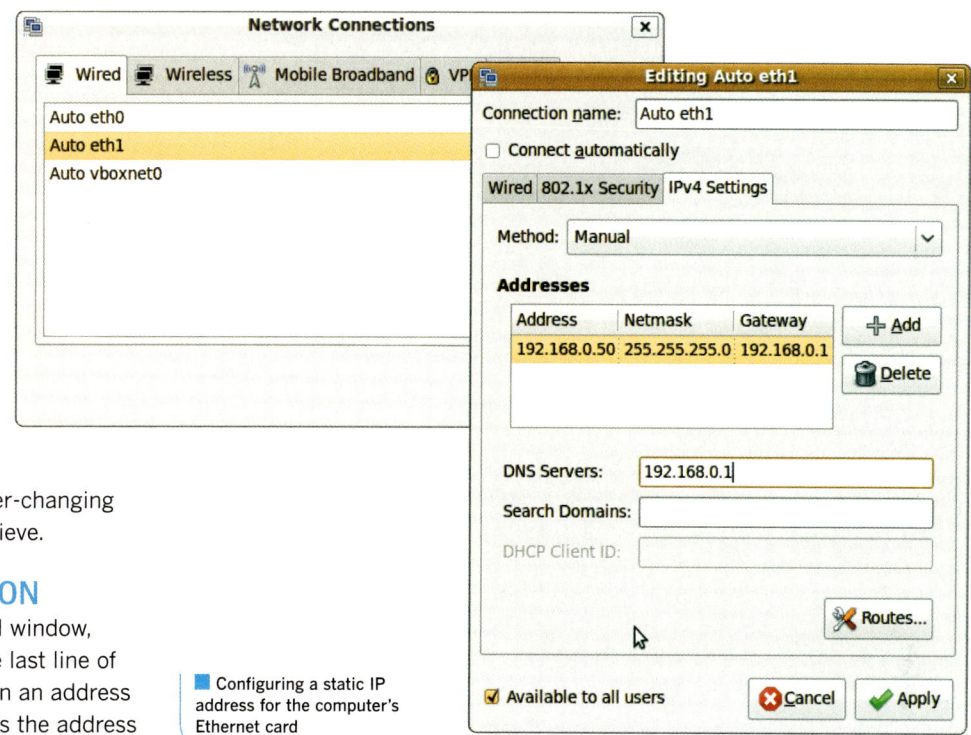

■ Configuring a static IP address for the computer's Ethernet card

GOING WIRELESS

Ubuntu has excellent tools for connecting to WiFi networks, making it a great low-cost choice for people on the move. We've used a cheap (about £14) Digitus Wireless LAN USB dongle bought from a local computer shop.

First, plug the dongle into a convenient USB port. Next, look for an icon on the right-hand side of the taskbar that looks like two flat-screen monitors. This is the Network Manager icon. Click this and a menu will appear listing all the networks that Ubuntu recognises, including any WiFi networks that are in range. Your wired network is selected by default, so choose your WiFi network and a window will pop up asking for the password. Enter this and a message will appear on the desktop to tell you that you're connected. To swap back to the wired network, click on the Network Manager icon again and select your network card.

Your WiFi network should automatically supply Ubuntu with details of security and other settings, but sometimes you may need to change these. You can do this by accessing Network Connections from the Preferences menu. Click the Wireless tab, select your network and press Edit. A second window will appear. The three

CHAPTER 5

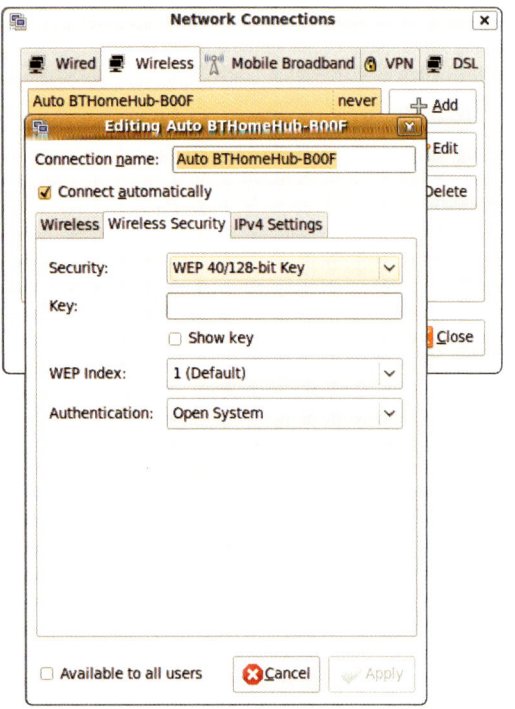

tabs allow you to enter any special details supplied by your ISP's technical support.

USING 3G MOBILE BROADBAND

Public WiFi hotspots are available in many towns and cities, but it's sometimes better to use your mobile operator's own 3G network. Linux used to struggle with new external communications hardware, but those days are long gone, and you no longer have to fiddle with the command line to make things work. To demonstrate how Linux has changed, we'll show you how to connect a Virgin Media 3G USB dongle.

Insert the dongle into a convenient USB port and the New Mobile Broadband Connection Wizard will appear. Click Forward to continue. Enter your country and your mobile broadband service provider, then press Forward again. The window will show a summary of the connection and ask you to give it a name.

Click Apply and you'll be able to open the Network Manager icon on the taskbar. Your new mobile option should appear in the list of known connections. Before you can connect, however, you need to enter your details to authenticate yourself to the mobile network. Reopen Network Connections and click on the Mobile Broadband tab. Select your 3G connection and press Edit.

■ Your WiFi network should provide the correct connection settings, but you can change them easily

■ The mobile connection wizard supports a wide range of 3G providers

Enter the username, password and any other settings your mobile broadband service provider has given you.

Apply your changes, close the Network Connections dialog box and select the mobile broadband connection from the Network Manager icon. You'll see a message that says 'GSM network connection established'.

USING NETWORK TOOLS

Ubuntu comes equipped with a range of network troubleshooting tools. For convenience, the most important tools have been gathered into a single multi-tab window. Open Gnome's System menu, select Administration and then choose Network Tools. The window that pops up has several tabs. Select a network device from the menu on the Devices tab and it will display its details and statistics.

The Ping tab lets you contact other machines on your local network and over the internet to test if they're working, and to discover how long packets take to reach them. To do this, the 'ping' command sends a stream of packets to the destination computer and waits for a response.

THE COMPLETE LINUX MANUAL

INTERNET ON LINUX

This is an incredibly useful network diagnostic tool (see the 'Ping commander' box below for more details). To use this tab, simply enter the DNS name or IP address of a destination computer and press Enter. The screen will slowly fill with a bar chart showing how long, in milliseconds, each of the five ping responses takes. If you're having trouble reaching a website, visiting this tab will tell you if the machine has crashed or if the connection is just very slow. It's a good way to verify that your network connection is working correctly.

The Netstat tab provides low-level routing information, but the Traceroute tab is far more interesting. If you enter the IP address or DNS name of a destination computer and press Enter, this tab gradually fills up with information about the route taken to get to it. Each entry is called a 'hop' along the route. It's fun to find out the route taken to get to your favourite websites, but if your network contains several subnets connected by routers and you have a connectivity problem, it will indicate where the problem lies by failing at that point.

The Port Scan tab is strictly for use on your own network. Port scanning tells you which of a target computer's ports are open and listening for traffic. Type in a DNS name or IP address and press Enter. If you try this on machines on the internet, you may trip an intrusion detection system and the site may complain to your ISP. This is because port scanning is a technique that hackers use to find vulnerable computers and services on the internet. If you're found using a port scanner over the internet, you may get banned from your ISP.

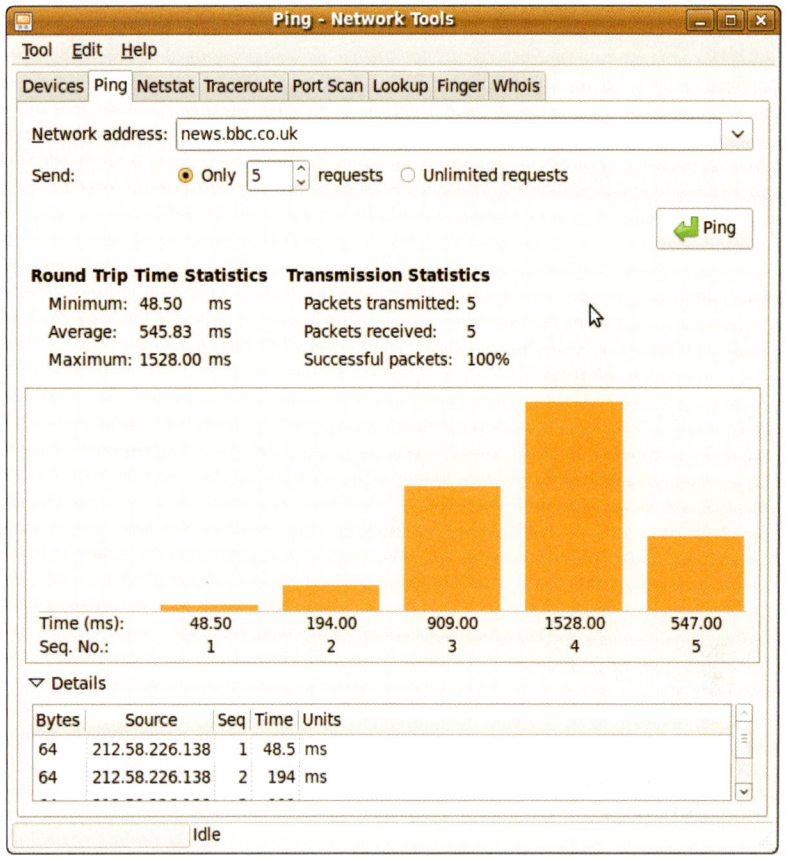

The Lookup tab lets you find details of public machines easily. Enter a DNS name or IP address and select the type of information you require. Related to this is the Whois tab. Enter a domain name (without the 'www' prefix) and the tab will contact a public Whois server to retrieve details of the domain's owner.

■ Pinging another computer is a good way of establishing where any connection problems lie

Ping commander Testing a network connection

Network administrators have a procedure for testing network connections that can quickly pinpoint a problem. Ubuntu's Network Tools make it easy to perform similar tests.

On the Ping tab, enter 'localhost' as the hostname. Localhost is a special machine name that refers to the computer you're using. When you send traffic to localhost, the network card detects that the address is local and responds itself, thereby proving that it's working properly.

Now ping the local machine's IP address. This traffic enters the network and comes straight back, proving that the local subnet to the hub or switch is working.

If you have two subnets, ping a computer on the other subnet to make sure the router between them is working properly. Finally, ping a website that's outside your local network, such as www.google.co.uk. If you can't reach it, check that your broadband router is working.

CHAPTER 5

Controlling the web

Linux doesn't come with all the technologies you need to view web pages, but you can add them easily. Here we show you how

Windows-based browsers have got to the point where they'll prompt you to add missing web components. The same's not true with Linux, and you may run into problems getting common websites such as YouTube to work properly. Over the next few pages, we'll show you how to get everything working.

The internet is filled with an impressive array of videos, applications and rich multimedia for you to enjoy – at least, it is if you have the right browser and addons. Ubuntu comes with just about everything you need to get going, including the excellent Firefox web browser. However, not everything will work straight away, and you may find that a few websites, such as YouTube, won't display video. Fortunately, these things are easy to fix.

Our instructions focus on Firefox, as it's currently the best browser for Linux. Internet

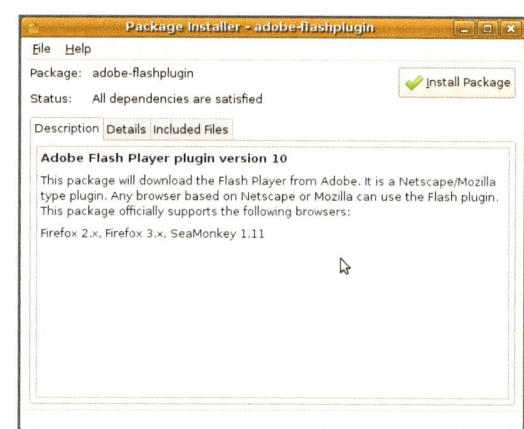

■ You can install Adobe's Flash manually. Once done, you'll be able to view videos on YouTube and use other Flash-enabled websites

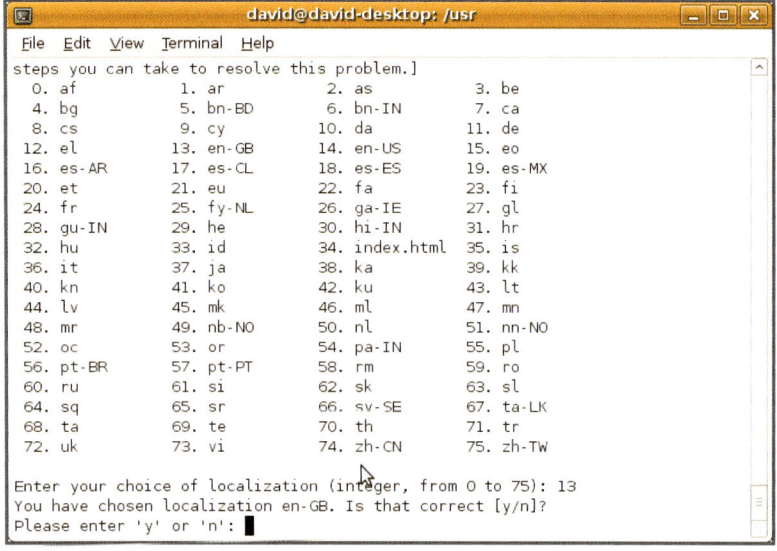

■ The installer lets you choose which language Firefox will use

Explorer is a Windows-only browser, and you can't install it on Linux unless you're prepared to mess around with the WINE Windows emulator (see the 'Don't bank on it' box on page 79 for details). Google's Chrome, which is also limited to Windows at the moment, has similar restrictions. You can get other browsers, but they're not very popular and don't have the same level of support as Firefox.

UPDATING YOUR BROWSER

The first thing you should do is make sure that you have the latest version of Firefox. Unfortunately, you won't simply be able to check this using Ubuntu's Software Centre on the Applications menu, so you'll need to update the software manually. This is easy to do with the free Ubuntuzilla application, which you can download from http://sourceforge.net/projects/ubuntuzilla/files.

Click on Files and download the .deb file for your operating system (32-bit or 64-bit). When the file has downloaded, find it on your desktop and double-click on it. Then click the

Install button. Once it has completed, you can use Ubuntuzilla to install Firefox. Bring up the Terminal from Applications, Accessories and type in the following command:

```
ubuntuzilla.py -a install -p firefox
```

If the installer says that it can't get a PGP key, try this command instead:

```
ubuntuzilla.py -a install -p firefox -g
```

Press y to accept the latest version of Firefox. Then type 13 to choose EN-GB as the language and press y to accept the choice. The new browser will be downloaded and installed on your computer automatically.

Once the installation has finished, you can launch the new version of the browser from the Applications, Internet menu. It will be called Firefox and the old quick-launch icon will also point to the new Firefox installation.

GONE IN A FLASH

Flash is one of the main internet technologies and is used for items as diverse as menus in websites and videos in YouTube. To use Flash, you need to install the Flash plugin. If you visit a site that requires Flash, you may be prompted to install it automatically, but this isn't always the case, so it's best to install it manually.

■ You can watch WMV movies in Firefox thanks to the gstreamer plugin

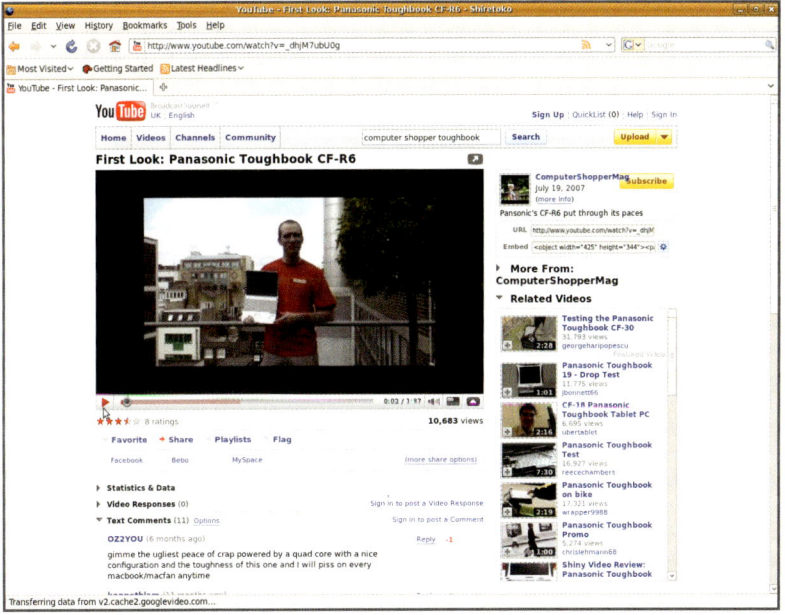

■ With Flash installed, you can view websites that use the technology, such as YouTube

To do this, open Firefox and go to **http://get.adobe.com/flashplayer**. From the drop-down menu, you can select different versions depending on your Linux distribution. For Ubuntu, select .deb for Ubuntu 8.04+ and click the Agree and Install Now button. The file will be downloaded to your computer's desktop. Once it's finished downloading, double-click on the install file (install_flash_player_10_linux.deb). Cancel any messages about a newer version being available and click Install Package. Type in your password when requested and Flash will install automatically. This will take a few minutes. Click Close to complete the installation.

Once the installation has completed, restart your browser. Shut down all your open browser windows, including the download manager, and start Firefox again. To make sure it's working properly, you should visit a website that uses Flash, such as YouTube. In YouTube, click any video. If it plays, then Flash is working; if you get an error message, you should download Flash again and reinstall it.

CUP OF JAVA

Java is another common web technology that is used by many websites. It's not always visible, as it's often used behind the scenes to make jobs such as filling out forms easier. Ubuntu comes with its own Java virtual machine (VM) installed,

CHAPTER 5

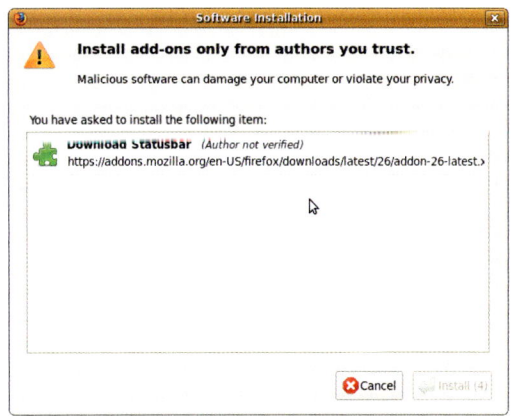

You can easily extend Firefox's capabilities by installing addons

but we found that it wasn't detected by Firefox 3.5, so it's best to install Sun's Java VM. Go to **www.java.com** and click Free Java Download. On the next page, select Linux (self-extracting file) for 32-bit Ubuntu and Linux x64 for 64-bit Ubuntu. Download the file to your desktop. To install it, open a terminal window. Remembering that you can press the Tab key to autocomplete file and folder names, type in the following:

```
cd /usr
sudo mkdir java
```

```
cd java
sudo cp /home/<your username>/Desktop/
    <name of file you downloaded>
chmod a+x <name of file you downloaded>
sudo ./<name of file you downloaded>
```

You'll then get a few pages of text containing the terms and conditions of use. Just press the spacebar to flick through the pages and type 'yes' when prompted. Java will install on your computer. Once it's done, you'll see a message onscreen saying 'Done'.

You now have to add Java to Firefox's plugins. To do this, go back to your terminal window. Type the following:

```
cd /usr/lib/mozilla/plugins
sudo ln -s /usr/java/jre<version>
    /plugin/i386/ns7/
    libjavaplugin_oji.so
```

This will install the Java plugin in Firefox. To test that it's working properly, shut down all your browser windows and launch Firefox again. Go to **www.java.com** and click on the 'Do I have Java?' link. A short test will run on your computer and you'll then be told that you have the latest

■ Install Java through the command line

```
inflating: jre1.6.0_14/man/ja_JP.eucJP/man1/pack200.1
inflating: jre1.6.0_14/man/ja_JP.eucJP/man1/unpack200.1
inflating: jre1.6.0_14/man/ja_JP.eucJP/man1/javaws.1
 creating: jre1.6.0_14/plugin/
 creating: jre1.6.0_14/plugin/i386/
 creating: jre1.6.0_14/plugin/i386/ns7/
inflating: jre1.6.0_14/plugin/i386/ns7/libjavaplugin_oji.so
 creating: jre1.6.0_14/plugin/i386/ns7-gcc29/
inflating: jre1.6.0_14/plugin/i386/ns7-gcc29/libjavaplugin_oji.so
 creating: jre1.6.0_14/plugin/desktop/
extracting: jre1.6.0_14/plugin/desktop/sun_java.png
inflating: jre1.6.0_14/plugin/desktop/sun_java.desktop
 creating: jre1.6.0_14/javaws/
  linking: jre1.6.0_14/javaws/javaws  -> ../bin/javaws
Creating jre1.6.0_14/lib/rt.jar
Creating jre1.6.0_14/lib/jsse.jar
Creating jre1.6.0_14/lib/charsets.jar
Creating jre1.6.0_14/lib/ext/localedata.jar
Creating jre1.6.0_14/lib/plugin.jar
Creating jre1.6.0_14/lib/javaws.jar
Creating jre1.6.0_14/lib/deploy.jar

Done.
david@david-desktop:/usr/java$
```

INTERNET ON LINUX

version of Java installed. Websites that use this technology should now work.

VIDEO ZONE

It's possible to get video working in websites that don't use Flash. Visit a website that you know has video and force Firefox into asking you to search for a relevant plugin. For example, to get streaming WMV video to work, go to www.football365.com. A video will attempt to load and fail, but a dialog box will appear that asks you if you want to search for a suitable plugin. You should then click Search.

When given the option, select gstreamer0.10-plugins-ugly and click Install. The plugin will download and install automatically. When it's complete, streaming WMV movies should play.

If you don't see this option, you can manually install all the plugins that you'll need. To do this, click on the Software Centre from the Applications menu. Search for Gstreamer and then install each of the Gstreamer plugins that appears in the results list.

EXTRA HELP

One of the best things about Firefox is that people can extend its capabilities by writing plugins for it. These are known as addons. The good news is that addons are often operating-system independent, so you can use the same ones in Windows and Linux.

To see what's available, go to www.getfirefox.com and click on Add-ons. Here you'll find the database of addons you can browse through and search. They all perform useful jobs; Download Statusbar, for example, displays your current

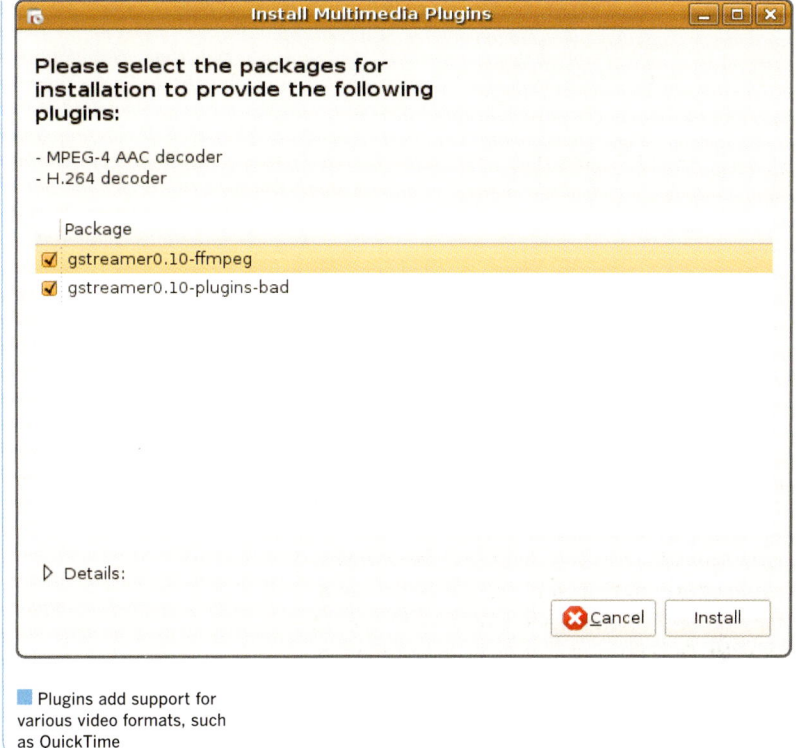

■ Plugins add support for various video formats, such as QuickTime

downloads in a handy status bar rather than using the entire download manager.

When you've found an addon you like, just click the green 'Add to Firefox' button. Then, when prompted, click Install. If there's no green 'Add to Firefox' button for an addon you like the sound of, it's probably because there isn't a Linux version of that particular plugin. You should search the addon database to see if there's something similar you can use instead.

Don't bank on it Why ActiveX websites won't work

Microsoft's ActiveX is a proprietary web technology for developing web applications. It used to be very popular, but many websites now refuse to use it because it's not secure. What's more, Internet Explorer is the only browser that supports it.

However, some websites, such as Egg Money Manager, still use the technology. This is a problem if you're running Linux, as you can't use Internet Explorer. It's not a problem that's easy to overcome, either. Internet Explorer can be installed using the Windows Emulator, WINE, but it's complicated and you also need to copy some Windows DLL files to get ActiveX working.

Because there's no ActiveX plugin for Firefox, you can't use ActiveX websites in Linux without a lot of hassle. If you need to do so, you can either search Google for help on getting Internet Explorer installed in Linux, or use a Windows PC for those times when you need to access that website.

CHAPTER 5

Configuring email

The Evolution email client lets you stay in touch with your family and friends. Here we explain how to set it up

After web surfing, the second most popular online activity is sending and receiving email. Ubuntu comes equipped with a range of email clients, as well as some impressive anti-spam measures. Here we take the lid off Linux email, and show you how easy it is to set up.

If you use Windows, you'll be familiar with the basic built-in client (Outlook Express or Windows Mail, depending on the version of Windows you have), but how do you go about getting your email in Linux?

The good news is that it's just as simple to use, and you get a better email client than Windows' built-in program. One of the email applications in Ubuntu is Evolution. On the taskbar at the top of the desktop, you'll see an envelope icon. When you click on this for the first time, Evolution will start by running its Setup Assistant Wizard to guide you through the basic configuration process.

To complete this, you'll need a few items of information, so it pays to make sure you have this to hand before you begin. These can be provided by your internet service provider, but you'll also be able to get them from your current email application's settings. You'll need to know the address of your ISP's mail servers, such as pop3.yourisp.co.uk. For incoming email, this is usually a POP3 server, but some email accounts, including Google Mail, use an IMAP server (see the 'Mail order' box on page 83). Make sure you get the type of server you're using right. You'll also need to find out if your email servers require any encryption (TLS or SSL are the common types).

Outgoing mail always uses an SMTP server such as smtp.yourisp.co.uk. Finally, you'll need to know the username and password of your email account.

EVOLUTION NOT REVOLUTION

The first page of Evolution's Setup Assistant is the welcome page. Click Forward to continue. The next screen can be used to restore Evolution's settings and email from a backup. For now, we'll assume that you're creating an account from scratch, so click Forward.

You'll be asked for your full name and email address. You can also specify an alternative reply-to email address, so that when someone replies to one of your emails, it will be sent here. Most people should leave this and the Organisation entry blank. Click Forward and you'll be prompted to configure how you receive email. Select POP or IMAP, depending on your ISP. Enter the name of the incoming mail server and your username. Select 'Remember password' to have Evolution store your password; if you don't do this, you'll have to enter your password every time you download mail. The next screen asks how often you want to check for new emails. This is a matter of personal choice,

■ The first step when configuring Evolution involves entering your details

INTERNET ON LINUX

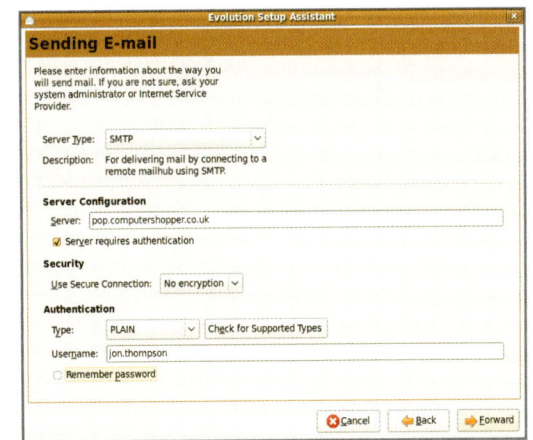

■ If your ISP's SMTP needs a username and password to send mail, tick the 'Server requires authentication' box

but the default of every 10 minutes is a good one, so leave this setting alone and put a tick in the 'Check for new messages every' box.

Click Forward to configure how you want to send email. Outgoing mail is handled by Simple Mail Transfer Protocol, or SMTP. Enter the name of your ISP's SMTP server in the server configuration box. If your provider's server requires authentication (a username and password) to send mail, tick the 'Server requires authentication' box. Most ISPs won't demand that you use a secure connection to the mail servers, but check first.

If your provider doesn't use encryption, set 'Use Secure Connection' to 'No encryption'; if you need encryption, select the type of encryption from the drop-down menu. Enter your username. If you put a tick in the 'Remember password' box, Evolution will log into your ISP mail account automatically when there's a message to send.

Clicking Forward again allows you to give the account a descriptive name. Click Forward again and enter your time zone. Finally, click Forward one last time and then Apply to finish the configuration process. Evolution is now ready for you to send and receive email, and to further customise your account.

To test Evolution, click the envelope icon on the taskbar. Hit Compose to create a new mail message, and address it to a webmail account. Enter a message, then press Send. Then go

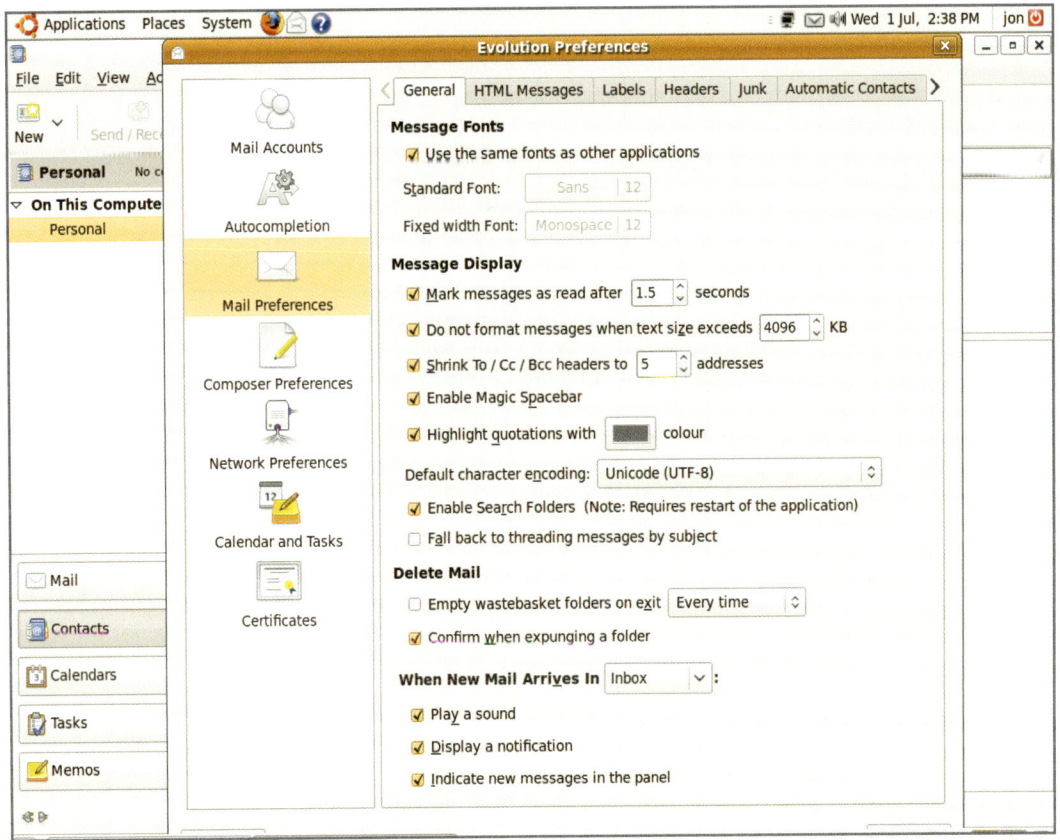

■ The main Evolution Preferences window is split into several categories

THE COMPLETE LINUX MANUAL 81

CHAPTER 5

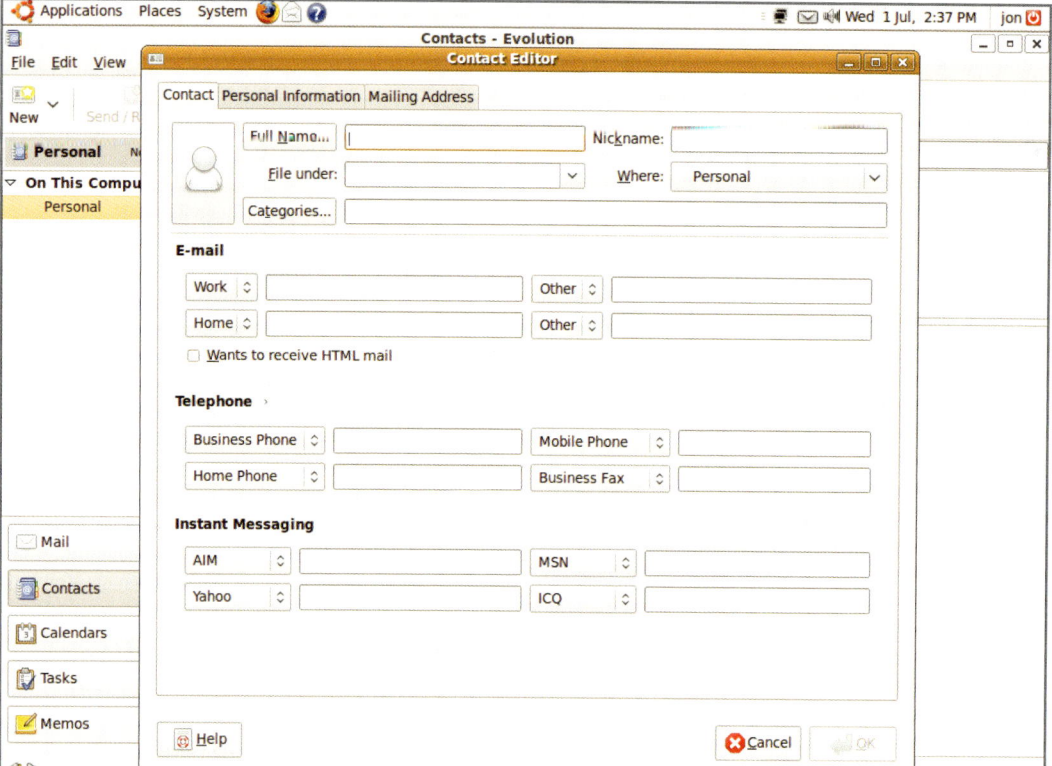

You can store so much data about a contact that Evolution can become a useful resource

to the webmail account. The message should have arrived. Reply, then check for new mail in Evolution using the Send/Receive button. This sends any mail left in your outbox and requests any unread mail from your ISP's mail server. The reply should download.

Once you've configured your email, you can add a new account or change your existing settings by selecting Preferences from the Settings menu. If you select the account you've just set up and press Edit, a second window will appear, displaying the data you entered in a set of tabs. If you move to a new ISP, or if your provider starts using a different connection method (an encrypted link, for example), you can change your server details here. Click OK.

ADVANCED CONFIGURATION

The left-hand pane of the configuration window has several categories. If you click Autocompletion, you'll be able to say whether you want Evolution to auto-complete any email addresses you begin entering. If you have a number of address books, you can select those to which this feature applies.

Then click the Mail Preferences category. The General tab lets you set the general look and feel of messages. To save disk space, you can tick the box marked 'Empty wastebasket folders on exit'. Just don't select this option if you're likely to need to recover any emails that you delete.

Next, click the HTML messages tab. This controls how you view HTML content. The default setting doesn't load images automatically and it's a good choice. If you select to load images from the internet, a spammer can authenticate that your email address is live. A useful trick to stop spammers is to change the HTML Mode to 'Only ever show PLAIN'. This will show you the full address of links in emails, so it's harder to get caught out by a phishing email.

Click on the Automatic Contacts tab and Evolution will automatically create a contact in the address book when you reply to a message. This tells Evolution that future incoming messages from that contact aren't spam, so they won't be junked by mistake.

The Composer Preferences category in the left-hand pane lets you define how you write new emails and replies. Here, you can specify

INTERNET ON LINUX

whether emails will be sent as HTML, whether Evolution will insert emoticon icons where you enter the relevant text, and if you'd like your recipients' email clients to respond by sending a receipt when messages are read.

With the default reply style of Quoted, the original message is quoted when replying to an email. Most people simply type their reply at the top of the quoted part, but if you have long email conversations, they're easier to read when laid out from top to bottom. Ticking 'Start typing at the bottom on replying' will place the cursor at the end of the message rather than the start.

You can also personalise your messages with a signature. Click the Signatures tab and press Add. Enter a name for the signature and the text. To finish, press Save and Close.

Back on the main interface, you can manage your email contacts by pressing Contacts at the bottom of the screen. This opens the address book. Double-click the upper pane to open a form for inputting the details of the new contact. This has three tabs for contact, personal and mailing information, so Evolution can be used for far more than just storing email addresses. To get back to your inbox, simply press the Mail button at the left of the lower screen.

BLOCKING SPAM

Stopping spam is easy using SpamAssassin, which is an intelligent and free utility for scanning your email. If you're downloading email from Google Mail or another webmail service, you don't need spam filtering as your messages will already have been filtered.

Before you can use SpamAssassin, you need to install it. Select Add/Remove from the Gnome desktop's Application menu. Type 'spam' into

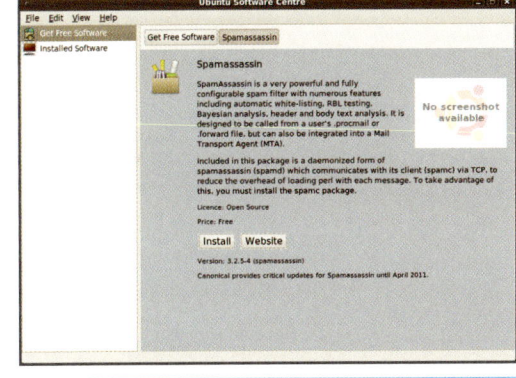

■ The SpamAssassin application can be found in Ubuntu's Software Centre, so installing it is a simple point-and-click procedure

the search box, double-click the SpamAssassin entry and click Install. Enter your password when prompted, and SpamAssassin will download and install on your computer.

You now need to enable SpamAssassin support in Evolution. Click on Preferences from the Edit menu, choose the Junk tab of Mail Preferences and select SpamAssassin as the Default junk plugin. You should see a message saying that SpamAssassin is available. Beneath this, if you tick 'Include remote tests' SpamAssassin checks online to see if a message has come from a known spam source.

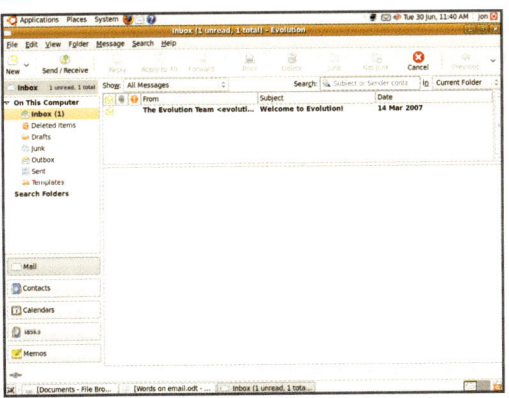

■ Once Evolution is configured and ready to send and receive emails, it will look like this

Mail order Email servers explained

Your ISP or email provider may give you a choice of POP3 (sometimes called POP) or IMAP servers, so which should you pick?

POP3 is the most common and easiest to use. Your email client connects to the server and downloads the email. Typically, it deletes the mail from the server when it's finished, leaving the only copy of your email on your PC. There's no more interaction between your mail client and server.

With an IMAP server, mail is stored on the server and accessed from the client. Any email you read on your PC is marked as read on the server, and vice versa. So if you're away and use webmail to read your email, when you get home, your client will show that your email has been read.

IMAP's the best choice if you have a lot of email storage space on a server, such as with Google Mail's current 7GB limit.

CHAPTER 5

Using VoIP

Real-time communication with your friends is easy with Ubuntu. Here we show you how to configure Skype for Linux

Skype may be best known as a voice-over IP (VoIP) application, but it also has some excellent text-based chat facilities. To keep in touch with non-Skype chat buddies, Ubuntu offers many other chat clients that are compatible with the protocols used by a wide range of chat services, including Microsoft's MSN and Yahoo! Chat.

Before you can use Skype, you'll need to download and install it. Open Firefox and go to **www.skype.com**, click on Download and then the Linux link on the right-hand side. Click the Download button and then select Ubuntu 8.10+, remembering to select the right version for your operating system (64- or 32-bit).

Once the download has completed, double-click the install file in the Firefox Downloads Window. This will start the Package Installer, which will display a dialog box that shows you more information on Skype. Click the Install Package button to start installing the application and enter your password when prompted.

Skype will now install automatically to your computer. You'll first see the licence agreement. Click Accept to continue and the Skype interface will appear. If you have a Skype username, enter it and your password, and click Sign In. Otherwise, you'll have to sign up for an account; click the 'Don't have a Skype Name yet?' link.

SKYPE'S THE LIMIT

Fill out the onscreen wizard to create a new Skype account, making sure you create a memorable Skype name so it's easy for your friends to find you. When you're done, click the Sign Up button. If your Skype name has already been taken, you'll need to type in another one.

Once your account has been created, you can log on to Skype. The first thing to do is test that Skype is working properly. In the main window, you should see Skype Test Call. Click the green phone icon and a call will be made. You'll hear a woman asking you to leave a message. Leave one and hang on until your message is played back. You can use this to make sure that your microphone and speakers work.

If you don't hear anything during this call, or if the call window says there's a problem with sound or your microphone, click on 'Configure your devices and Skype's behaviour'. This opens a configuration window.

Click on the Sound Devices option in the left-hand pane. The reason you have no sound may be that all the options are set to 'default device'. Click the Sound In, Sound Out and Ringing options, and select a sound device. You can press the 'Make a test sound' and 'Make a test

■ Create a memorable Skype username so it's easier for your friends to find you

INTERNET ON LINUX

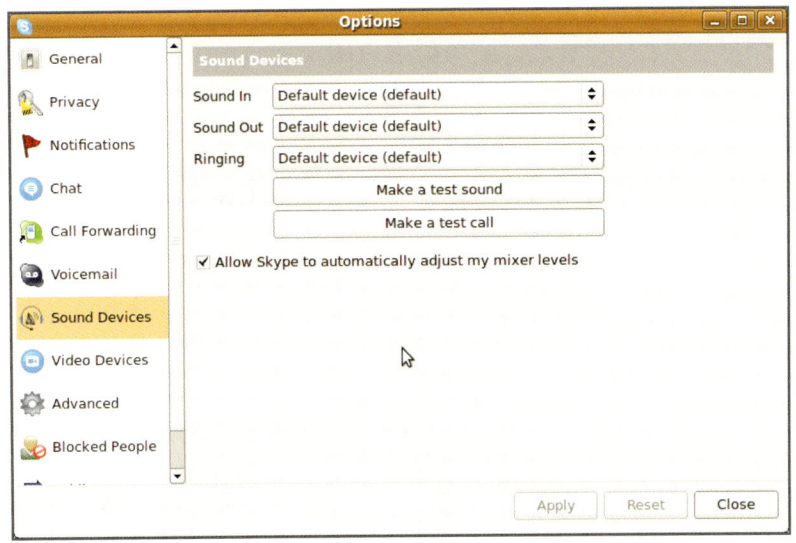

■ The default sound device may be the underlying cause of failed test calls

call' buttons to test your modified configuration. If you want to change your details to make it easier for people to contact you, click on your name in the main Skype window and then click the Edit Profile button. Add any extra information that you want to divulge.

When you're done, you can start to add friends. This is done by clicking on the small green icon at the bottom of the main Skype user interface. This opens up the Add Contact dialog. Enter as much information as possible about the person you want to add. As a minimum, you'll need to know their name, but adding the country, email address or Skype name will narrow the search. Press the Search button, and Skype will respond with a list of people. Click on the one you want and press Add Contact.

A new window will open, with a short message that will be sent to the contact. Edit this and press OK. Once you've been approved by your contact, they'll appear in the main Skype window. When they're online, a green tick will appear next to their name.

IT'S GOOD TO TALK

To call a contact, select their name from the main Skype window and click the green phone icon. You'll be able to have a conversation with the other person when they answer. Click the video camera icon to add video to the call if you've got a webcam.

Alternatively, if you have SkypeOut credits (log into your account at www.skype.com to buy credits), you'll be able to make calls to landlines. Click the Call Phones or Send SMS button at the bottom of the main Skype window. Select the country you're calling from the drop-down list, type in the phone number and press the green telephone icon to make the call. You can right-click a contact and select 'Remove from contacts' to delete it from your friends list, and select Block if you want to stop someone contacting you.

You can also use Skype for text-only chatting. Press the blue speech bubble next to the contact's name and a chat window opens. Type in a title for the chat topic and press Enter. The cursor moves to the input box at the bottom of the interface. Enter a line of text and press Enter to start a conversation.

To change your status, click the green and white tick logo next to your name. If you don't want to be disturbed, you can select Invisible or Offline. The 'Skype Me' setting invites people on your contacts list to call you for a chat.

If you get bombarded with strangers calling or sending you messages, Skype can block incoming connections from anyone you don't know. Click on the Skype button at the bottom of the main Skype window, and select Options. Click on Privacy and choose 'only people I have allowed' for 'Allow calls from…' and 'Allow chats from…'. Click Apply and Close to apply the settings. You can also use the Options dialog box to change the way that Skype behaves and to manage people that you've blocked.

■ Stop people you don't know from contacting you by using the privacy options

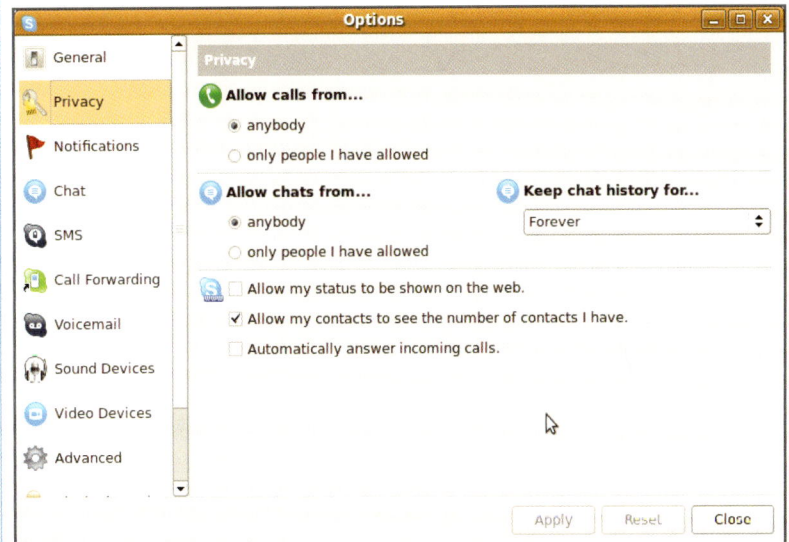

THE COMPLETE LINUX MANUAL 85

CHAPTER 5

Using instant messaging

Sometimes you don't need to make a phone call, but an instant response is required. Instant messaging makes this easy

Sometimes calling people isn't as easy as sending instant text messages. Although Skype has built-in messaging, there are times when you may need to contact people using other clients, such as Google Talk, Windows Live Messenger or AOL Instant Messenger (AIM). Fortunately, Pidgin lets you use a single client and talk to your friends no matter which service they use. It's easy to set up, too.

Pidgin isn't installed by default. To install it, search for Pidgin in the Software Centre in the Applications menu and install Pidgin Internet Messenger. You'll then find it under Internet in the Applications menu. When the software starts, you'll be prompted to add new accounts, so click the Add button. On the next screen, you'll see a dialog box to add an account. Select the service you want to talk to from the Protocol box.

To use an IM service such as Google Talk, you'll need an account. If you haven't already got one, you'll need to create one. The basic information you need to set is your username and password, but some protocols have extra options you need to set. We'll take you through setting up the main services: Google Talk, AIM and Windows Live Messenger.

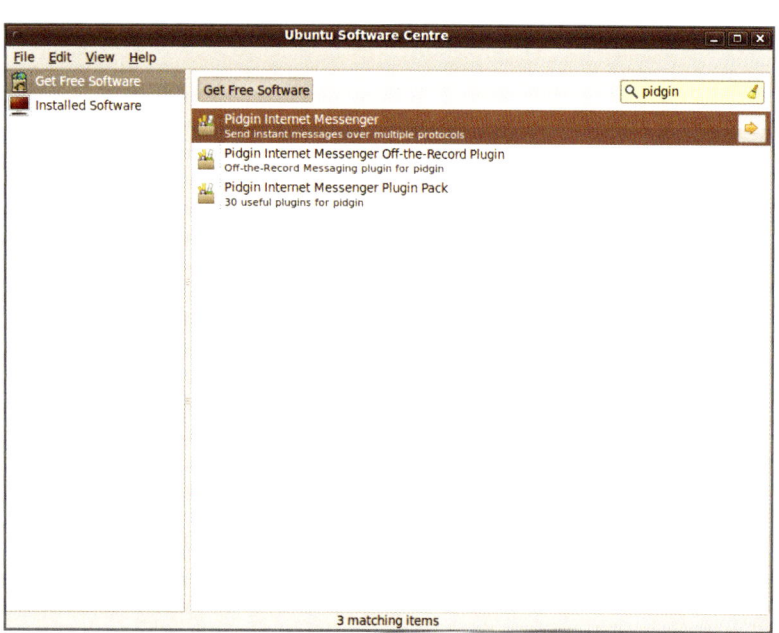

■ You can add new Pidgin plugins quickly and easily

SETTING UP

Google Talk is easy to set up. Your username should be the first part of your Google email address before the '@' sign. The domain is the part after the '@' sign, such as googlemail.com. Enter your Googlemail password and click Add. On the next screen, click Add to add another account.

AOL Instant Messenger (AIM) is one of the most popular instant messaging services, but in our experience it's also one of the least reliable and most difficult to configure. Don't be surprised if you can't sign in to your AIM account occasionally, as this seems normal for the service. That said, there are things you can do to make it more reliable.

After you've entered your account details, click the Advanced tab. You'll see extra settings that define how Pidgin connects to AOL's IM servers. Change the Port option to 443 and click Use SSL. Select 'Allow multiple simultaneous

INTERNET ON LINUX

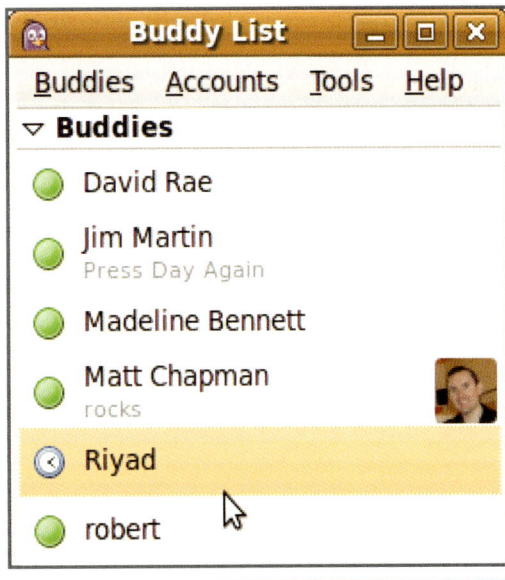

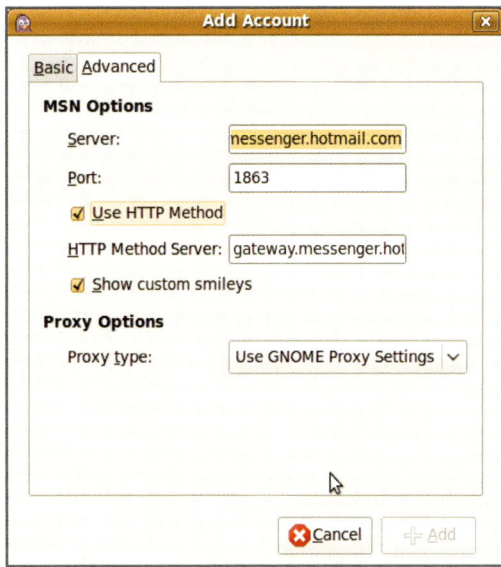

▪ You need to change the way Pidgin connects to Windows Live Messenger to get the best connection

▪ You can organise your friends and set your online status easily

logins' and leave the Proxy type setting alone. Click Add to add the account.

Windows Live Messenger is called MSN Messenger (its old name) in Pidgin. We've found that the connection can fail unless you alter the advanced settings. Enter your Windows Live Messenger account details and then click the Advanced tab. Click Use HTTP Method and leave all the other settings alone. Click the Add button when you're done.

STARTING OUT

Once you've added all your accounts, click the Close button and Pidgin should start up and connect to your accounts. You'll be able to see the online status of your friends, no matter which IM service they're using. If you get any error messages, you can check your account settings by clicking on Manage Accounts in the Accounts menu.

To talk to a friend, simply double-click on their name and starting chatting by typing. You can also right-click on friends and change settings such as their name (Alias), so they're easier to find. Select the 'Send file' option to transfer a file directly to your friend.

Adding new friends and organising them is just as easy in Pidgin as in other IM applications. Click on Buddies, Add Group to add a new group. Type in a name for it and click Add. You can then drag and drop your friends into the new group.

You can also add new friends. Click Buddies, Add Buddy, then select the service your friend is on, type in their name and click Add. You can change your status by clicking the bar at the bottom of the Pidgin window. The same options also appear at the top-right of the desktop.

PLUGIN AND PLAY

One of the best things about Pidgin is that you can use plugins to add extra features. It comes with a set built in, but you can add more. Click on System, Administration and Synaptic Package Manager. Type 'pidgin' into the search box and click Search to reveal a list of available plugins.

We like the Pidgin Encryption plugin, which encrypts your communications with other Pidgin users, stopping anyone from eavesdropping. Put a tick in the pidgin-encryption box and click Apply. The plugin will be downloaded and installed automatically.

Once the installation has completed, shut down Synaptic Package Manager and go back to Pidgin. Click on 'Plugins' from the Tools menu. Scroll down and select Pidgin-Encryption and click Close. Your client is now ready for encryption. When you talk to a friend, you'll see a padlock icon at the top of the chat window. This will be locked if your friend is using Pidgin and has encryption enabled, and unlocked if they don't. You can click the icon and turn on encryption, but your friend will just receive gibberish if they don't also have the plugin.

CHAPTER 5

Connecting a webcam

Chatting with friends is so much easier when you can see them. Luckily, Skype's video call features are easy to use with Linux

There are times where making a voice call with Skype simply isn't enough and you want to be able to see the person you're talking to. Fortunately, this is easy as Skype is designed to support video calls. All you need to do is have a webcam as well as a microphone and headset.

INSTALLING A WEBCAM

Getting a webcam working should be as simple as plugging it in and letting Linux install a driver automatically. In most cases, this is all you have to do, but you can make life easier by buying a webcam from a well-known manufacturer, as Ubuntu is more likely to recognise it and work. Cameras from Logitech, Creative, Microsoft or Philips are usually good choices.

To test if your webcam is working properly, log on to your Skype account (see page 84 for more details). Click the Skype button at the bottom and click Options. Click the Video Devices button on the left and you should see a video window. Click the Test button in the middle of that window and you should see a preview of the video from your webcam.

If you don't see a preview, or the video looks corrupted, there's a problem with your webcam. However, if the video's there but green, it's a common Skype problem that can usually be fixed by editing the command line that runs the application. To do this, click on System, Preferences, Main Menu. Click on Internet, Skype and select Properties. Change the Command to:

```
bash -c 'LD_PRELOAD=/usr/lib/libv4l/
    v4l1compat.so skype'
```

Click Close to apply the settings and restart Skype to see if this has fixed the problem.

■ You may need to change Skype's command line to get video calls up and running

■ A webcam should work the second you plug it in to your Linux computer and will allow you to make video calls

OTHER PROBLEMS

Fixing the problem isn't always as easy as it sounds, and depends on the make and model of your webcam. More importantly, it depends on the real make and model of your webcam, not the brand on the front. Linux provides an easy way to find this out. Get a terminal up from the Applications, Accessories menu and type:

```
lsusb
```

This will bring up a list of all the USB devices connected to your computer, including the manufacturer's name and the type of product. If you scroll down the list you should see an entry that contains the name of your webcam. For example, a common make and model of webcam is the Microdia PC Camera (SN9C201).

Armed with this information, you can look for the necessary Linux driver, if there is one. This can get a bit complicated, and we can't cover how to install every driver. Fortunately, there's plenty of help out there. Our best advice

INTERNET ON LINUX

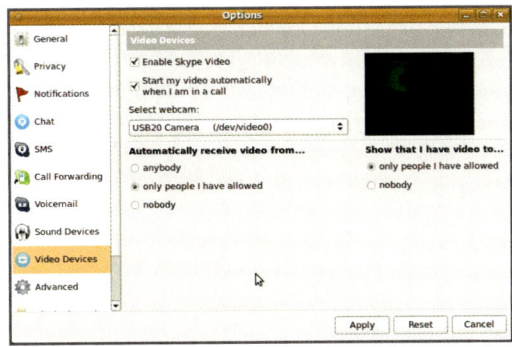

■ If your video is corrupt or missing, you have a problem with your webcam

is to type the name of your camera into Google followed by the version of Ubuntu you're using. It won't take long to find some instructions on how to download and install a driver.

Webcam drivers need to be compatible with the Linux kernel that you're using, so it's important to find instructions for your exact version of Linux or they won't work. If you can't find any drivers or the instructions won't work, you should think about buying a new model that has support. Have a look at models from Logitech, Creative or Philips. Before you buy one, search Google for that model plus the version of Ubuntu that you're using. This will let you know if it will be compatible or not.

USING YOUR CAMERA IN SKYPE

Using your webcam to make a call in Skype couldn't be easier, but before you start bothering your friends you should make sure that your camera is working correctly. First, follow the instructions in the first paragraph to make sure your webcam is working correctly. When it is, you can make a test call to a friend. Note that they don't need to have a webcam installed on their computer for this to happen; if they don't

■ Once you're in a video call, you can see your friends and your own video feeds

■ To get your webcam working, you may first need to find out its make and model

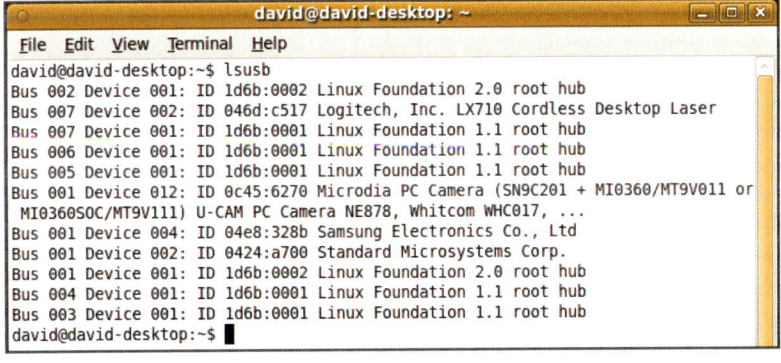

have a webcam they'll be able to see your video, but you won't be able to see them.

To make a video call, select the person you want to call from the list of your friends. Click the Green call button to initiate the call. When you're on the call, click the video camera icon at the bottom of the window and select Start My Video. This will bring up a main video window to show you the person you're talking to (if they have a webcam), with a smaller video of yourself, so you can make sure you're in the frame.

CHANGING SETTINGS

If you primarily make video calls, there's no need to initiate a video call manually every time. Click on the Skype logo at the bottom of the main Skype window and select Options. Click on Video Devices and select 'Start my video automatically when I am in a call'. This will turn on video chat the moment you call someone. Click Apply to alter these settings.

THE COMPLETE LINUX MANUAL

INTERNET ON LINUX

Firewalls and internet security

Linux may be more secure than Windows, but it's not completely immune to attack. Here we show you to protect your system

Linux is widely considered to be more secure than Microsoft Windows. This is partly because of its open-source nature, which allows anyone to spot and report programming errors and vulnerabilities in the operating system and its applications instantly.

It's not immune from attack, though. Over the next few pages we'll show you how to boost your computer's security by configuring Linux's built-in firewall and installing anti-virus software.

Hackers are entirely motivated by money, and they'll use any trick they can to get information that they can either sell or use to make cash. While Linux has been relatively immune to attacks, as its install base was too small, its increasing popularity means that hackers now have the OS in their sights.

As such, you need to boost the security of your computer. For starters, every computer on the internet needs a firewall to protect it from unwanted intrusions by hackers, for example. Increasingly, Linux also needs anti-virus protection. Security companies are now waking up to the threat posed to Linux operating systems by malware, and have begun supplying basic Linux versions of most of their products.

THE FIREWALL

The purpose of a firewall is to inspect every data packet attempting to enter or leave the computer, and decide whether or not to allow it on its way or to block it. Firewalls are very closely connected to the operating system itself and have to be capable of running at top speed without introducing any significant drain on resources or network performance.

A number of commercial firewalls include a vast range of features. However, at their most basic, firewalls simply need to decide whether to allow or 'drop' packets based on a set of rules. Configuring a firewall is therefore a matter of writing these rules to tell it which types of network traffic to let through, and which to block.

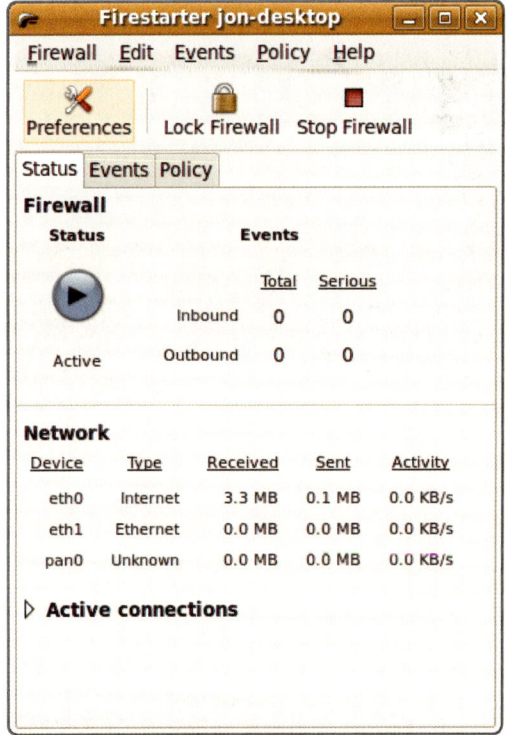

Firestarter's main interface The Lock Firewall button is for use in emergencies only

CHAPTER 5

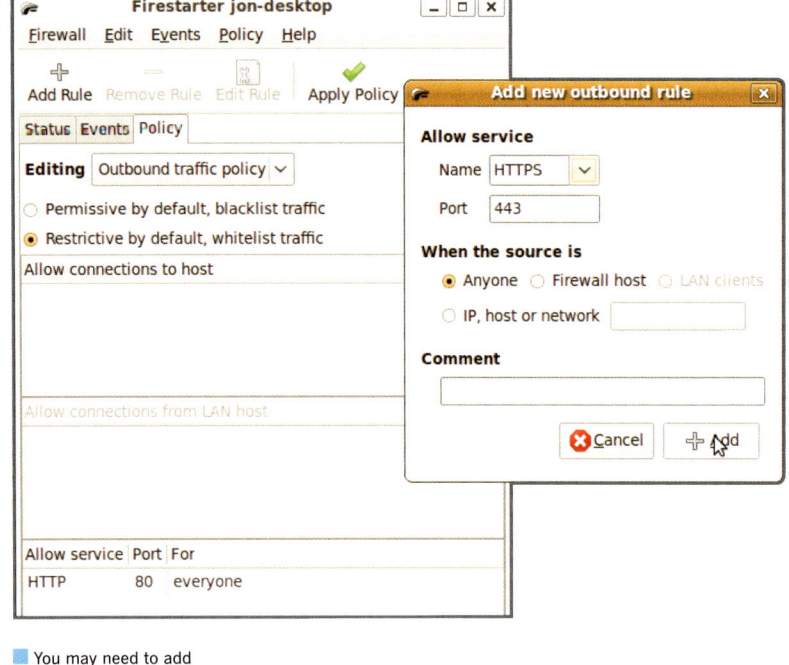

◼ You may need to add specific rules to allow HTTP and HTTPS traffic through the firewall for web browsing

Linux traditionally comes with a firewall called iptables that requires system administrators to set it up using extensive configuration files. For the rest of us, however, there's a far friendlier firewall called Firestarter. Like most firewalls commonly used on Microsoft Windows, this is an entirely graphical application that makes configuration very simple.

INSTALLING FIRESTARTER

Firestarter is a free application. To install it, first click on the Applications menu and select Ubuntu Software Centre. Type 'firestarter' in the search box and press Return. The Firestarter application should appear in the list below the search box. Click the Install button to begin the installation process.

You may be asked for your password in a subsequent pop-up. If this happens, enter it, click OK and Ubuntu will download and install the latest version of Firestarter. Once this process is complete, click Close. Firestarter should now be installed and ready to protect your computer.

CONFIGURING THE FIREWALL

To open Firestarter's user interface, click on the Administration option on the System menu. The first time you run it, after entering your password to confirm you want to make changes to the system, you'll see a configuration wizard. Click Forward to continue.

The next screen on the wizard allows you to assign the firewall to a specific network connection. This should default to Eth0 if you have a single wired connection, which is correct, so leave it as it is. If you're using a wireless network card, it'll either be set as the default option or will be available on the pull-down list.

Your internet gateway usually assigns all PCs on your network an IP address when they boot up. Unless you've chosen to disable this and assign IP addresses manually, tick the box marked 'IP address is assigned via DHCP' before clicking the Forward button again.

There's no need to enable connection sharing on your Ubuntu machine, so you can safely press Forward again and finally click Save. The main Firestarter control panel will now pop up. The firewall status pane should show it as being active.

ACTIVE CONNECTIONS

There are two important buttons on the Firestarter control panel. The first is Lock Firewall. When you hit this, Ubuntu's firewall immediately blocks all incoming and outgoing traffic and the status icon changes to a padlock. It's the button you should click if you think something suspicious is happening. Clicking this button for a second time unlocks the firewall and it continues allowing traffic to pass through it as usual – subject to its security rules, of course, which we'll come to in a moment.

The second important button on the control panel is Stop Firewall. When you press this, the status changes to Disabled. This isn't a recommended setting to use other than briefly when you believe there's a problem with the firewall blocking legitimate traffic.

Another useful part to the control panel is Active Connections. Click the arrow button next to this and the display extends to show the connections you have to the outside world. Open tabs in Firefox, run Skype or an instant messenger application, and all your external connections will be listed here.

DIFFERENT MODES

Firestarter works in two modes. The first is called Permissive and is the default setting. This allows all traffic to enter and leave the

THE COMPLETE LINUX MANUAL

computer except for the ports the user tells it to block. The second mode is called Restrictive, which blocks all traffic except for the dataflow present on the ports you explicitly allow.

For the best security, Firestarter should run in this second mode so that it blocks all traffic except the stuff you explicitly allow. It blocks only outgoing traffic, not incoming traffic, but this is enough to stop hackers compromising your security as it prevents your computer from replying to any malicious packets.

To put Firestarter into Restrictive mode, first click the Policies tab just under the Lock Firewall button. Now click the Editing pull-down menu and select Outbound traffic policy. This causes two radio buttons to be displayed directly underneath the menu. Select the second, marked Restrictive by default, whitelist traffic. Press the Apply Policy button at the top of the window and open a web browser.

After a few seconds of trying to connect, the browser will return an error message because Firestarter is blocking all outgoing traffic. You now need to allow HTTP and HTTPS traffic through the firewall so you can browse the web.

In the lower pane of the Policies tab, and with Outbound traffic policy selected, right-click on the window's bottom pane and select Add Rule. This produces a small pop-up window. Select HTTP from its pull-down menu. Under the option 'When the source is', choose Anyone. Click the Add button to add your new rule to the list and it will automatically be activated.

Do the same for HTTPS (the secure version of the HTTP protocol used when buying things online). When both HTTP and HTTPS rules have

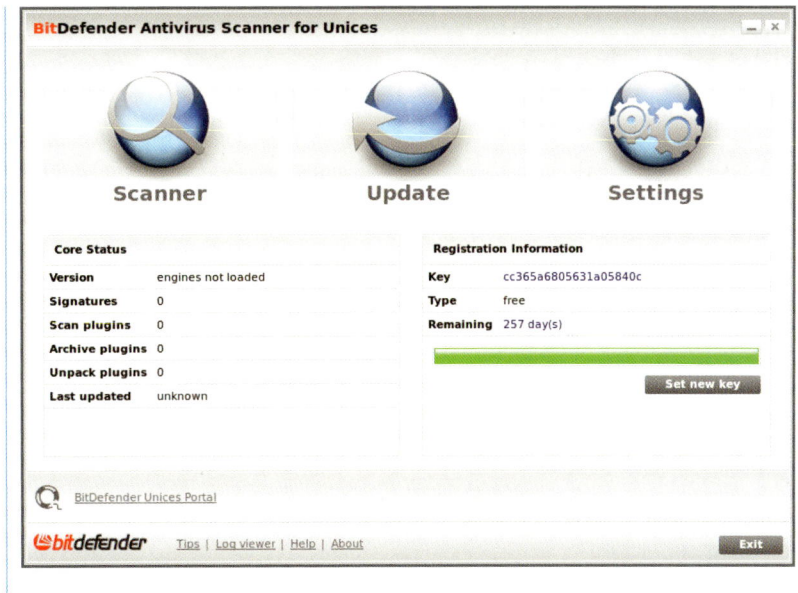

■ BitDefender's interface looks pretty simple, but it's a fully functional virus scanner

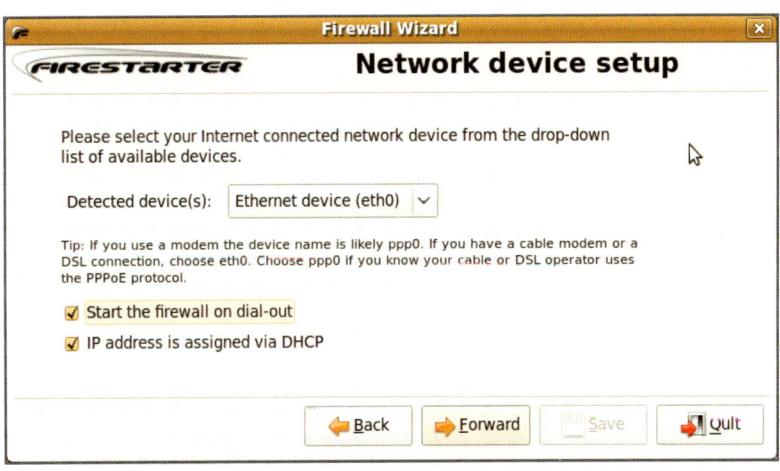

■ Firestarter's configuration wizard makes it easy to alter the relevant settings

been created, press Apply Policy. Try surfing again and everything should work smoothly.

If you normally send and receive email from Ubuntu and you find that it now doesn't work, you'll need to add rules to the list for SMTP and POP3. You'll also have to add a rule for Samba if you mount Windows shares. If you need to add a rule for a port that's not named on the list, simply enter its number in the input box. To find out the port number for a particular type of traffic, visit http://tinyurl.com/portnumbers.

ANTI-VIRUS SOFTWARE

Because of its increased popularity, Linux is beginning to need virus protection. We're going to show you how to download and install the popular BitDefender Anti-Virus package. This offers manual scanning, but with some nifty options. The installation process requires you to use the command line, but by following our instructions, it'll still be a simple process.

First, you need to obtain a free personal use licence from http://tinyurl.com/ydun6v. Click on Request Free License, enter your name, email address and country, click the tick box to confirm you're a private user and hit Send. Your licence key will be emailed to you.

Next, go to http://tinyurl.com/dymsjb and click the i586.deb.run package if you have a 32-bit machine. Otherwise, click the amd64.deb. run package. This opens the download manager. Select Save file and finally click OK.

CHAPTER 5

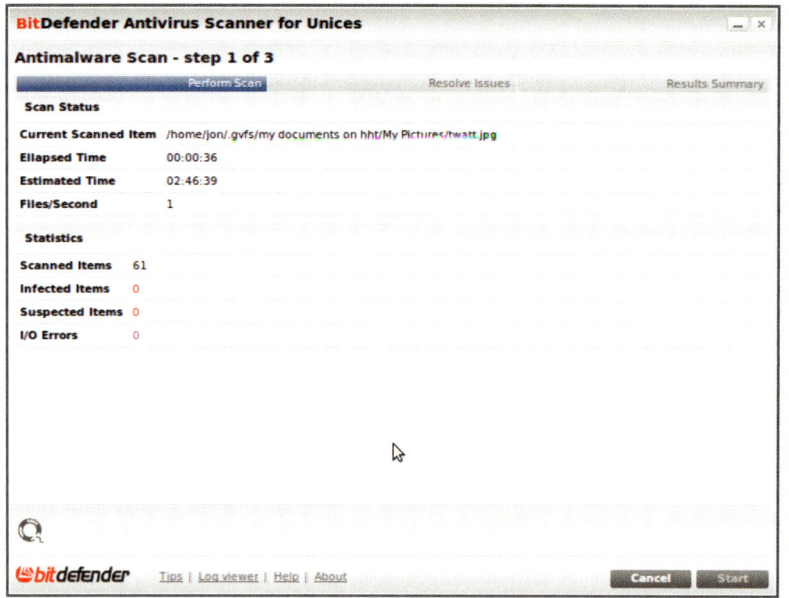

Once downloaded, click on Accessories on the desktop's Applications menu and select Terminal. This opens a terminal window. In it, enter the following command:

```
cd /Desktop
```

Now enter the following (noting the capital B of 'Bit'), but instead of clicking Return, press the tab key. This will fill in the long filename for the downloaded BitDefender package:

```
sudo sh Bit
```

Hit Return and you'll be asked for your password. Enter it and the BitDefender licence agreement appears. Hit the space bar to scroll through it a page at a time. Once at the bottom, you'll be asked to enter the word 'Accept'. Do so and BitDefender installs itself. The installation process will also ask if you want a GUI installed. Enter the upper-case letter Y and press Return.

Once installation is complete, using BitDefencer is very simple. Open it from the System Tools menu of the desktop's Applications menu. Press Set New Key and enter the personal licence key emailed to you earlier. Now press the Update button to download the latest virus definitions. To scan a directory structure for malware, press the Scanner button, select the directory and finally click Open.

■ To scan a file or folder for viruses and malware, simply open it and let BitDefender do its stuff

CONFIGURING BITDEFENDER

Hit the Settings button and you'll see various basic, but useful, options. Of these, the General Settings pane is the most useful. The option to keep the application running in the background ensures that the anti-virus engine remains active after you've closed its control panel. This makes subsequent scans faster, but increases memory and processor usage. Allied to this setting is 'Pre-load anti-virus engines on startup'. This loads various malware detection modules and keeps them loaded between scans rather than loading them for each one.

You can either exit or simply hide the BitDefender control panel when not in use with the two buttons at the bottom right of the screen. When hidden, the red BitDefender logo appears on the right of the desktop's menu bar. Click this and the interface opens again.

If you opt for 'Hide main window on startup', the BitDefender icon will appear on the desktop's menu bar. This is useful if you use the 'Enable file drop zone' option.

With this option activated, you'll see a large BitDefender icon on the desktop. Drag and drop the file or directory you want scanning on to this and it provides a convenient method of carrying out scans. Nothing's actually moved; it's merely a way of telling BitDefender what to scan.

If you enable 'Scan on drop', then when you drag and drop a file or directory on to the Drop Zone icon, it'll instantly be scanned. Otherwise, the Drop Zone accepts files for scanning and displays a numeric tally as you add more. If you want to, you can right-click on its icon and select 'Start scanning' to scan the lot in one go.

■ A small but useful set of configuration options allows you to use BitDefender's Drop Zone for quick scans

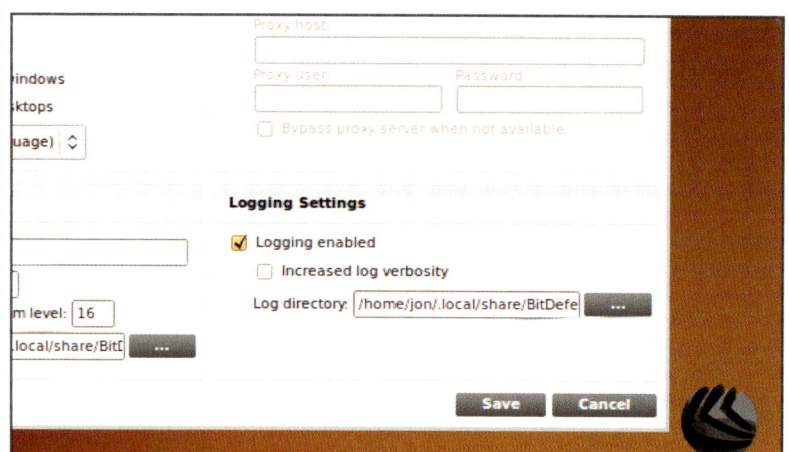

TRY COMPUTER SHOPPER
WITH 3 ISSUES FOR £1

As a technology enthusiast you already know how satisfying it is to get the most from your PC. Why not save time and effort when it comes to looking for new products and software by adding the **UK's best-selling computer magazine** to your monthly read?

Computer Shopper puts you in a great position to negotiate when buying anything to do with PCs. Every issue features **more industry advertisers then any other PC magazine**. So you can compare prices quickly and easily, to make sure you get the best deal.

Find out more with for 3 issues for £1
Right now you can claim the next 3 issues for just £1! It's a 100% risk free offer because if after 3 issues you're not completely satisfied you can write to cancel your subscription and you **won't pay any more than the £1 already debited**.

YOUR GREAT DEAL
- **3 issues for £1** to start your subscription
- If you're not satisfied, simply cancel and **pay no more than the £1** already debited
- **Save up to 26%** on the shop price
- **FREE delivery** to your door
- Get every issue **before it hits the shops**

CALL NOW ON 0844 844 0031
Order securely online at www.dennismags.co.uk/computershopper entering offer code G0905CRM or return the invitation below

---

COMPUTER SHOPPER 3 ISSUES FOR £1 OFFER [UK ONLY]

☑ **YES!** Please start my subscription to Computer Shopper with **3 issues for £1**. I understand that if I'm not completely satisfied, I can write to cancel during my introductory period and pay no more than the £1 already debited. To keep receiving Computer Shopper, I don't have to do anything – my subscription will automatically continue at the LOW RATE shown. The 3 issues for £1 are mine to keep, whatever I decide.

YOUR DETAILS – Please complete in BLOCK CAPITALS

MR/MRS/MS FORENAME
SURNAME
ADDRESS
POSTCODE
DAYTIME PHONE YEAR OF BIRTH
MOBILE NO.
E-MAIL

Dennis Publishing (UK) Ltd uses a layered Privacy Notice, giving you brief details about how we would like to use your personal information. For full details please visit our website www.dennis.co.uk/privacy/ or call us on 0844 844 0053. If you have any questions please ask as submitting your details indicates your consent, until you choose otherwise, that we and our partners may contact you about products and services that will be of relevance to you via, direct mail, phone, e-mail and SMS. You can opt-out at ANY time via www.subsinfo.co.uk or privacy@dennis.co.uk or 0844 844 0053.

Direct Debit Payment – 3 issues for £1, then £21.99 every 6 issues (SAVE 26%)

Instruction to your Bank or Building Society to pay by Direct Debit

Please complete and send to: Freepost RLZS-ETGT-BCZR, Dennis Publishing Ltd, 800 Guillat Ave, Kent Science Park, Sittingbourne ME9 8GU
Name and full postal address of your Bank or Building Society

To the manager: Bank name
Address
Postcode
Account in the name(s) of
Branch sort code
Bank/Building Society account number
Signature(s)
Date

Originator's Identification Number: 7 2 4 6 8 0

Ref no. to be completed by Dennis Publishing

Instructions to your bank or Building Society
Please pay Dennis Publishing Ltd. Direct Debits from the account detailed in this instruction subject to the safeguards assured by the Direct Debit Guarantee. I understand that this instruction may remain with Dennis Publishing Ltd and, if so, details will be passed electronically to my Bank/Building Society.

Banks and building societies may not accept Direct Debit instructions for some types of account

You will be able to view and amend your subscription details online at: www.subsinfo.co.uk

PLEASE RETURN TO:
Freepost RLZS-ETGT-BCZR, Computer Shopper Subscriptions, 800 Guillat Avenue, Kent Science Park, Sittingbourne ME9 8GU

Offer Code: G0905CRM

CHAPTER 5

Storing files online

Online storage is an efficient and secure way to back up your files. It's also incredibly easy using the free Dropbox service

Being able to store files securely online has become very popular. As well as providing a safe location for backups that can't be damaged in your home or physically stolen, online storage is also incredibly convenient, allowing you to access your files from anywhere.

Dropbox is a free online service for Linux. The software lets you synchronise files with multiple computers over the internet. When you save a file on one computer it gets automatically updated on all the others. Dropbox also has 2GB of free online storage (up to 100GB of storage can be paid for), which you can use for standard online storage. It also has a dedicated Linux client for it. Here, we'll show you how to use it.

INSTALLATION
To install Dropbox, download the installation package from www.getdropbox.com. Click on the Download button, making sure that you select the right version of Ubuntu and the type (32-bit or 64-bit). When the file has downloaded, double-click it in Firefox's Downloads window.

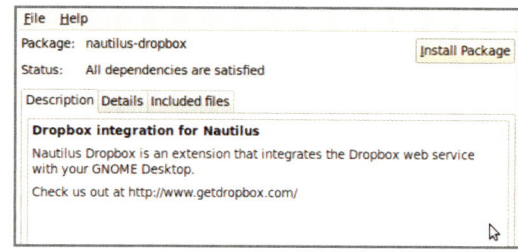
■ You have to install Dropbox manually, but it's a simple procedure

This will launch the Package Installer. Click Install Package and Dropbox will be installed on your computer. Once it's finished, click the Close button and shut down the Package Manager.

Click on Applications, Internet, Dropbox, and you'll see a dialog box warning you that you need to install a proprietary daemon. Click OK and this will be downloaded automatically from the internet to your computer. It should take only a few minutes.

GETTING UP AND RUNNING
Restart your computer when the installation has completed. Next time your computer starts you'll notice a new icon in the top-right of the screen for Dropbox. If you click it, a window will appear asking if you have a Dropbox account. Select 'I don't have a Dropbox account' and click Next. Fill out all the required details. You'll be asked which type of Dropbox account you want (2GB,

■ Dropbox lets you synchronise files between multiple PCs

■ Dropbox has to install some proprietary software in order to work properly

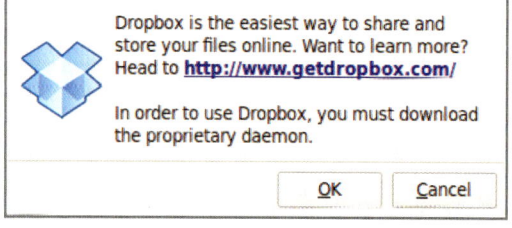

INTERNET ON LINUX

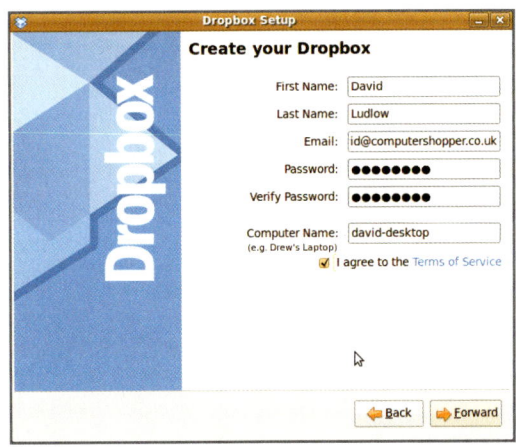

You can create a free Dropbox account and use the service with 2GB of free online disk space

25GB or 50GB). Select 2GB for now, as you can always upgrade at a later date if you really like the service and run out of storage space.

After you've created your account, you'll be told a bit more about how Dropbox works. You'll also be asked if you want to select where your Dropbox folder will be stored. There's no need to change this, as the default location of your Home folder is fine, so click Finish. Your Dropbox folder will be opened automatically.

USING DROPBOX

Your Dropbox folder is stored in your Home folder and called Dropbox. To upload files to it, simply drag and drop them into this folder. When they have a green tick next to them, it means they've been successfully uploaded.

When you download the Dropbox client to another computer (Linux, Windows or Mac) and log on with the same account details, the online files are synchronised with that computer. Any changes, such as a file or folder being deleted or new files being created, are mirrored on all computers connected to the same account.

As the Dropbox folder appears as a normal folder, too, you can use it as the destination for backups. This will automatically write your files to Dropbox's secure servers.

WEB ACCESS

You don't have to access Dropbox through a special folder stored on your computer, as you can also log on to your account using a web browser. This lets you see all the files and folders you have stored online and lets you manipulate them, too. You can delete files and folders, create folders and upload new files.

One feature that the website gives you over the desktop client is that it lets you create a shared folder that you can invite other people to use. Changes to that folder and its files are replicated for everyone with access to it, making it a great way to collaborate on projects.

You can also share files and photos with people that don't have Dropbox accounts using the special Photos and Public folders. Anything dropped into the Public folder can be shared with the outside world with read-only access. You simply right-click the file or folder you want to share and select Dropbox, Copy Public Link, and then email this to your friend.

A similar thing works for photos. Just create a folder inside the Photos folder and add pictures to it. Right-click the folder you want to share and select Dropbox, Get Public Gallery Link. Send this link to your friends, and they can view your high-resolution photos.

■ Files and folders with green ticks next to them have been uploaded to your web space

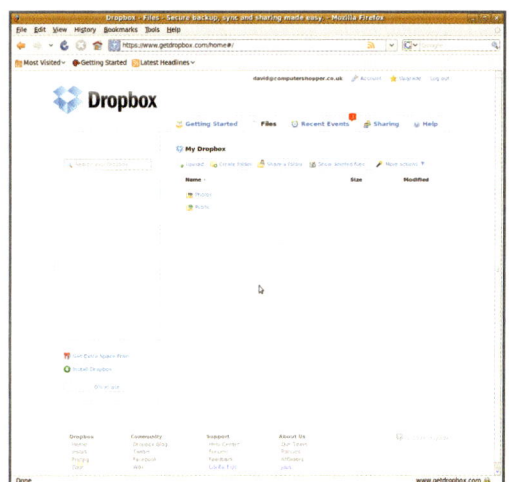

■ You can also access your Dropbox account through the service's website

CHAPTER 5

Uploading files with FTP

If you have your own website, you may need to upload files to it via FTP. Linux has built-in support for FTP, but using FileZilla is easier

The File Transfer Protocol (FTP) is used by the vast majority of web-hosting providers to let you upload and download files to and from your website. The graphical FileZilla FTP client – the same software as available for Windows – is the best way to use FTP.

INSTALLING FILEZILLA
FileZilla can be downloaded from the internet, but it's actually easier to install it directly from the command line. Start a terminal window from the Applications, Accessories menu, and type:

```
sudo aptitude install filezilla
```

Press Enter. Type in your username and press Enter again. When prompted, type Y (note this is upper case) and Enter then, when prompted, Y and Enter again. This will cause the latest version of FileZilla to be downloaded from the internet and installed on your computer. Once the installation has completed, you can close the terminal window. FileZilla can now be accessed through the Applications, Internet menu.

USING FILEZILLA
FileZilla is an incredibly easy application to use. When you start it for the first time, you'll be presented with a list of files stored on your computer's hard disk, listed under 'Local

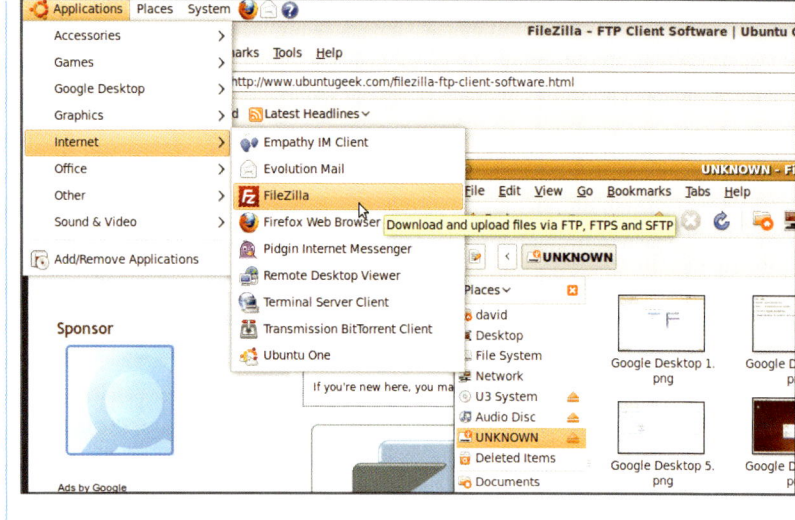

■ FileZilla can be launched like any other application

■ FileZilla can be installed quickly and efficiently from the internet by using a terminal window

site'. There'll also be a blank window called 'Remote site'. When you connect to your web-hosting service, the Remote site window will be populated with its files; you can then drag and drop between the two.

ADDING SITES
Click the Site Manager icon (the first icon in the toolbar) to bring up a new window. This lets you specify logon details for all the FTP sites you use, so that you can access them quickly without having to enter your details every time.

To add a new site, click the New Site button and enter a memorable name for the site to which you want to connect. Type in the Host name (the address of the site, such as ftp.mywebsite.com). Leave the Port option blank, unless otherwise told by your web host. Change the Logontype to Normal and type in your username and password. Click OK to save the settings or Connect to connect straight away.

INTERNET ON LINUX

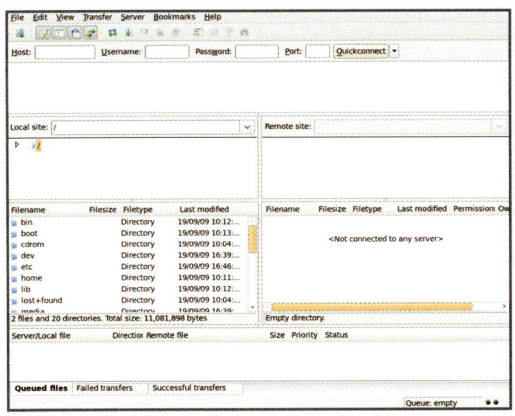

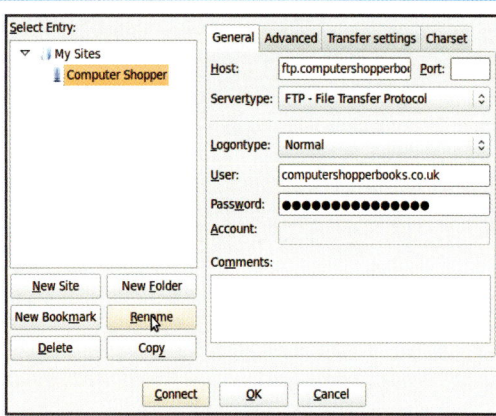

■ FileZilla can remember all the FTP sites to which you connect

■ FileZilla is easy to use and lets you transfer files between your PC and your web host in the same way that you manage local files

To connect to a site in future, simply click on the Site Manager icon, select the site to which you want to connect and click Connect. If you're having trouble connecting and you're sure you've entered the connection details correctly, try selecting your site and clicking on the Transfer settings tab. Change the Transfer mode from Default to Active and try again; if you still don't have any luck, try selecting Passive instead. Sometimes FTP sites will work with only one of these options selected.

TRANSFERRING FILES

Once you're successfully connected to a remote website, you can easily transfer files between the two. The Remote site window will now be populated with folders on your FTP site. Double click on a folder to view the files it contains. When you've found the files or folders you want, you can navigate to a specific folder on your home computer using the list under Local site.

You can then simply drag and drop files or folders between the Local and Remote sites (or vice versa). When you do this, a bar at the bottom of the main FileZilla window will show you how the transfer is progressing.

You can also drag and drop files directly from Ubuntu's normal File Browser into the Remote site (and vice versa) to start a transfer. This is often quicker and easier than using FileZilla to navigate through your local hard disk.

ADVANCED FEATURES

Don't worry about accidentally overwriting a new file with an old copy, as FileZilla will check for this. If a duplicate file is detected, you'll see a warning dialog box asking you what you want to do. You can choose the Skip the file, Overwrite (there are lots of options for choosing when to overwrite, such as if the file you're trying to copy is newer than the one you're trying to overwrite) and Rename. You can also choose whether to apply the same option every time, only for uploads or only for the current set of files you're transferring ('current queue only').

Finally, FileZilla will automatically check for updates, downloading the latest version to your computer and installing it. It checks every time you start the application, so you'll quickly be informed if there's a new version available.

■ You can just drag and drop files between your local computer and the remote FTP site

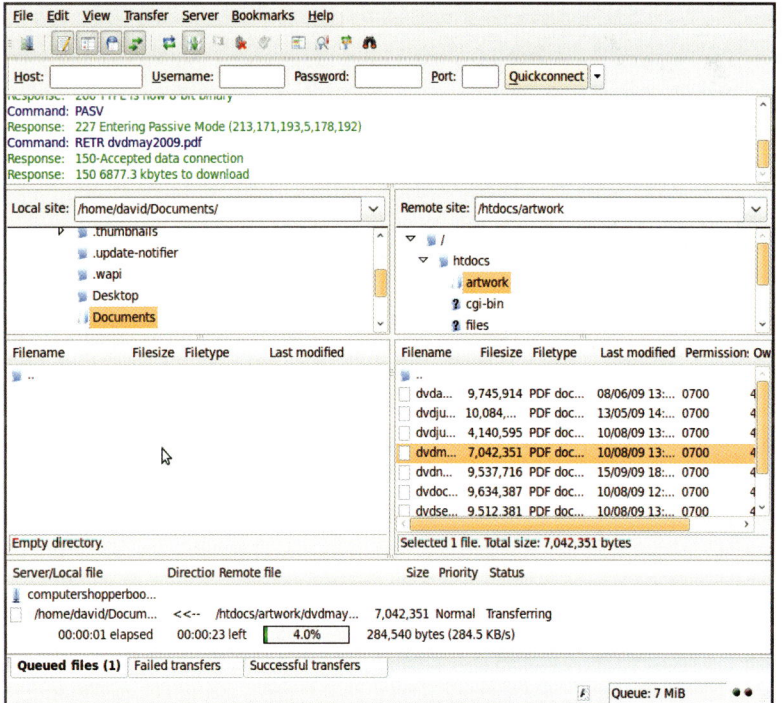

THE COMPLETE LINUX MANUAL

CHAPTER 6

System health

Just as with a PC running Windows, it's important to make backups on Linux so that you don't lose any important files. Here we'll show you how to back up individual files regularly so that your work is always safe, and make a complete image of your computer so that you can restore it in the event of a serious problem.

Choosing a backup destination	102
Making backups	104
Making an image of your system	109

CHAPTER 6

Choosing a backup destination

There are lots of places you can store your important files and folders. Here we take a look at the most popular options

Making a backup of your data is the only way to make sure it's safe. If you copy all the files on your PC to an external storage area, it doesn't matter if your computer is stolen or breaks down, as your data can be restored to a new PC.

There are lots of different ways to make backups and plenty of options when it comes to storing them, too. Here, we'll look at the some of the most practical solutions for storing your precious files so you can be sure your data is safe should the worst happen.

ONLINE

Online storage is rapidly becoming more popular as broadband speeds increase. Systems such as Dropbox (see page 96 for details on how to use this service) work by providing you with storage space that you can use over the internet for a monthly charge. The main benefit of a system such as this is that you don't have to buy any physical storage devices.

This means that your backups can't be stolen along with your computer, and can't be burnt down with your house. The companies providing these services make sure that your data is backed up again, so it's the most secure method of backup that you can make.

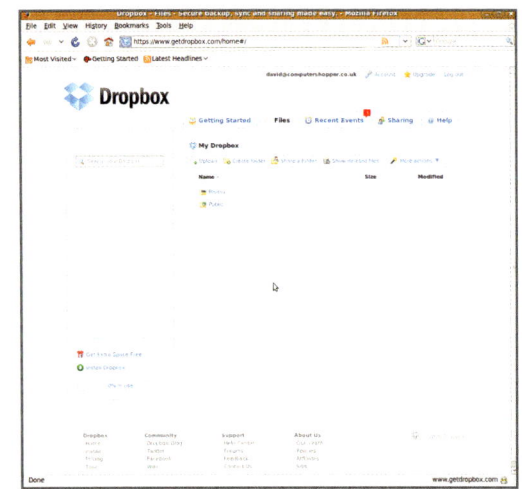

As online storage can be accessed from anywhere with an internet connection, it's a good method for people with laptops, as you can back up your data while on the move, combating laptop theft, loss or malfunction.

The biggest problem with these services is in the amount of internet traffic they create and the speed at which they work. All broadband connections have slower upload speeds than download speeds, and the fastest upload speed you can get is around 1Mbit/s (122KB/s). To put this into context, if your documents, pictures and videos folders amount to 30GB of data, this would take you almost three days at maximum speed to save all your data online. As most broadband upload speeds are slower than this, you're probably looking at a lot longer.

To get the most out of online storage, you need to choose the files you want to back up carefully so as to save on bandwidth. Office files are typically the smallest in size, and therefore are the quickest to upload.

Finally, be aware of how much data you've backed up; if you have a problem and have to restore it all, it could take a few days. You could also download so much data as to break your ISP's fair usage policy and incur extra charges.

PRO Backups safe from local disasters
CON Slow; can breach your fair-usage policy
BEST FOR Important files or mobile backups

SYSTEM HEALTH

CD AND DVD

Almost every modern PC includes an optical drive that can write files to disc, and using it to make backups may seem a good idea. Media is cheap (CDs cost less than 15p each and 8.5GB dual-layer DVDs cost around 60p) and capacities are high. Before you start making backups to CD or DVD, though, consider what kind of data you'll be backing up, how often you'll do it and how frequently the files will change.

You can only write to a CD or DVD once, unless you buy pricier rewriteable discs. This means that making a copy of your documents folder will require a new disc each time.

These discs can still be useful, though. Once you've edited your photos, it's unlikely you'll go back and change them again. The files can be copied to disc and stored. This is called archiving, and it's different to backing up.

If you're serious about your digital photos, take two copies of each set and keep one at home and store one with a friend or who lives at a different address. This way, if the worst should happen and your PC is stolen, you'll still have a copy of your pictures.

> **PRO** Cheap and easy
> **CON** Hard to update backups
> **BEST FOR** Archiving files such as photos

NETWORK STORAGE

If you have more than one computer, a network-attached storage (NAS) device can store your backups. A combination of an external disk and a network port, a NAS device can be accessed from any network-connected PC in your home. The whole family can share files and store backups centrally. You can even access some NAS devices over the internet.

Prices are reasonable, with 500GB devices currently available for around £80. NAS devices can also be placed out of the way, such as in the loft. This makes them harder for criminals to steal.

Look for a device that contains multiple hard disks and supports RAID 1 (mirroring) or RAID 5 (parity). These will protect your data against a single disk failing in the NAS, so you always have some protection against mechanical failure.

> **PRO** Lots of people can back up at once
> **CON** Can be hard to configure; relatively slow
> **BEST FOR** Homes with multiple computers

EXTERNAL HARD DISK

An external hard disk is easy to connect to a PC and, because it's external, you can quickly plug it into another computer. As they live outside your PC's case, they're immune to problems such as a faulty power supply, which may damage your internal disks. External hard disks are also great value, with 500GB of storage costing around £55.

External disks usually connect via USB or eSATA. USB is the most common. You simply plug your disk into a spare USB port on your computer, and it will be automatically detected. USB is pretty quick, too, beating both CD and DVD drives when it comes to speed.

For quicker transfers, an eSATA drive is your best bet. Provided that your computer has an eSATA port, you can get the fastest transfer rates available. The eSATA system is essentially SATA with a slightly different connector, so an eSATA disk can be as fast as an internal hard disk. You can convert an internal SATA port to eSATA using a blanking plate costing around £3.

The main benefit of using a hard disk for backup is that data can be rewritten, so you can leave the drive plugged in and make regular backups to it. The danger is that they are attractive to thieves and offer no protection if your house burns down. That said, for regular and convenient home backups, they're a great choice.

> **PRO** Simple to connect
> **CON** Works on only one computer at a time
> **BEST FOR** Backups on a single PC

THE COMPLETE LINUX MANUAL

CHAPTER 6

Making backups

Keeping your files safe is incredibly important no matter which operating system you use. Fortunately, backing up in Linux is easy

File backups are in incredibly important way of protecting your data. You should make them regularly to make sure you don't lose any important files in the event of a disaster. Fortunately, setting up a file backup strategy in Ubuntu is incredibly easy.

Before you start, there are some things to consider. First, a backup is only as good as the information that you give it; if you don't tell your computer to back up some files, it won't. For that reason, it's worth making sure that your computer is well organised and that you keep your data in neatly ordered folders and not spread out all over the hard disk.

Ubuntu, like Windows, sets up predefined folders for each user, including ones for Documents, Music, Pictures, Videos and Downloads. We think it's worth keeping your documents in these folders, so that you know exactly where they're located. This makes setting up your backup regime easier and ensures that you won't accidentally overlook any documents and lose data in the event that your computer suffers a catastrophic failure.

BACKUP TYPES

There are two types of file backup that you can make: full and incremental. A full backup, as its name implies, backs up all your files regardless of when they were last modified. You should make at least one full backup a week, so that you've got a copy of every file that you need.

The downside with full backups is that they take up a lot of disk space. If you ran only full backups you could end up backing up exactly the same files time after time. For this reason, there are incremental backups.

These back up only the files that have been modified since the last time that you made a backup, and so require a lot less disk space. To perform a full restoration of your data from an incremental backup, however, you'll also need a copy of a full backup. Incremental backups should be made more regularly; we suggest doing this at least once a day.

TREAT YOUR MEDIA WITH CARE

From the previous two pages, you'll have worked out which type of backup media you're going to use. Regardless of the choice, it's important that you protect your backup media and treat it carefully; dropping your backup disk isn't only expensive, but may cause you to lose all your data. For really important data you should even consider making two backups and storing one set away from your house, such as with a friend.

Ubuntu has a backup utility called Simple Backup, which is incredibly easy to use and configure. Here we'll show you how to use it.

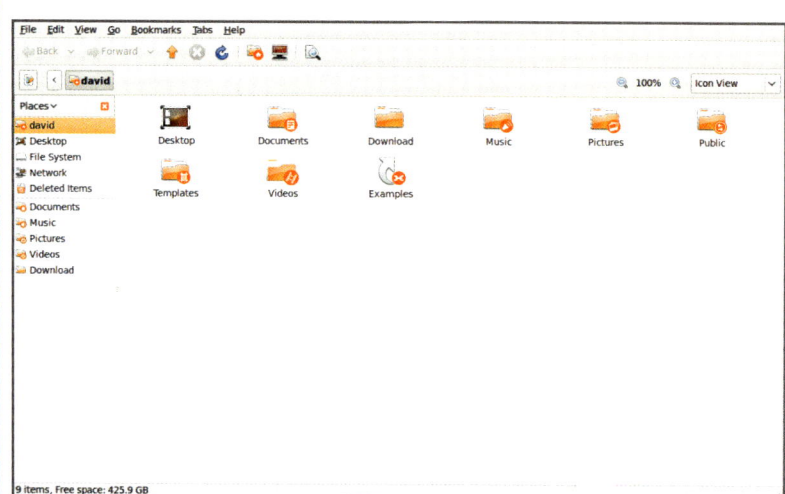

■ Ubuntu has default folders for all your data; it's worth using them to make backing up easier

104 THE COMPLETE LINUX MANUAL

SYSTEM HEALTH

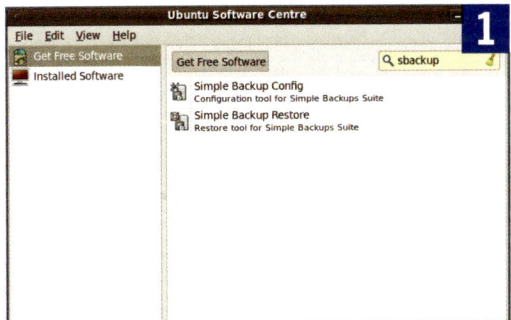

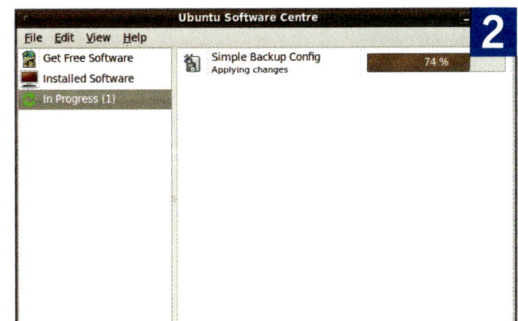

1 To install Simple Backup, click on Ubuntu Software Centre from the Applications menu and type sbackup into the search bar.

There are two applications available: Config and Restore. Click on either one and then click the Install button. It doesn't matter which one you choose, as hitting the Install button will download and install both applications.

2 Enter your password when prompted. Installation should be a fairly quick process and will take only a couple of minutes, depending on the speed of your computer and internet connection. Once the software has been installed, click Close. Simple Backup is now available to use.

3 You can run Simple Backup's configuration from the Administration menu under System. When it starts, you'll see the first screen, which lets you choose the type of backup you want to make. 'Use recommended backup settings' does quite a good job, but we think it's best to select 'Use custom backup settings' instead. That way you can choose exactly when you want your computer to be backed up.

Don't use 'Manual backups only', as you'll have to remember to perform a backup every time that you want to.

4 After selecting 'Use custom backup settings', click the Include tab. This lists the files and folders that will be backed up. The default settings are pretty good and include all the default document folders. Click Add Directory to add a new folder to be backed up if you store important files elsewhere.

Be careful when using the Add File option, as this lets you manually specify a single file that should be backed up, not the contents of the folder that it's in.

5 Click on the Exclude tab to leave out any files you don't want to back up. Here you can add specific folders that don't contain any useful data, such as the predefined /var/cache/ folder. The File types option lets you select files

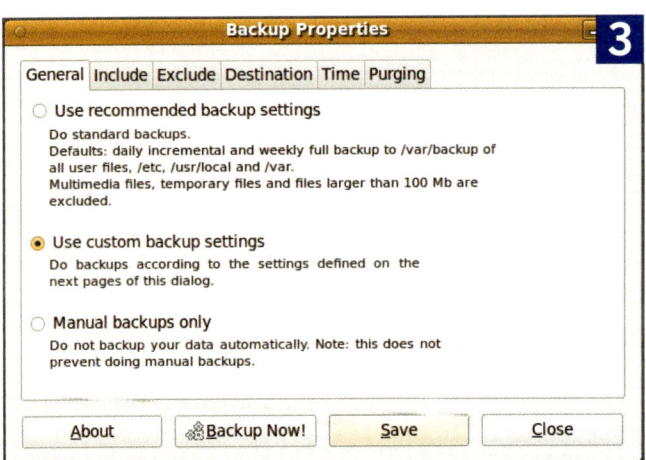

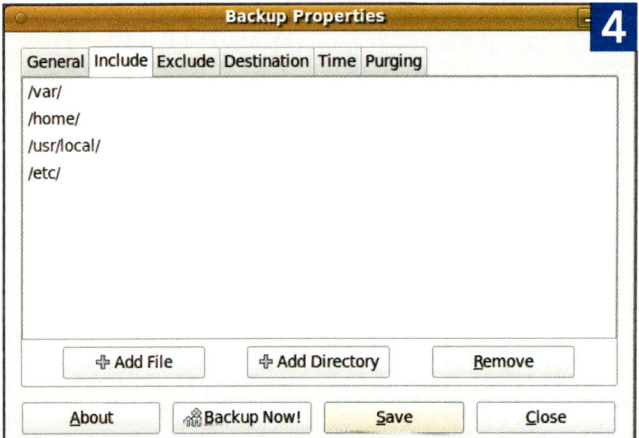

THE COMPLETE LINUX MANUAL 105

CHAPTER 6

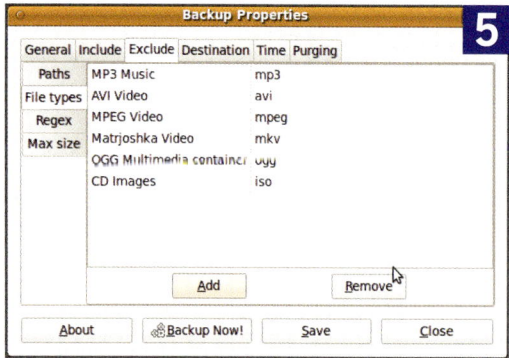
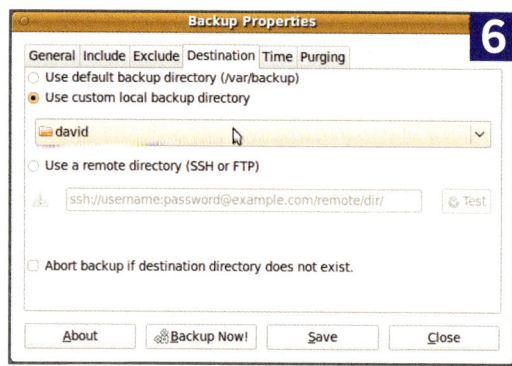
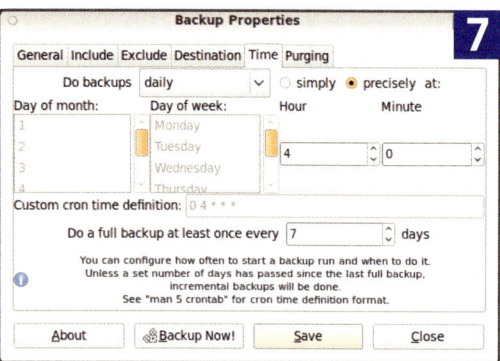
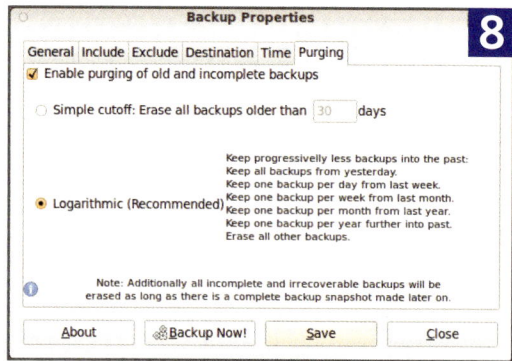

you don't want to back up. By default, MP3 files are listed here. If you want to back up your music, make sure that you select this option and click Remove. Repeat this process for any other file types that you do want to back up. Alternatively, you can add file types that you don't want to back up by clicking the Add button. This lets you specify files by typing in their extensions.

Finally, click Max size to see the maximum individual file size that will be backed up. The default 10MB limit should be fine, but if you want to back up everything, including large video files, increase this number to the size of the largest files you want to back up.

6 Click the Destination tab to tell Simple Backup where you'd like the backups to be placed. By default, it's configured to back them up to your hard disk. Click 'Use custom local backup directory' and then click the drop-down menu to select an alternative hard disk.

Alternatively, you can select 'Use a remote directory (SSH or FTP)' and upload your files over the internet. Note that you can't use online web-hosting space for this; you'll need a dedicated FTP server.

7 Click the Time tab to decide when your backups should take place. The default option is to back up once a day. You can change this to hourly, weekly, monthly or even set a custom schedule. Daily is a good choice, though, although hourly could be useful if you work on lots of very important documents. If you change the option from Simply to Precisely, you get to specify at what time the backup runs.

Finally, you can change how often to perform a full backup. Every seven days is a good choice, but have them more regularly if you prefer.

8 Click on the Purging tab to work out when to delete old backups in order to save disk space. You can either force Simple Backup to delete all your old backups after a set amount of time – say, 30 days – or leave it on Logarithmic. This keeps more of the newest backups and leaves fewer old backups around. It's the best option for most people.

9 Once you've made your changes, click Save to apply the settings. Your computer will automatically be protected according to the schedule that you set. However, it's best to run a backup now to make sure that you've

SYSTEM HEALTH

backed up all your documents in case your computer suffers from a disaster now.

Click the Backup Now! Button. You'll see a message saying that your backup is being run in the background. You should also hear your hard disk as it's accessed to back up files. Click Close on the dialog box and Close on Simple Backup. Depending on how many files you have, the backup process can take a few minutes to a few hours to complete.

10 If your PC suffers a disaster, you'll need to restore your files. If it's a complete system failure, you may need to reinstall Simple Backup following the instructions in Step 1. To restore your data you'll need to use a different application, which is installed automatically. Click on System, Administration, Simple Backup Restore. Enter your password and click OK. By default the restore program is set to look for backups in the default location; as we changed this, you'll need to click Use custom. Click the Folder icon and navigate to where you backed up your files and click Open. Click Apply.

11 Once you've selected the backup location, you can select the backup you want from the drop-down Available backups list. This will list backups by date, so you can find the most recent one quickly or a backup from a specific date if you need a particular version of a file.

Select the backup you want and you'll see a list of Files and Folders to restore. These are the folders that you manually specified in your backup regime. You can expand these folders in order to find a specific file.

Each top-level folder, and all the files and folders it contains, can be restored individually. Just select it and click Restore. Alternatively, select the individual file or sub-folder that you want to restore and click Restore.

12 Restoring an old file will overwrite any existing files with the same name. If you want to compare an old file to a new one, or restore an older version of an existing file to examine, select it and click Restore As. You can now call the file anything you want and select the folder to which you want to restore it.

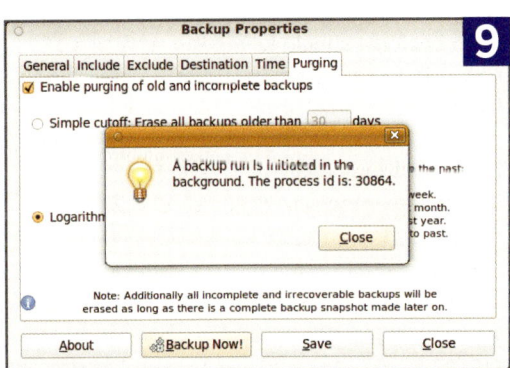
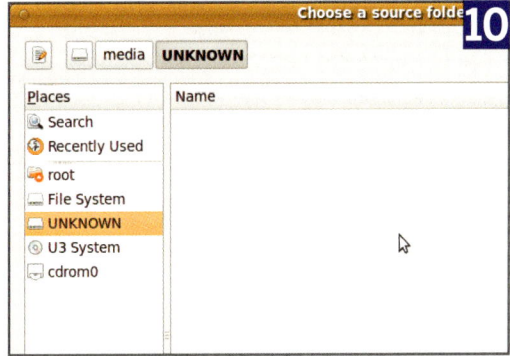
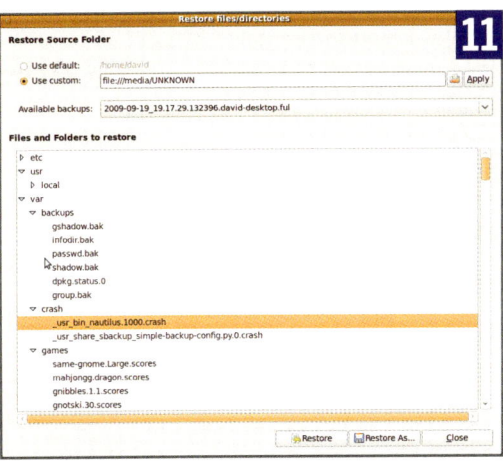
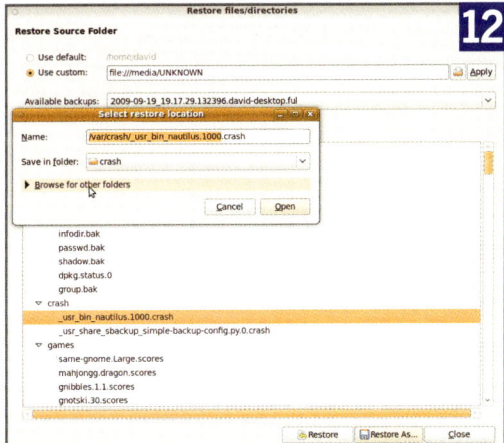

THE COMPLETE LINUX MANUAL

SYSTEM HEALTH

Making an image of your system

A system image is the most complete backup you can perform, as it makes a copy of your operating system, applications and files

Now you've got Ubuntu working the way you want it and downloaded all the drivers and extra software you need, you know just how much hassle it is to get a computer up and running from scratch. Imagine the pain you'd feel if your PC decided to fall over tomorrow, taking your hard disk with it. More likely, as time goes on, is that you'll suffer from a problem. All those extra applications and hardware you've installed and uninstalled can cause problems or just make your system bloated. Reinstalling from scratch doesn't sound like a huge amount of fun.

This is where using a disk-imaging program can save you a world of trouble. These applications take a complete copy of your hard disk, including the operating system, your applications, all your settings and every file on your hard disk. It's the most complete backup that you can make of your PC.

NO MORE REINSTALLING
When restored, the image will take your computer back to the day that the image was made. The advantages of this are obvious: instead of having to reinstall Ubuntu when it's no longer working the way you want it, you can just flash the image back and return to the days when you first installed it, complete with all your settings and applications. So, instead of hours of work, with a disk-imaging application it takes only a fraction of the time.

The best thing is that you're not just limited to taking one image. With the right software, you can also schedule images to occur regularly, so

■ If your PC completely fails, a system image can help you recover quickly

that you're constantly making a backup. If your PC fails in some way, you can just restore your computer back to the last good image; a bit like a super System Restore.

Imaging programs also include standard file backup options, so you can take fewer images, which use a lot of disk space, but still protect all your data.

HARD DISK
Ideally, you should store images on an external hard disk so that you don't lose them if your main hard disk should fail (these images are too big to store on other media such as DVDs). This also means you can restore the image to your hard disk (or to a new one in the case of a major problem), getting up and running again in short period of time. You could also back up to a secondary partition on your primary hard disk.

CLONEZILLA
While Windows users are spoiled for choice when it comes to disk-imaging software that runs in the OS, it's not as simple in Linux. With Ubuntu there are no applications that run from the desktop. Instead, you'll need to download the free CloneZilla utility and burn it to a spare CD or DVD. This disc can be used both to back up and restore an image.

As you can't clone from inside the operating system, you'll want to run these kinds of backups less often. You should therefore run them before you make major system changes or install new hardware, and combine image cloning with file backup for the best protection.

CHAPTER 6

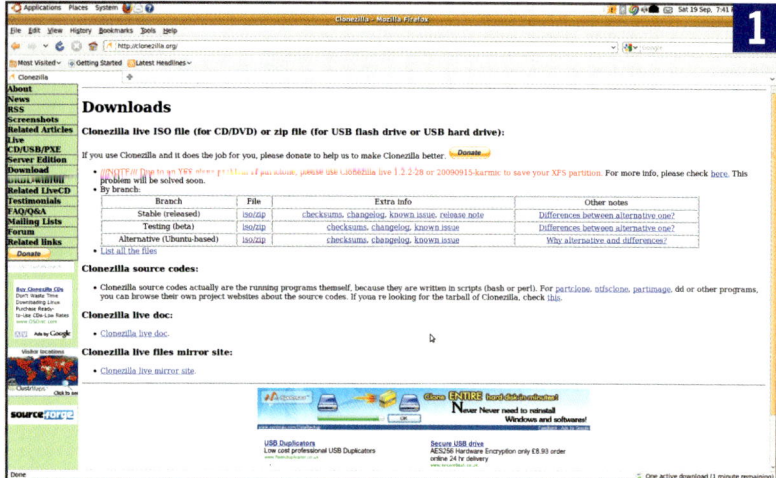
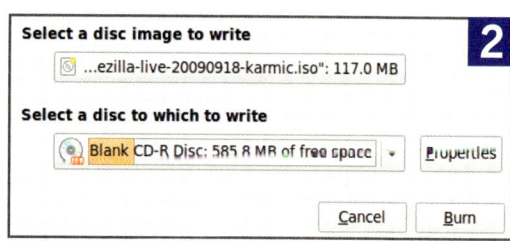

1 CloneZilla is an excellent free application for taking an image of your computer. It runs from its own CD, so you need to download the necessary image first. Visit **http://clonezilla.org** to download the latest version of the software. Click the Download link and select iso/zip under Alternative (Ubuntu-based). Select the .iso file download and wait for the download window to appear. Click Save File. Depending on the speed of your internet connection, the 117MB file should download in around 15 minutes.

2 Once the file has downloaded, right-click on it in Firefox's Downloads window and select Open Containing folder. Right-click on the file and select Open with Brasero. Put a blank CD or DVD into your computer's optical drive and click Burn. A CD is all you need to use, as CloneZilla is a small application. The file should take only a few minutes to write to disc. When it's completed, click Close.

3 To make an image of your computer, you'll need to restart it and boot from the disc that you've just created. This is because the software needs to make sure there are no locked files in order to make a complete copy of your hard disk and all its contents.

Before you restart your computer, make sure you've saved all your work and select Restart from the menu at the top-right of the screen. When your computer restarts, make sure the BIOS is set up to boot from the optical drive first or your normal operating system will start first. When your BIOS is configured properly, CloneZilla will boot from its disc automatically; you won't need to press any keys.

4 When the CloneZilla boot menu appears you'll see a choice of startup options, depending on the graphics mode that you want to run the software in. The first choice should work for most people, but if the screen appears corrupted on your computer, restart and choose an option that runs at a lower resolution. Don't worry if the resolutions sound low, as CloneZilla

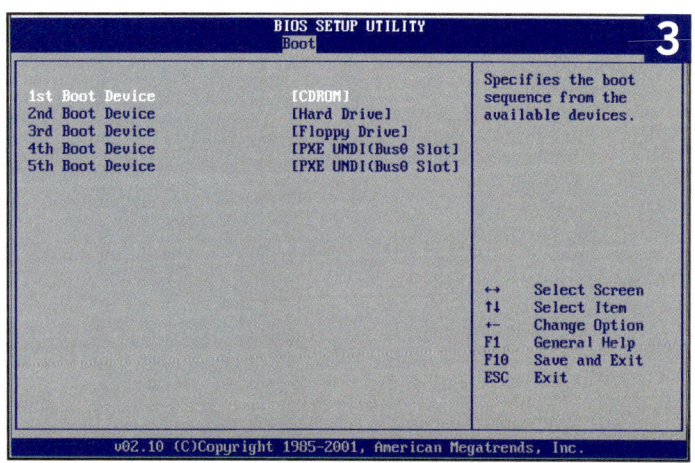
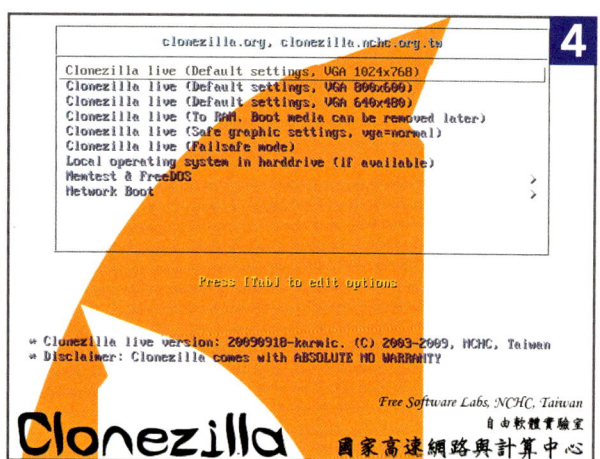

THE COMPLETE LINUX MANUAL

SYSTEM HEALTH

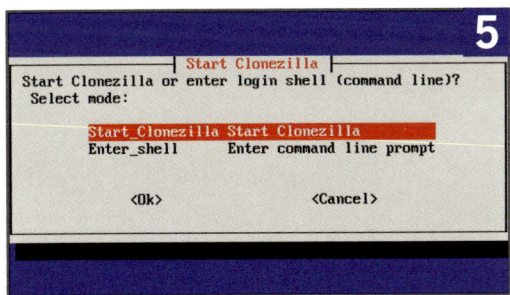
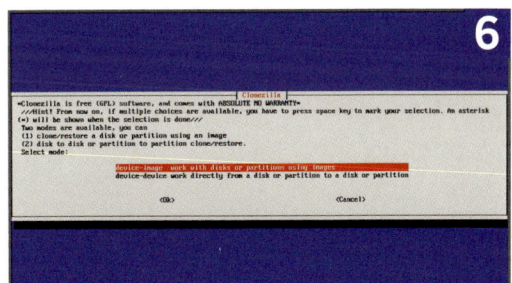
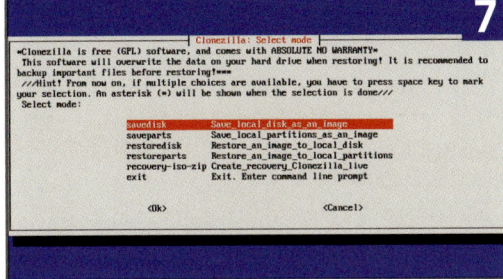
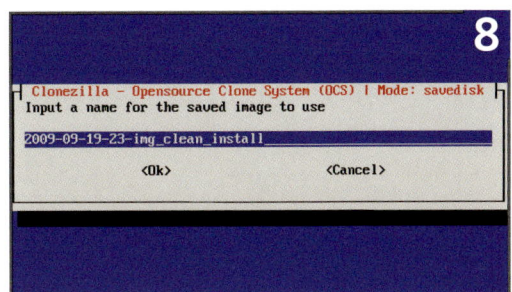

uses simple menus that are easy to see at any resolution, and there's no fancy graphical interface. When you're ready, select the first option and press Enter.

5 CloneZilla will now load a version of Linux, which it runs from and uses both to back up and restore your computer. This process of loading the operating system will be quick. When the OS has finished loading, you'll see a simple graphical menu system that you can use to back up your hard disk. On the first menu, select English as the language, then choose not to adjust the keymap (this is for non-standard keyboards). When the next menu pops up, choose to start CloneZilla.

6 You'll be a given an option of the type of session that you want to run. Device-to-image lets you back up to an image file; Device-to-device lets you copy one hard disk to another, and is useful if you're upgrading your disk. Select Use local device. You'll then get a message telling you that if you want to use a USB drive you should insert it now and wait five seconds before continuing so that CloneZilla can detect it. When you're ready, press Enter. You'll get a list of hard disks in your system and need to select one to store the information about system images. The first hard disk (HDA1 or SDA1) will be the hard disk with the operating

system on it and the one that you want to back up; HDB1 or SDB2 is the second hard disk, and most likely the one that you want to back up to. Select this. On the next screen select Top_directory_in_the_local_device and hit Enter. Press Enter again.

7 On the next screen, you can select the mode in which you want to run CloneZilla. Beginner will suit most people and will give you the options that you need. Select this and press Enter. On the next screen you need to select what you want to do. Savedisk will take a copy of your entire boot disk, including the operating system and all of its files. Select this option and press Enter.

8 You'll now need to give your image a name. It makes sense to give it a descriptive

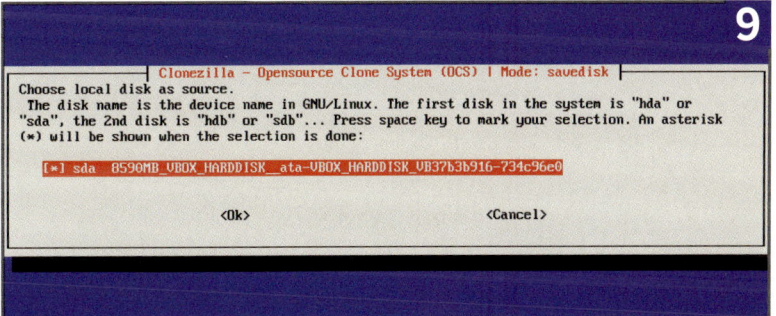

CHAPTER 6

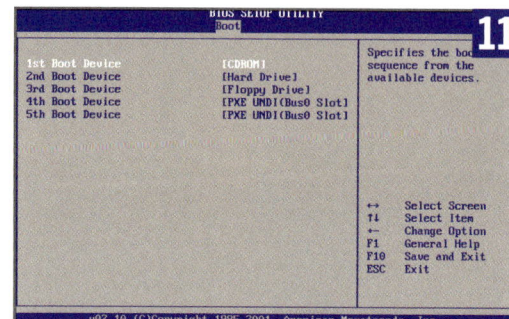
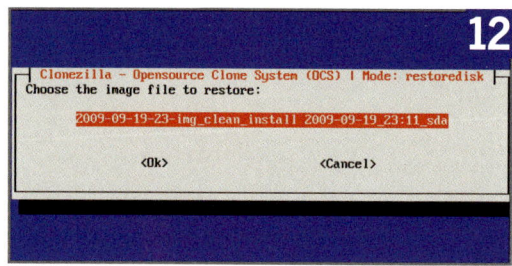

name and a date, so that when you come to restore an image you know exactly when it was made and what it does. For example, 2010-01-23-fresh-install will help you identify what that particular image does. The date part should be filled in automatically, so just give the image a descriptive name following this and press Enter.

9 You'll now need to choose which disk you want to make an image of. This should be easy, as there will probably be only one hard disk listed now, as the backup hard disk isn't listed on this screen. If not, you'll most likely want to back up SDA or HDA, as this is the first hard disk in your computer and the boot hard disk. Select this and press Enter.

10 Press Enter when you're prompted and CloneZilla will check your hard disks to make sure that everything's in order. It will then ask if you're sure that you want to continue. Type 'y' and then Enter and the software will begin the imaging process. Depending on how big your hard disks are and how much data you have, the process can take anything from a few minutes up to a few hours.

When it's completed, reboot your computer, take out the CloneZilla disc and start your operating system as normal. Remember to make regular image-based backups.

RESTORING AN IMAGE

11 If your PC suffers a problem, you'll need to know how to restore an image. Fortunately, this is an easy process using CloneZilla, too. It uses the same disc that you used to create the image, so make sure that you keep this somewhere safe. Put the disc into your computer and make sure that the BIOS is set to boot from it. Then, follow Steps 2 through 7, but don't select the Savedisk option.

12 Select the Restoredisk option and you'll be presented with a list of available disk images. This is why it's important to call the images something constructive, otherwise it could be hard to tell which image to restore.

Look at the date of the images you have. If you've suffered a problem recently because of new hardware or software, select the image that's closest in date to the last time your computer worked properly. If you just want to clean out your computer, select a suitable image that removes the applications and features you want to get rid of.

When you're ready, press Enter. Select HDA or SDA as the target disk, and press Enter to confirm. Type 'y' and Enter both times that you're asked if you want to continue. The image will be restored to your computer, and when you reboot you'll have everything back to how it was when the image was created.

112 THE COMPLETE LINUX MANUAL

CHAPTER 7

Network storage

Linux isn't just a desktop operating system; it also comes in versions that do a specific job. FreeNAS is one excellent example, as this operating system will turn your computer into a fully functional network attached storage (NAS) device that will enable you to share your files and documents all over your house. In this chapter we'll show you how to install and configure FreeNAS.

Making your own NAS 116
Configuring FreeNAS 120

CHAPTER 7

Making your own NAS

If you have an old PC sitting around doing nothing, you could turn it into network storage using the powerful FreeNAS system

An old PC can easily go to waste, but with FreeNAS you can make good use of it and turn it into a powerful network-attached storage (NAS) device. Best thing of all is that FreeNAS, as its name suggests, is completely free.

Unlike many commercially available NAS devices, FreeNAS has a wealth of features and, as you're using a PC, the ability to support a lot of hard disks. Here we'll show you how to install it and share files, while on pages 120 to 123 we'll be covering advanced configuration options.

To install FreeNAS on an old PC, you'll need a computer with at least one hard disk in it and an optical drive. The best installation of FreeNAS uses a USB flash drive. You'll need a drive with at least 64MB of disk space; you can buy 1GB models for around £3 if you don't have one.

To start, download the ISO CD image of the operating system from **www.freenas.org**. You need to download the LiveCD version. There are two versions for download: one for Intel processors and one for AMD 64-bit processors. Make sure you select the right version, and download the ISO file to your PC. This file is an image of a CD that needs to be written to a blank disc (see page 46 for details on burning a disc). For Windows PCs, use the free CDBurnerXP (**http://cdburnerxp.se**).

GIVEN THE BOOT

Once the files are on a CD, you can boot from the disc on the computer that you'll use for FreeNAS. Before you do, though, there are some configuration options you need to think about. First, for the maximum flexibility you should install FreeNAS on a USB flash disk, leaving your hard disks completely free for data storage. For this to work, you need to set your BIOS to boot from USB devices.

To do this, turn on your FreeNAS PC, plug in your USB flash drive and enter the BIOS (normally you have to press Delete, F10 or F12, but look out for a message telling you which key to press). Typically the USB boot options are under Advanced BIOS Features. There may be an option to boot from USB drives, you may have to select a USB flash drive from the Boot Device menu or the option may be called Boot Other Devices. In our BIOS the USB drive was detected as a hard disk and we had to select it as the first device in the Hard Disk Boot Priority menu.

If your PC can't boot from USB flash drives, you can install FreeNAS to one of your hard disks, but this makes configuration harder later on and prevents you from using this hard disk in a RAID array.

Alternatively, you can connect the flash drive to a USB port and boot the PC from the FreeNAS Live CD. Your settings will be saved automatically to the flash drive, so there's no

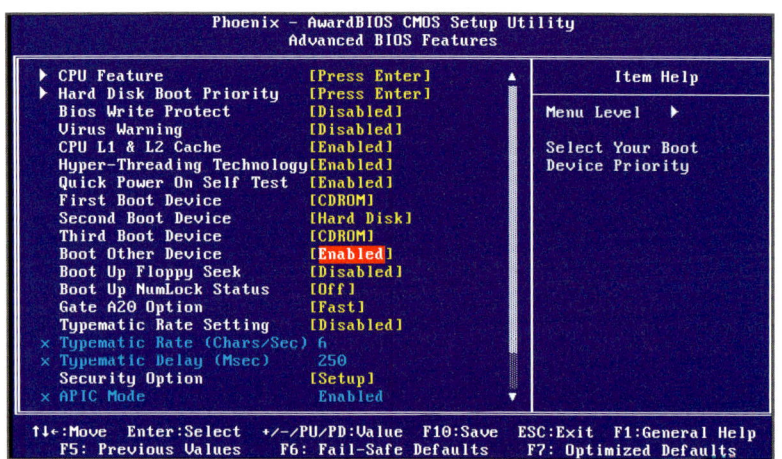

■ You need to enter the BIOS and set your computer to boot from a USB disk for the optimal FreeNAS installation

NETWORK STORAGE

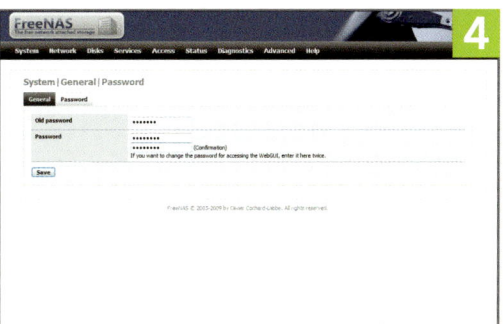

installation at all. However, this makes it trickier to upgrade to the latest version of FreeNAS.

While you're in the BIOS, make sure you disable the option to halt on keyboard errors, as your FreeNAS PC won't need a monitor or keyboard connected to it when it's ready.

The other configuration option to consider is whether you want to use RAID or not. FreeNAS lets you use all common types of RAID (see http://tinyurl.com/raidlevels for details). You'll need at least two hard disks to use RAID. The benefits are increased speed and reliability, and you can add extra hard disks to your PC later to increase storage. The alternative is to use each disk separately; this is your only choice if you have one hard disk. We'll show you how to use both methods in our step-by-step instructions.

CONNECTING YOUR PC

You're now ready to install the operating system on your computer. Before you start, however, make sure you remove all USB flash drives or you'll get an error (if you're planning to start FreeNAS from a CD each time, start your computer and go to Step 3).

1 Boot from the disc you created. When the Console setup menu appears, insert your USB drive into a spare port, type 9 and then Enter to install FreeNAS to your computer's hard disk. Select option 1 and press Enter. FreeNAS will confirm the partitions that it will create and warn you that your entire USB flash disk will be wiped.

Press Enter to continue. Select your optical drive from the list and press Enter. Finally, select the flash drive to which you want to install the OS (it will have a name that starts 'da') and press Enter again.

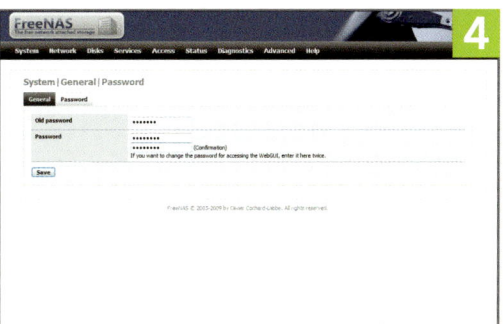

CHAPTER 7

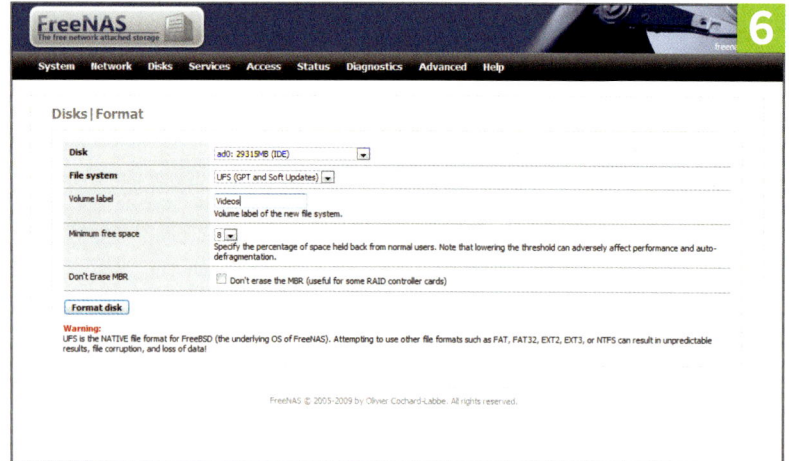

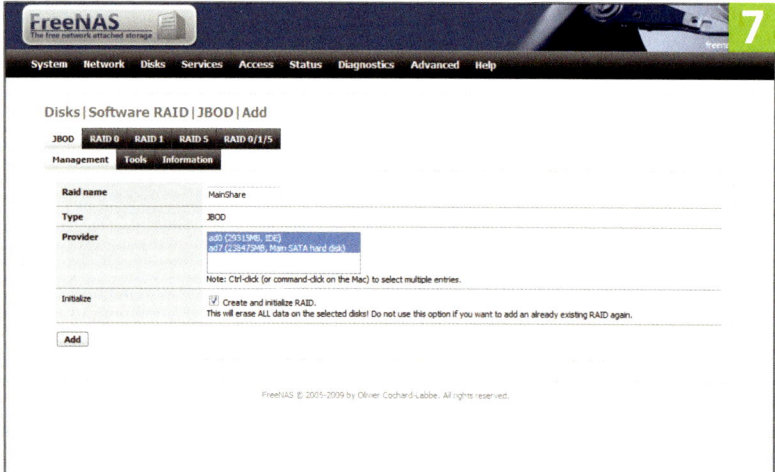

2 FreeNAS will install itself to the flash drive, which should take only a few seconds. When it's finished, you'll get a message telling you that you can remove the optical disc and restart your computer. Follow these instructions and make sure your computer is set to boot from USB devices.

3 When your computer restarts, you'll see a similar Console setup menu to the one in Step 1. Type 1 and then Enter to pick the network interface you want to use. Pick the one with (up) in brackets and press Enter. Go to Finish, exit the configuration and press Enter, then Enter again.

Next, set the IP address that you want your FreeNAS computer to use by typing 2 and then Enter. You'll be asked if you want to use DHCP. If your router has an option to fix the IP address it gives to a specific PC (many do), select Yes.

Otherwise, select No. In this case you'll have to select an IP address to use manually.

The easiest way to find a safe address is to follow your router's instructions to access the web-management page from your main PC and view the DHCP server settings. The page you'll see will contain a start address, such as 192.168.1.1, and either an end address, such as 192.168.1.50, or a number that says how many addresses it hands out, such as 50. In this example, 50 IP addresses would give us a range between 192.168.1.1 and 192.168.1.50.

All you have to do is pick an IP address outside this range. To be on the safe side, we recommend picking an address that's 10 higher than the last DHCP address. So, keep the first three numbers the same and add 10 to the last number – in our example, that would be 192.168.1.60 – and write down this address, as you'll need it later.

Enter the address into FreeNAS and press Enter. You'll be prompted for the subnet mask that your network uses. You'll most likely have a network that uses 255.255.255.0, so type 24 and press Enter. On the next two screens you'll need to enter a Gateway and a DNS address. Both are your router's IP address. Type this in both dialog boxes and press Enter. Finally, say No to IPv6 and press Enter. You'll then get a confirmation that the IP address has been configured.

4 FreeNAS is now running, so you can switch to its web-based interface for further configuration. In a web browser on another computer, type the IP address of your FreeNAS server into the address bar. The default username is 'admin' with the password 'freenas'.

The first job is to change the password. Click on the System menu and select General. Click on the Password tab, type in the old password and then your new password twice. Click Save and you'll be prompted to log into the management page again with your new password.

5 Next, it's time to set up file-sharing. Click on Management in the Disks menu and then click the big plus sign. Select a hard disk from the drop-down Disk menu (hard disks start with 'ad') and type in a description. We recommend leaving the other settings alone, except for S.M.A.R.T., which is used to monitor your disk's health. Put a tick in this box and

NETWORK STORAGE

click Add. Repeat this step for each hard disk in your system, and then click Apply Changes on the Disks, Management screen.

6 Your hard disks need to be formatted in order to be used. To do this, select Format from the Disks menu. If you're going to use each disk individually, leave the File system option on its default value of UFS, type in a Volume label and click Format disk. Repeat this procedure for all your disks and go to Step 8.

If you want to use RAID, select Software RAID from the File system menu and click Format disk. Repeat this for all your hard disks and go to Step 7.

7 To create a RAID array, select Software RAID from the Disks menu. Select the type of RAID array you want to create from the tabs and click the plus icon. Type in the RAID name (no spaces are allowed), select the hard disks you want to use in the Provider menu, select Initialize, click Add, then Apply Changes.

You have to format your new RAID array, so select Format from the Disks menu. Choose your RAID array from the drop-down Disk menu, type in a Volume label and click Format disk.

8 Now you need to share your disk. Click on Disks and then Mount Point. Select a hard disk or RAID array from the drop down Disk menu. Type in a Share name and Description, then click Add. Click Apply Changes and your share is ready to be used.

In order for computers to be able to access the share, you need to enable the file-sharing service. Click on CIFS/SMB from the Services menu and put a tick in the Enable box. You shouldn't need to change many of the settings, but there are some you can: NetBIOS name is the name that will appear when computers browse the network, Workgroup is the Windows workgroup in which your server will appear, and Large read/write should be enabled if your computers run Linux, Windows 2000 or later. When you're ready, click Save and Restart.

Finally, you need to select which files you want to share. Click on the Shares tab. Type in the name you want the share to be known by and a comment, and then click the button next to Path. Select the mount point that you created at the start of this Step (individual hard disks

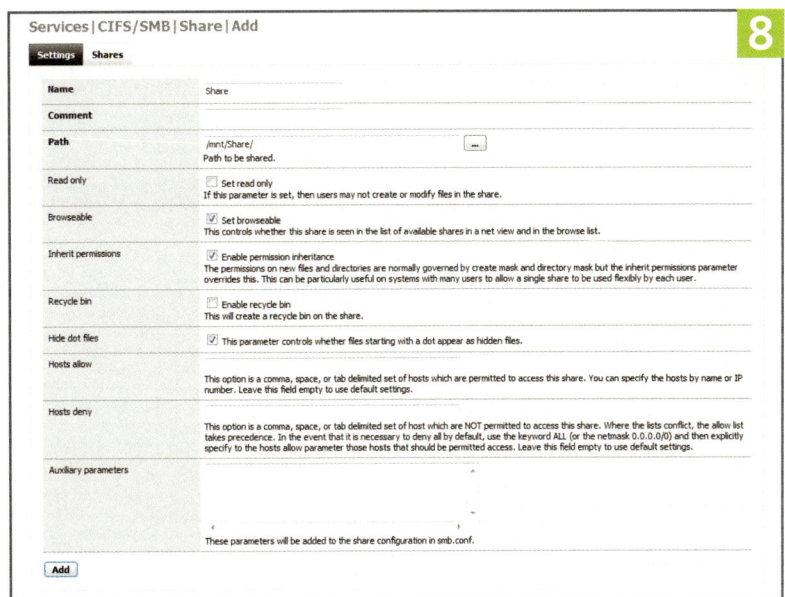

will have one mount point each and a RAID array has one mount point) and click OK. Click Apply Changes. Repeat for all mount points.

9 On a Windows PC, get a Run command up (Windows+R) and type \\<*ip address of your FreeNAS server*> to access shared files. Right-click a folder and select Map network drive to create a network drive that you can access just like a normal hard disk.

In Ubuntu, select Connect to Server from the Places menu. Select Windows Share from the menu and type the IP address of your FreeNAS computer. To save the connection, select Add bookmark and give it a name. Click Connect to access shared files. You Bookmark is now available in the Bookmark menu under Places.

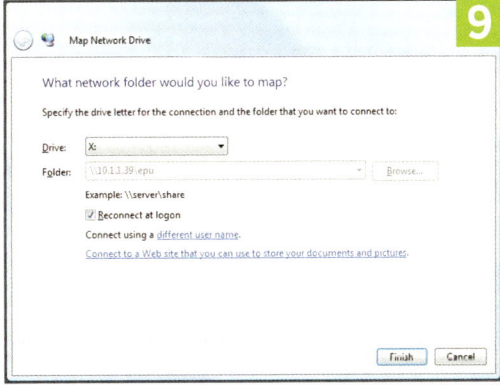

THE COMPLETE LINUX MANUAL 119

CHAPTER 7

Configuring FreeNAS

FreeNAS's advanced features let you add security, share files over the internet and share media with other computers

On the previous four pages we showed you how to install FreeNAS and turn an old computer into a network-attached storage device. However, we only scratched the surface of what FreeNAS can do. Here we'll take you through some of its more advanced features so that you can use the application to its full potential. We'll cover how to configure security, as well as advanced types of file-sharing such as creating your own media and FTP server that you can access from anywhere on the internet.

The first place to start is security. Your default installation of FreeNAS doesn't have any usernames or passwords, so anyone could access the computer. While this is fine on a local network, if you're going to use more advanced features that are accessible over the internet, such as the FTP server, you'll need to know how to set up users and groups.

At the time of writing, the current version of FreeNAS doesn't let you choose which users have access to each particular service. This means that anyone with a username and password can access every feature and every share. For home use this shouldn't make any difference, unless you're really keen to restrict access for members of your family.

BACK UP YOUR CONFIGURATION

If your system develops a problem and you have to reinstall FreeNAS, you'll need to restore it quickly. If you don't back up your configuration, you risk losing every file stored in your RAID array.

To do this, log on to FreeNAS's web-based management and click Backup/Restore from the System menu. Click Download configuration and save the file to your PC. If you need to

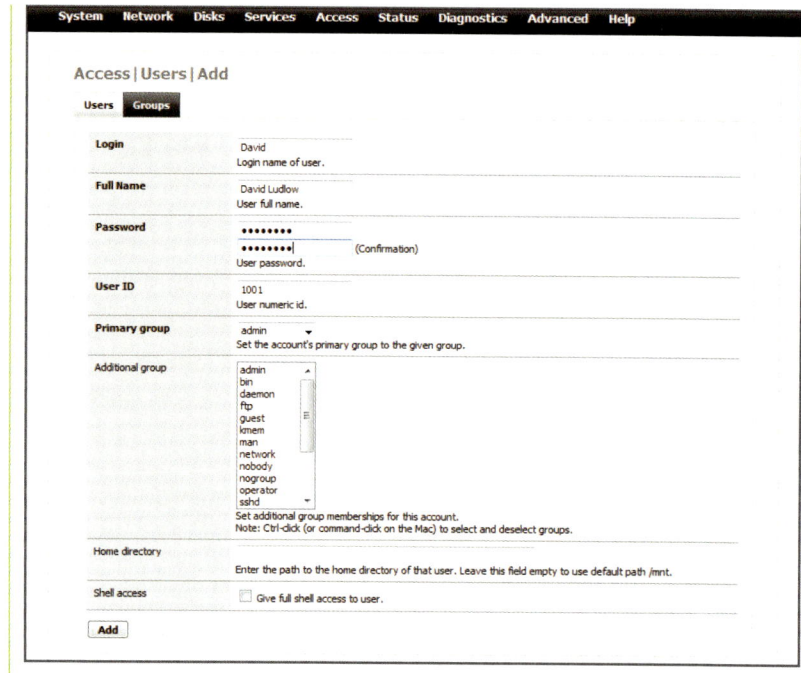

Adding users to your FreeNAS computer can help increase security

restore your configuration, use the same menu, but click the Browse button, select the configuration file you backed up and then click Restore configuration.

It's also worth checking that you have the most up-to-date version of FreeNAS. Go to **www.freenas.org**, click the Download link and select the latest version in the FreeNAS Images list (not the LiveCD list). This will download a .img file. In FreeNAS's web-management page, select Firmware from the System menu. Select Enable firmware upload, click Browse, select the .img file you downloaded and then click Upgrade firmware. This will automatically upload the file and upgrade your FreeNAS computer, restarting it when it's completed.

NETWORK STORAGE

ADDING A USER

To add a new user, go to FreeNAS's web-based management page and log on. Click on the Access tab and select Users and Groups. Click the blue Plus button and you'll be prompted to add a user by typing in a username and password. It's best to type in the same names and passwords that are used to log into your PC, as this way you'll automatically be able to access network shares from Windows PCs (Linux users will have to authenticate).

You can also assign users to groups. At the moment, all users have access to every service; however, when this is updated in a later version of FreeNAS, it will make security easier to deal with as you'll be able to allow or deny a whole group of users access to a service. For now, though, we've put all our users in the 'admin' group. When you've created one user, click Add, then Apply changes. Click the blue Plus button to add another user.

TURNING ON SECURITY

Now you have users, it's time to use them. Select CIFS/SMB from the Services menu. To turn on security, select Local User from the Authentication menu and then click Save and Restart. When you see the message, "The changes have been applied successfully", all your network shares are secure and only authorised users can access them.

Now when you access the share it will be protected. In Linux, you'll have to type in a username and password. If you created a username and password that matches your current Windows user, you'll be able to access the shares; if you didn't, you'll be prompted to type in a valid username and password.

SMARTER SHARES

On the previous four pages we showed you how to share an entire mount point (hard disk or RAID array), but this isn't always the best use of disk space. It often makes more sense to share only a particular folder. For example, you could give each user their own share to use. A similar argument goes for other services here.

To share a folder, you first need to create one. FreeNAS has a built-in file browser that lets you do this. Click on Advanced and select File Manager, then log on with the same username and password that you use to log on to FreeNAS's web-management page. You'll see an Explorer-style file browser that you can use to view every file and folder. To create a new folder to share, you need to know where to put it.

Unlike Windows, which has different drive letters for each hard disk, FreeNAS is based on Linux. On pages 116-119, we explained that for each hard disk or RAID array you have to create a mount point, and it's the mount point that you need to access. These are stored in the 'mnt' folder, so click on this. Here you'll see a list of folders with the same names as the mount points that you created, each one referring to a hard disk or RAID array. Click on one to access it. Select Directory from the drop-down menu, type in a name and click Create to make a Folder.

The new folder will have the wrong permissions and won't allow users to write files to it. To change this, click on the link under the Perm's column next to the folder you've created (it will look something like drwxrwxr-x). Put a tick in the 'w' box under the Public heading and click Change.

To use your new folder to create a share, click on CIFS/SMB from the Services menu of the main web interface window, and click on the Shares tab. Click the blue plus icon, type a name for your new share (we've chosen the name of one of our users) and a description. Click the button next to Path and navigate to the 'mnt' folder. Click the mount point name where you created your new folder, then click your new folder. Click OK, then click Add followed by Apply changes. Your new share will then show up when you access your FreeNAS computer through Windows or Linux file-sharing. It may be prudent to stop sharing the main share, which

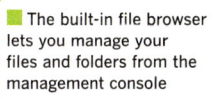

■ The built-in file browser lets you manage your files and folders from the management console

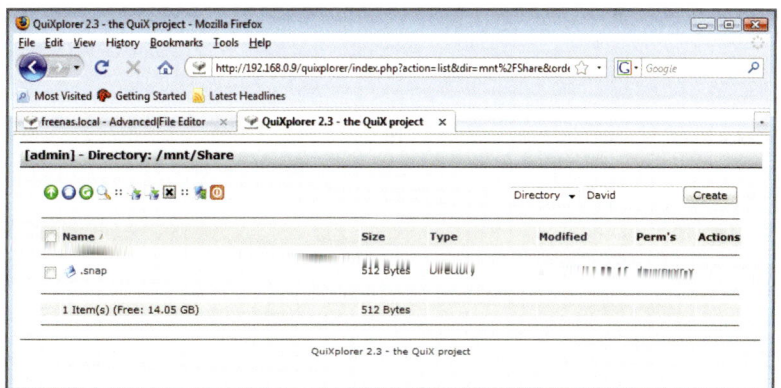

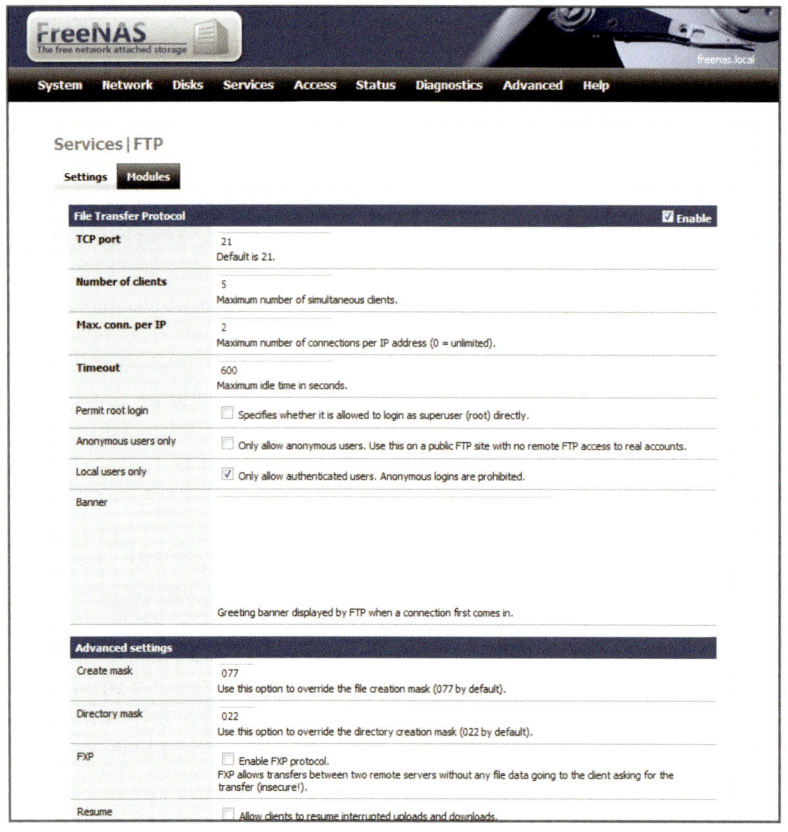

You can access your FreeNAS server over the internet using FTP

gives users access to an entire drive, by clicking the red minus icon next to a share's name.

SETTING UP FTP

The problem with network shares is that they're not easy to share over the internet. Fortunately, FTP provides a way for all users to access their files from anywhere. Be warned, though, that FreeNAS's FTP settings are quite basic and give users access to the 'mnt' folder and, therefore, access to every hard disk and RAID array you have installed.

To turn on FTP, select FTP from the Service menu (don't select TFTP, as this is a very basic form of FTP). Put a tick in the Enable box and a tick in the box marked 'Only allow authenticated users. Anonymous logins are prohibited.' This will let only authenticated users access FreeNAS.

You can leave the other settings as they are, although you may want to turn on Resume, which lets users continue downloading a file if it's interrupted, and SSL/TLS, which allows users to make secure connections to your server. However, this latter option will place a bit of an overhead on your server, so turn it off if performance becomes an issue. When you're done, click Save and Restart.

To test that it's working, open your web browser and type ftp://<ip address of your FreeNAS computer>. When prompted, type in a valid username and password, and you'll be able to browse all the files on your PC. This access is very basic, so for more control you're better off with a dedicated FTP client such as FileZilla (see page 98).

INTERNET ACCESS

The next step is to give access to the computer over the internet. The first problem to overcome is that your home has an external IP address that's shared by all the computers on your network. This IP address can change, making it impossible to access your home network. Fortunately, with Dynamic DNS you can create a simple URL that's updated regularly so that it always points to your home.

The only point to make is that if your router doesn't support DynDNS.org (the best free Dynamic DNS service), FreeNAS does, so you don't need to download any other software. Just select Dynamic DNS from the Services menu, click Enable and type in your DynDNS.org account details.

With Dynamic DNS up and running, you need to configure your router so that it knows to send incoming FTP requests to your FreeNAS computer. This is fairly straightforward and involves configuring port forwarding (called virtual servers on some routers). You need to

To access your FreeNAS PC over the internet you'll need to use port forwarding

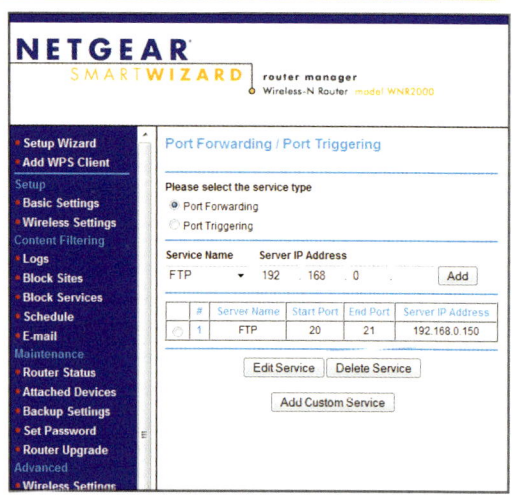

NETWORK STORAGE

You can stream music from FreeNAS to iTunes easily

configure a new rule that forwards all incoming traffic on Port 21 to the IP address of your FreeNAS computer. Your router's manual will tell you how to do this, and www.portforward.com has lots of information about it as well.

Once that's done, you can access your FreeNAS computer from over the internet. In a web browser, you type ftp://<name of the DynDNS.org URL you created>, such as ftp://computershopper.homeftp.net. You can also use your DynDNS.org URL in a dedicated FTP client, such as FileZilla.

ITUNES AND UPnP

If you want to share your media files, FreeNAS makes this easy. It has support for iTunes sharing, which lets you share music files with computers running iTunes and some media streamers, and UPnP, which lets you share music with a wide range of media streamers. Both services work in the same way, so we'll just explain how to use UPnP.

First, you need a folder in which to store all your media. This can be an existing folder in a share or you can create one specifically using the instructions above. In either case, make sure that you have network access to this folder so that you can copy new files to it, by creating a new share if necessary.

To turn on the UPnP server, select UPnP from the Services menu and select Enable.

Click the button next to Database directory and choose a folder in which to create the media directory. This can be stored anywhere, but for convenience we put ours in a directory called Media, which we used to store our media files. Click Add, which is next to Content, and add the directory that houses your media. You can add multiple directories by repeating this step.

If you have a media streamer with limited format support, you can use transcoding to turn one file format into another. Put a tick in the Transcoding box, and FreeNAS will convert files into a compatible format. However, this operation is processor-intensive, so turn it off if your PC's performance suffers. If you do turn on this feature, select a Temporary Directory in which to store the transcoded files.

Finally, select Enable web user interface, click Save and then restart. Your server will now be working. You can click on the URL link to view a web page with the status of your server.

To turn on iTunes sharing, select iTunes/DAAP from the Services menu and follow these instructions. The only difference is that you need to set a password for the administrator's web page, and click the Zeroconf/Bonjour link at the bottom of the page to make sure these two network services are selected and turned on, otherwise iTunes won't detect your NAS.

Your FreeNAS computer can share media files using its built-in UPnP server

THE COMPLETE LINUX MANUAL

CHAPTER 8

Troubleshooting

Although we've thoroughly checked the advice in this book and made the steps as easy to follow as possible, you may occasionally run into problems. Perhaps your computer is crashing or a piece of hardware isn't working as it should. Don't worry: we're here to help. Over the next few pages we'll guide you towards finding the best solutions to any problems.

Troubleshooting	126
How to use your free Ubuntu 9.10 CD	128

CHAPTER 8

Troubleshooting

When things go wrong, Linux can seem impossible to fix, but it isn't. Here we'll help you find the answers to any problems you may have

Although Linux is a lot easier to use now than it used to be, when you run into problems it can seem just as confusing as ever. Don't panic, though, as getting your PC working again isn't as hard as you think.

FIND OUT WHAT HAPPENED
The first step to fixing a problem is knowing what went wrong and why. It could be that Ubuntu fails to load one day through no fault of your own, but it's more likely that installing a new piece of hardware or software caused the issue. Remember any changes you've made, so you'll be able to find the help you need and avoid making the same change in the future.

IS IT A HARDWARE PROBLEM?
A problem with your computer could easily be an issue with hardware as well as software. If

■ Make a complete system image of your computer so that you can restore it quickly after a problem

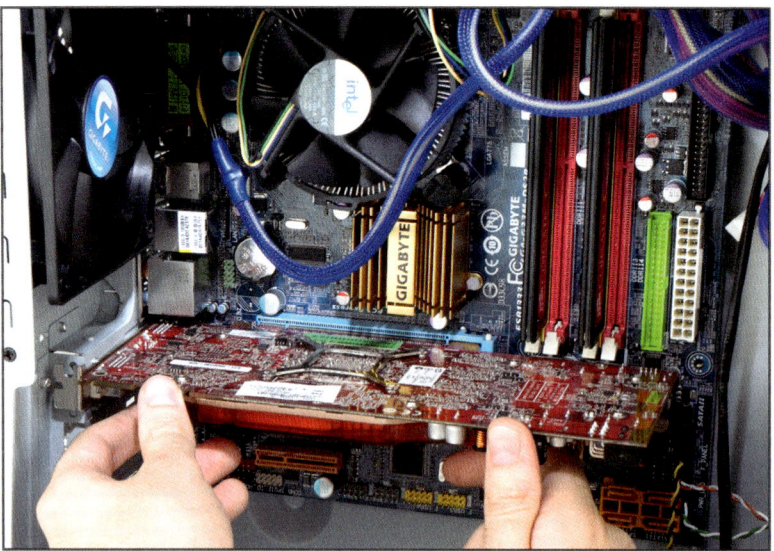

■ What appears to be a Linux problem may actually be a hardware problem

your computer won't turn on or there's nothing onscreen, there's probably something wrong with your hardware, rather than Linux.

If you've just installed some hardware, remove the new bit of kit and see if that makes a difference. If you've upgraded your PC recently, make sure that the memory, expansion card or processor are all fitted correctly.

HAVE A BACKUP READY
If your computer has completely broken and you can't even start Linux, don't worry about trying to fix it. Instead, reach for a system backup (see page 109). A complete system image enables you to restore your computer back to a working point before the trouble started. It's the easiest and best method of fixing a problem, and highlights why you should make a backup before making any major system changes.

FOLLOW ONSCREEN INSTRUCTIONS
Linux can be frustrating as it often doesn't provide a graphical way of fixing a problem. However, you'll often see an onscreen message telling you the command that you need to type. Look out for any helpful messages and then try typing them into a Terminal window (or directly

TROUBLESHOOTING

onscreen if Ubuntu won't even load the graphical interface). If the command won't run, try using 'sudo' in front of it. This will run the command with higher-level privileges. You'll be prompted to type in your password when using sudo.

KNOW THE DETAILS
Ubuntu has lots of different versions that aren't compatible with each other. In fact, the differences between 'point' releases, such as 9.04 and 9.10, can sometimes be so great that software and hardware that worked on one won't work on the other. For this reason, make sure you know exactly which version you're running. Also know the exact product name or software version that you're having problems with. All this information together will make sure you get the right help; following advice for the wrong version of Linux will often not work.

READ THE DOCUMENTATION
There's official documentation for each version of Ubuntu on the operating system's website (https://help.ubuntu.com). Make sure you click the right link for your version of the OS (9.10 if you installed from the free CD with this book).

In the documentation you'll find detailed step-by-step instructions on how to perform tasks, as well as explanations. Make this your first stop when you're trying to troubleshoot a problem.

VISIT THE OFFICIAL FORUMS
One of the best things about Linux is that the users form a community. Many of these members are so passionate about the OS that they'll do anything to help someone that's struggling. At **http://ubuntuforums.org** you'll find the official forums dedicated to helping people that are having problems with Ubuntu.

Before you post a question, search the forums to see if there's an existing answer to your problem, remembering to follow the advice in 'Know the details' above. Finally, don't worry about the occasional person who posts a rude or unhelpful remark to one of your questions; other users will soon appear and hopefully give you the help you need.

Do read the Forum FAQ and Code of Conduct first so that you don't post messages in the wrong place or use the wrong type of language. These documents are helpful guides on how to ask for help in the right way.

■ Look out for onscreen messages that tell you how to fix your problem

SEARCH GOOGLE
The official forums and documentation don't have the answers to everything, so searching Google can be your last resort. Remember, you need to provide the exact details that you're looking for in the search in order to get the best results (see 'Know the details', above).

You'll probably find many forums that contain information related to your problem. Read through a few to find the best answers; we find that comments from other users can really help track down the best answer.

DON'T PANIC
Many troubleshooting solutions require you to edit a file or use strange-sounding commands. Don't worry about these. If you're interested you can look up what they do, otherwise find a solution where people have verified it's correct and follow the advice.

■ Forum threads are a sure-fire way to find and ask for help

THE COMPLETE LINUX MANUAL **127**

CHAPTER 8

How to use your free Ubuntu 9.10 CD

MISSING DISC? If your Ubuntu 9.10 CD is missing, please ask your newsagent.

To make things as easy as possible, we've included a free CD of the full version of Ubuntu 9.10 with this book. Here's how to use it

1 INSERT DISC

Your free disc is a complete Ubuntu 9.10 installation CD that contains no other software. You can boot your computer directly from it and choose one of two options: either run a test version of Ubuntu without installing it so you can try it out, or install Ubuntu on your hard disk by following the guide on page 12. First, you need to turn on your computer and insert the CD into your optical drive. If it doesn't boot from the disc, go to step 2; otherwise skip straight to step 3.

2 SET YOUR COMPUTER TO BOOT FROM DISC

To use the disc, your computer needs to be set up so that its optical drive is the first boot device. To do this, you need to press the key to enter the BIOS when your computer first powers on. This is likely to be the Delete, F2 or F12 key, but look out for a message onscreen.

In the BIOS, find the Boot options, which is likely to be under Advanced Options. Select the 1st Boot Device as CDROM. When that's done, save the changes and exit the BIOS.

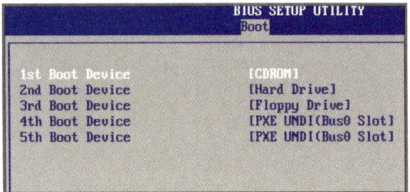

3 INSTALL LINUX

Your computer will now automatically boot from the CD. On the first menu, select English as your language and you'll see the Ubuntu menu. From here, you can select 'Try Ubuntu without any changes to your computer' to run the OS from the CD. This lets you give Linux a try without making any changes to your computer.

When you're ready to give it a proper go, select Install Ubuntu from the main menu and follow the steps on page 12.

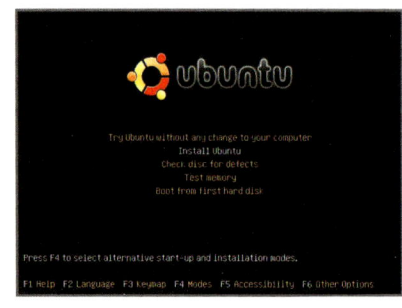

LINUX: THE COMPLETE MANUAL

EDITORIAL

Editor
Jim Martin

Contributors
David Ludlow, Jon Thompson

Design and layout
Anand Parmar

Production
Steve Haines

COVER ILLUSTRATION
lewing@isc.tamu.edu

PHOTOGRAPHY
Danny Bird, Jan Cihak, Pat Hall, Timo Hebditch, Andrew Ridge

Digital Production Manager
Nicky Baker

MANAGEMENT

Magbooks Manager
Dharmesh Mistry

Publishing Director
John Garewal

Production Director
Robin Ryan

Managing Director of Advertising
Julian Lloyd-Evans

Newstrade Director
Martin Belson

Chief Operating Officer
Brett Reynolds

Group Finance Director
Ian Leggett

Chief Executive
James Tye

Chairman
Felix Dennis

MAGBOOK
The 'Magbook' brand is a trademark of Dennis Publishing Ltd, 30 Cleveland St, London W1T 4JD. Company registered in England.

All material © Dennis Publishing Ltd, licensed by Felden 2009, and may not be reproduced in whole or part without the consent of the publishers.

ISBN 1-906372-69-1

LICENSING
To license this product, please contact Winnie Liesenfeld on +44 (0) 20 7907 6134 or email winnie_liesenfeld@dennis.co.uk

LIABILITY
While every care was taken during the production of this Magbook, the publishers cannot be held responsible for the accuracy of the information or any consequence arising from it. Dennis Publishing takes no responsibility for the companies advertising in this Magbook.

The paper used within this Magbook is produced from sustainable fibre, manufactured by mills with a valid chain of custody.

Printed by BGP, Bicester, Oxon

Please note: Due to the fact that Ubuntu is constantly updated, you may notice slight differences between the screenshots in this book and what you see on your screen. However, any changes will be minor and shouldn't affect the step-by-step guides.